Fancy
Goldfish

Fancy Goldfish

A Complete

Guide to Care

and Collecting

by Dr. Erik L. Johnson, D.V.M., *and* Richard E. Hess

photographs by Fred Rosenzweig

with contributions by
Jackie and Louis Chan,
Jeffrey Hunter, *and*
Izhak Kroshinsky

NEW
HOLLAND

First published in 2001 by
New Holland Publishers (UK) Ltd
London ● Cape Town ● Sydney ● Auckland

Garfield House
86 Edgware Road
London W2 2EA
United Kingdom

80 McKenzie Street
Cape Town 8001
South Africa

14 Aquatic Drive
Frenchs Forest, NSW 2086
Australia

218 Lake Road
Northcote
Auckland
New Zealand

ISBN 1 85974 957 7

Dedicated to Fred Rosenzweig

Translation of chapter 8 by Andrea Lingenfelter. All photographs by Fred
Rosenzweig unless otherwise attributed. Photographs of pathogens, diseased fish,
and veterinary techniques and equipment in part 1 by Dr. Erik L. Johnson.

EDITOR'S NOTE: The terminology for Goldfish varieties can be confusing,
since many originally Chinese varieties are called in the West by their
Japanese names, and Chinese names and variety categories are not used at all.
Since this is the widest current usage, however, we have followed it. Japanese
names have been used for varieties that are distinctly Japanese. For example,
the Japanese version of a Calico Oranda is called an Azuma Nishiki, and the
Japanese Calico Ranchu is called an Edo Nishiki.
The many different attributes that Goldfish may possess also complicate
naming. We have tried to follow an order of color—attributes—variety. But
which is the attribute and which is the variety? For example, it is a Blue
Telescope Butterfly Tail or a Blue Butterfly Tail Telescope? While our choices
may be arbitrary in this matter, we hope at least they are consistent within this
book. Fortunately, this is a wonderful problem to have, because it is indicative
of the enormous variety of characteristics Goldfish possess.

Book and cover design by Liz Trovato

Printed in China

Page 3: Calico Ryukin (left) and group of young Lionheads (right); pages 4–5:
Black Bubble Eye; facing; page 6: young Ranchu bred in the United States;
page 7, Calico Telescopes; page 8, Calico Hamanishiki; page 9, Red-and-
white Pompom Celestial; page 66, Gold-and-black Oranda; page 80, Dr. Erik
L. Johnson and assistant performing surgery on a Koi; page 83, Red-and-black
Oranda; page 84, Red Bubble Eyes. All photos in chapter 10 are of Ranchus
bred by Izhak Kroshinsky.

Contents

Foreword

Richard E. Hess

LIONHEADS.

Goldfish have enchanted mankind for over a thousand years. Their variety of shapes and colors and their graceful movement through the water make them living works of art, and their tameness makes them enjoyable pets; no wonder that people have always found pleasure in collecting them. Today the passion for Goldfish collecting is greater than ever, and all over the world the fraternity of collectors grows day by day.

This book is the culmination of research compiled by dedicated experts in their fields. I believe it is the finest, most accurate, and most complete gathering of information about Goldfish that has ever been assembled in one source. I'm greatly indebted to my great friend and coauthor, Dr. Erik Johnson, for his expertise in and his dedication to the field of Goldfish and Koi health. His persistent research to find and develop new techniques to keep our Goldfish healthy is always on the cutting edge, and his section on Goldfish health, which makes up part 1 of this book, will not only be of tremendous help and interest to hobbyists but is a major contribution to the professional literature.

We were fortunate to gain the cooperation of world-renowned Goldfish photographer Fred Rosenzweig. Fred is a creative and sensitive photographer, and his stunning photography presents each fish at its best. Fred has spent decades photographing the finest specimens of every Goldfish variety, and the fruits of his efforts speak for themselves in these pages.

My thanks go to Jackie and Louis Chan, too, for sharing with us their unique professional knowledge of choosing high-quality Goldfish. The Chans are the proprietors of the Tung Hoi Aquarium Company in Hong Kong, and have a vast, and in English as yet untapped, knowledge of fine Goldfish. Goldfish originated in China, and China is the main exporter of fancy Goldfish today. With a thousand-year tradition of Goldfish keeping, collecting, and appreciation, our Chinese "mentors" have much to teach us, and the Chans' essay is a unique look at the Chinese aesthetics of Goldfish. This is the first time anything like this has been published in English.

Izhak Kroshinsky has spent twenty years developing the finest strain of Ranchus in the United States.

The establishment of a top strain of fancy Goldfish requires careful attention to detail, patience, and dedication, and we are fortunate to be able to learn from Mr. Kroshinsky's many years of hands-on experience, so generously shared in his contribution, simply by reading.

I want to thank Dr. Streamson Chua for sharing his expertise with us on hand spawning and raising Goldfish fry.

I would also like to express my admiration and sincere gratitude to Jeff Hunter, who not only edited this volume but also wrote the contribution on Japanese Goldfish culture. His many years as a resident in Japan and his language ability have allowed him to provide our readers with information about Japanese Goldfish otherwise unavailable in English. The whole project would have been impossible without his unfailing assistance.

I hope that this unique book will be of use to all collectors for many years to come, helping them to care for and enjoy their Goldfish to the fullest. I also welcome readers' feedback and comments, and I invite you all to visit me at the Goldfish Connection (goldfishconnection.com) and share our excitement about these most beautiful and entertaining pets.

BLUE BUTTERFLY TAIL TELESCOPE.

PART ONE

Goldfish Health and Disease

Dr. Erik L. Johnson, D.V.M.

Doc Johnson here. I'm a companion-animal veterinarian with a special interest in the treatment of fish diseases. I was born in 1965 and I've kept fish since I was six years old. As with most hobbyists, I'm sure, I've seen many of my pets die; since becoming a veterinary professional, however, I hope that I have been able to tip the balance a little bit in my favor, and I want to share that experience and learning with you. That's one of the great things about being human beings: we can learn from the mistakes of others. One of the great things about being a veterinarian specializing in fish medicine is the tremendous advances we have seen in the field in the last decade, and being able to share them with you.

If you read this book carefully, absorb the information in it, and apply it systematically in your day-to-day Goldfish husbandry, you will become an expert Goldfish keeper. Some of the chapters of this part of the book are basic to your success with Goldfish, while others are more advanced, and you may not use the

MATTE RED-AND-WHITE RYUKIN.

information for many years. Still, I hope you will read through every chapter and master the information before attempting to diagnose and treat your fish. A single health disorder of a Goldfish can have several symptoms and causes, and so this disorder must be discussed in several ways and in several contexts. This creates a certain amount of redundancy, but I am confident it will make this part of the book more useful to the reader.

A few ground rules. Though most of the information in this book applies universally, my main frame of reference is Goldfish keeping in the United States, where I live and practice. We use Fahrenheit degrees and U.S. gallons.

In the first chapter after this brief introduction, I review the proper environment for keeping healthy Goldfish and basic husbandry techniques, with a strong emphasis on water quality. Though many hobbyists are eager to medicate at the first sign of trouble, more often than not something is wrong with the Goldfish's environment—the water—and it is there that you should start.

Chapter 2 presents the basic diagnostic techniques you need to acquire in order to find out what ails your fish. Most of these can be mastered by the hobbyist, such as visual examination, basic microscopy, and biopsy. You will find these invaluable in identifying Goldfish diseases, and proper identification is the first and crucial step toward treatment and cure. Other techniques are more advanced, and can be provided by professional services. I have tried to present information to help you find and use such services to your advantage.

I also include specific health management techniques in this chapter, such as injection, anesthesia, and quarantine—one of the easiest but most important ways you can protect your fishes' health when you add new Goldfish to your collection.

Chapter 3 presents all of the major pathogenic (disease) threats to Goldfish, organized into parasites, bacterial infections, fungal infections, and viral pathogens. Within this categorization, individual pathogens are ordered alphabetically to help you find them quickly.

But disease-inducing organisms are not the only threats to your pets' health. In fact, in my clinical experience, environmental disorders—your aquarium water—are the culprits in many if not most cases of Goldfish "disease." I cannot emphasize this enough, but I have tried to make it very clear in chapter 4, which treats this and related topics, including the various types of accidents to which our fancy Goldfish are prone.

Chapter 5, the Formulary, presents all the medications you will need to treat Goldfish diseases, with detailed information on uses, dosing, and precautions. I have categorized these treatments into bath treatments, which are placed directly in the water; topical treatments, applied to the fish's surface; injected treatments, which represent one of the greatest advances in fish medicine, in particular for treatment of bacterial illnesses; and finally, oral treatments, or medicated foods.

Chapter 6, "Symptoms, Causes, and Solutions," may actually be the one you turn to first when your fish are sick. It presents brief descriptions of conditions—not diseases—to help you identify the problem. After locating the probable causes of your fish's symptoms, you must turn back to the sections on the proper diseases and medications and study them carefully before treating.

I have added a final section to chapter 6 describing several surgical procedures that I use in correcting certain medical problems that afflict Goldfish. This section is directed mainly at veterinary specialists, but it also provides the hobbyist a vision of the latest in ornamental fish medicine and an idea of the help available from veterinary professionals.

I have appended a brief appendix to help with dosage and other calculations.

In closing let me say that one of the greatest dangers in treating sick Goldfish is that the cure can be worse than the disease. Be very careful to use the correct dosages of any drug or chemical, and to make sure that you fully understand the instructions, in context, before you treat your fish. Take the time to be sure your mathematical calculations for dosages are correct. Countless fish have been killed through overdoses of medications which, when used correctly, are benign.

CALICO RANCHU.

Chapter 1

Goldfish

Keeping

and

Husbandry

BLACK RANCHU.

The Goldfish belongs to the Cyprinid class of fish and is scientifically referred to as *Carrassius auratus*. It is unparalleled as an ornamental fish, with more colors and body types than any other species. Hundreds of varieties of Goldfish have been bred, and many of them are described in detail in other sections of this book.

Goldfish may be one of the hardiest of ornamental fishes, too; they can withstand temperatures as low as thirty-three degrees Fahrenheit and as high as the low hundreds.[1] Goldfish can also withstand very poor water quality for long periods of time if other conditions are acceptable. They are not especially fussy about their diet and they are not aggressive. If well kept they may live many years. In Asia, their place of origin, they have been kept and bred in ponds and tubs without high-tech equipment for centuries.

The modern Goldfish hobby ranges from a tank of

pet fish purchased at the local fish store to the breeding and showing of pedigreed champions of the rarer varieties, "living jewels" that can be a source of great pride and satisfaction to their owner. But regardless of where you fall on this scale and what variety of Goldfish you keep, the requirements for keeping Goldfish alive and healthy are very similar.

Housing

Goldfish may be housed in containers of just a few gallons on up to lakes and pools of many thousands of gallons. As a simple rule of thumb, you should provide at least ten gallons for each mature fish, and more for especially large varieties.

Most hobbyists house their collections of ornamental Goldfish in aquariums. Goldfish are large and relatively messy fish, producing considerable quantities of bodily wastes. The larger the aquarium you choose for

1. All temperatures in this book are given in degrees Fahrenheit.

your collection, the better your results will be. This bears repeating: Get the largest tank you can afford if you want the best possible results with your Goldfish. Large tanks not only provide more space and oxygen, but also more stable water conditions.

Of course, Goldfish can be kept outdoors in ponds or other containers as well—throughout the year in mild climates. Ponds present their own set of advantages and disadvantages. They offer natural food and light, which often results in larger, more brightly colored Goldfish. Because ponds are generally larger than aquariums, they also tend to have more stable water chemistry. But they also present a challenge in both disease and predator management, because the hobbyist has less control of the aquatic environment.

Lighting

Lighting has several effects on fish that can contribute to your success or failure in keeping Goldfish. Anyone who is experienced in this hobby will agree that full-spectrum illumination or, better yet, sunlight will enhance and improve skin condition and color in Goldfish. Full-spectrum lighting with sufficient intensity and spectrum will also stimulate the growth of healthy green algae on the inner surfaces of the aquarium. Algae benefit the fish in numerous ways including: (1) providing edible phytoplankton for the fish to consume; (2) providing for the reduction of nitrate in the environment; (3) raising dissolved oxygen by photosynthesis during the photo-

period; and finally, (4) the algae layer is slick and protects and cushions the fish when they come into contact with the aquarium sides. I strenuously encourage the hobbyist to allow as much sessile green algae to remain on the ornamentation and sides of an aquarium as is aesthetically tolerable.

Lighting also provides the fish with certain metabolic capabilities. Without a full-spectrum light source such as natural sunlight or full-spectrum fluorescent bulbs, the fish will not be able to activate Vitamin D in their skin cells and will eventually suffer calcium abnormalities, which may stunt growth or depress the immune system.

Darkness is just as important as lighting. Though they do not close their eyes, fish require sleep, and a lack of sleep contributes to the cumulative effects of chronic stress. Fish that are deprived of a natural cycle of light and dark do not perform as well as fish that are allowed to sleep in darkness. Indeed, fish deprived of darkness still sleep, although they do not derive anything near the benefits that fish with a night-and-day cycle do. The best light cycle is sixteen hours of bright light followed by eight hours of darkness. The longer photoperiod will ensure a healthy carpet of green algae and, therefore, lower nitrate levels, which will be discussed in detail later.

Temperature

The temperature at which we should house our Goldfish collections is the subject of debate. While it's

WHITE RYUKIN.

true that Goldfish of most varieties are extremely adaptable to a wide range of temperatures, there is considerable evidence that Goldfish do best in water in the mid to high seventies. This temperature range has several clear advantages.

First, it ensures that the water still carries sufficient oxygen. Water warmer than this carries far less oxygen.

Temperatures in the seventies also ensure adequate function of the nitrifying bacteria in the biological filter. Colder temperatures jeopardize the efficiency and capability of the nitrogen cycle.

Since Goldfish are "cold-blooded" animals (poikilotherms), this temperature range ensures the proper functioning of fish metabolism and normal levels of activity without unduly increasing their oxygen demand.

Different varieties of Goldfish also demonstrate different degrees of adaptability to temperature. The hardiest varieties, including Comets, Shubunkins, and Wakins, will survive winter in North America unless the pond freezes solid. The more highly selected varieties such as Orandas, Ryukins, and Ranchus may survive a temperate winter in North America when left outside, but in my experience they do this with less and less success as they mature. For further discussion of temperature, see chapter 5.

On the other hand, Goldfish will not spawn naturally unless they are subjected to a seasonal temperature drop—though it doesn't have to be as cold as Ontario in January to be "winter" for Goldfish. There is also evidence to suggest that the lengthening of the days in the spring also plays an important role in egg production and the onset of breeding behavior.

Filtration

Filtration is very important in Goldfish keeping, primarily because Goldfish are fun to feed. They can eat a prodigious amount of food if allowed, and the wastes they produce present a challenge to filtration technology. The filtration system you choose will depend upon the size of your collection and your budget, but the fundamental methods and goals of filtration are the same, whatever technology you select.

Filtration occurs on two levels. The first is mechanical, the removal of visible impurities and particles by a mechanical baffle or screen. The second level of filtration is the chemical reduction of nitrogenous waste in the water. The nitrogenous waste products come from the proteins that the fish ingest. They are released into the water in the form of ammonia, which is reduced by bacteria living on the surfaces of the filter media. We will discuss this again, in more detail, in the section on the nitrogen cycle.

A wide variety of filters are available today, including hang-on filters that are suspended from the aquarium, undergravel filters, canister filters, wet-dry filters, bead filters, sponge filters, sand filters, and even algae filters.

Filtration also creates water current and oxygenates the aquarium water. The ancestor of the Goldfish is a river fish. Though they can adapt to almost any body of water as long as it is sufficiently oxygenated, Goldfish tend to be more energetic and active with dynamic water current and plenty of aeration. Varieties such as Bubble Eyes and Tosakins, which are not able to move with agility because of their highly selected body shapes, cannot cope with strong water current, but most other varieties seem to enjoy it as long as there are also quieter areas in the tank where they can rest and sleep.

Ultraviolet Sterilization

Ultraviolet sterilization can be regarded as another kind of filtration. It is done by pumping water into a cylindrical chamber that contains a high-intensity ultraviolet bulb protected by a glass sleeve. The intense ultraviolet rays shine through the water, and their wavelength actually disrupts the DNA of any microorganism passing through the chamber. The ultraviolet sterilizer does not perform any mechanical or chemical filtration but can be very useful in achieving water clarity by killing suspended bacteria and algae that cloud the water. Ultraviolet sterilizers are available in varying strengths. Stronger ultraviolet sterilizers kill more pathogens, including larger pathogens such as *Ichthyophthirius multifilis* ("ich," or white-spot disease).

For water clarification, including killing suspended green algae, the ultraviolet sterilizer is unsurpassed. Several manufacturers now offer small, aquarium-sized units.

With an ultraviolet sterilizer, you can achieve crystal-clear water without the use of chemicals. In addition, ultraviolet sterilizers do not harm the green algae attached to the interior of the aquarium, which helps in nitrate control.

Ultraviolet sterilizers are also helpful in caring for sick fish, because they can decrease bacterial populations in the aquarium and limit the spread of pathogens from one fish to another. I strongly recommend ultraviolet sterilization for clear, cleaner, healthier water.

Feeding

I consider feeding time the most enjoyable activity in keeping Goldfish. So do many other hobbyists, which can result in overfeeding.

The number of feedings per day depends upon the age of the fish and the condition the keeper is trying to achieve. Smaller fish are in their growth phase and need many small feedings throughout the day for optimal growth and performance. Feed all they'll consume in less than five minutes several times a day.

Larger fish that are not being groomed for breeding should be fed a variety of foodstuffs once or twice per day. Feed the amount they will eat in five to seven minutes. Breeders need more frequent meals of high-protein foods, but in smaller quantities. The feeding of fry is beyond the scope of this chapter.

In spite of the fact that Goldfish have been in cultivation for at least one thousand years, there is wide disagreement about what to feed them. Fortunately, they are very adaptable in their nutritional requirements, as one might expect of a species that has existed for tens of thousands of years in the wild sifting mud for tiny rotifers and crustaceans. Still, there are some facts of Goldfish nutrition that all hobbyists need to be aware of.

Variety is the spice of a Goldfish's life, and a fish which is fed nothing but flake food all its life will be small, badly formed, and poorly colored. It will probably also develop cataracts by the time it is five years old. Fish fed a variety of flake, pellet, and frozen foods will have the deepest bodies, most impressive body shape, and most brilliant color. They will also be the most prolific breeders.

Contrary to the advice of older works on Goldfish stating that Goldfish are vegetarians and need little protein, large amounts of high-quality protein are very important for growth and health. I strenuously advocate the use of a wide variety of proteins, including animal, fish, and invertebrate sources. A mixture of pellet and frozen foods is important because it is more likely to provide a full and balanced profile of amino acids, the building blocks of proteins.

Vegetable food is also important, perhaps more so in older Goldfish. Many flake and pellet foods offer good-quality vegetable nutrition, and hobbyists report success with peas and other garden vegetables, prepared appropriately.

Storage of your Goldfish food is critical. Refrigerate but do not freeze your fish foods. In the freezer, the fats in the foods may be "freezer burned," damaging the fat-soluble vitamins A, D, E, and K. When food is refrigerated, spoilage is reduced without the risk of the destruction of fats and their vitamin cargo.

Speaking of vitamins, a good vitamin profile in manufactured foods is important, but liquid or any other vitamins put into the water are a waste of money. The fish will not absorb them in any useful form.

Overfeeding is the most common mistake made by hobbyists. We love to watch our fish eat. There are several negative effects of overfeeding Goldfish. First, the excess nitrogen can quickly exceed your filter's capacity to reduce it, and ammonia and nitrite accumulations will swiftly result, followed by sick fish. Second, the excess food in the environment can also stimulate the bloom of opportunistic bacteria. This results in cloudy water, which, again, may be followed by illness. Finally, excessive feeding can cause fish to become fat.

Water Quality

Maintenance of water quality is perhaps the most important aspect of Goldfish husbandry. The main parameters that must be controlled are ammonia, nitrite, nitrate, carbonate hardness, pH, oxygen, and temperature.

THE NITROGEN CYCLE

Ammonia, nitrite, and nitrate are intricately related in what is called the nitrogen cycle. An understanding and a mastery of the nitrogen cycle are probably the key elements of water-quality management. The nitrogen cycle refers to the process through which beneficial bacteria reduce fish wastes and excretions into environmentally harmless compounds. First they reduce ammonia into nitrite, then nitrite into nitrate. Plants then use the nitrate as fertilizer, or the hobbyist reduces it through regular water changes.

Ammonia (NH_3) is the primary waste product of fish, and the initial fuel of the nitrogen cycle. Vented waste makes up 25% of fishes' ammonia excretion; the other 75% of the fishes' ammonia excretion takes place via osmosis through the gills. Ammonia is not actively excreted, but leaves the fish because a higher level of ammonia exists in the bloodstream than in the surrounding water. When the water contains high ammonia levels, the ammonia does not leave the fishes' bloodstream and they die of ammonia poisoning.

Ammonia is removed naturally from the environment by beneficial bacteria of the *Nitrosomonas* species that lives on all underwater aquatic surfaces and in the filter. *Nitrosomonas* pares off ammonia's hydrogen ions (H+) and replaces them with oxygen (O_2) molecules, creating a nitrite (NO_2) molecule.

The need for oxygen in this reaction is illustrated in the following equation:

$$NH_3 + (O_2 \text{ required}) \rightarrow (Nitrosomonas) \rightarrow NO_2 + 3H+$$

Both ammonia and nitrite accumulation can be detected by simple water-test kits readily available at your local fish store. A cycled tank should always have readings of zero for these two compounds.

As we have seen, the beneficial bacteria *Nitrosomonas* convert ammonia into nitrite. Nitrites are broken down by another beneficial bacteria, *Nitrobacter* species. *Nitrobacter* is extremely sensitive to water quality. It will go on hiatus if the water is too low in dissolved oxygen, too warm, too cold, or if it has been treated with almost any additive or medication, including salt. When the *Nitrobacter* stop or slow down, you can expect to see an accumulation of nitrite in the system. In addition, the conversion of nitrite to nitrate is only half as efficient as the conversion of ammonia to nitrite, which can also contribute to nitrite accumulations.

Nitrate is the final product of the nitrogen-reduction cycle. It is at this point in the cycle that reduced nitrogen can return to the food chain by becoming available to plants. Nitrate, in the presence of phosphates, makes a vitally important fertilizer for plant life of all kinds. Perhaps the most relevant plant in this regard is the simple algae. Many a garden pond has been clear all

winter, and then in the spring, as the *Nitrobacter* bacteria "warm up" and begin to reduce the winter's leafy wastes, the pond becomes pea-soup green. Fish tanks which have completed the nitrification cycle may also turn green at the six-week mark, as the ammonia finishes its path from nitrite to nitrate.

Again, nitrate levels can be determined through simple water tests. It is recommended that you keep nitrate levels below 50 PPM, which you can do by regular water changes.

PH

The symbol pH stands for "potential of hydrogen." It is a measurement of the free hydrogen ions in a system. Neutral pH is assigned a numerical value of 7.0. As there are less and less free hydrogen ions in the water, that numerical value rises; as they accumulate, it drops. Water with a pH higher than 7.0 is called alkaline, and water with a pH lower than 7.0 is called acid. Aquatic life requires a pH from 5.5 to 9.5. The pH of fish (and human) blood, and coincidentally the ideal pH for Goldfish, is 7.4. The pH can be measured with a simple test kit.

Numerous factors influence pH. As we have seen above, *Nitrosomonas* bacteria produce hydrogen ions by stripping them away from ammonia to produce nitrite. These hydrogen ions accumulate in the water, resulting in a lower pH. Minerals and carbonates tend to remove hydrogen ions from the water, which drives pH upward. Unsealed driftwood and other sources of organic molecules tend to bind up those minerals and carbonates, so that they can't grab onto hydrogen ions; at the same time, these organic materials generate hydrogen ions as they decay, and these two factors combine to contribute to a lower pH. Plants use carbon dioxide during their exposure to light, and this raises the pH. At night, plants give off carbon dioxide, which lowers the pH. Fish and bacteria all use oxygen and produce carbon dioxide twenty-four hours a day, which lowers the pH. Combined, these biological processes tend to have the net effect on a fish tank of causing the pH to move downward into the acidic range. Fortunately, there are molecular "checks and balances" against this effect.

CARBONATE HARDNESS

The molecule responsible for stabilizing the pH against these influences is called the carbonate molecule. A measurement of carbonate molecules is expressed as the total alkalinity (TA), or the carbonate hardness (KH).

Carbonates come from several places. In nature, they come from the slow dissolution of natural minerals in rocks. In particular, limestone and gypsum are rich in

carbonates, as are seashells and corals. As they dissolve, they release minerals such as calcium and magnesium, as well as carbonate molecules, into the water.

The carbonate molecule exists in a balance with the environment. When hydrogen ions become abundant, such as through biological processes, the carbonate molecules pick up the extras, which prevents the pH from falling. When hydrogen ions become scarce, the carbonate molecules will liberate some hydrogen ions. The net effect of the carbonate molecules on the water is to hold the pH at some constant level, which is why they are often called a buffer or buffering agent. Because of the importance of this buffering capacity of carbonate molecules, there is a benefit in having a quantitative measurement of carbonate activity in your aquarium water.

The carbonate levels in a system are measured by a test of the total alkalinity. Most major garden centers, pet shops, and pool-supply stores carry affordable total alkalinity test strips. Test results will vary depending upon regional conditions. For example, water in the eastern United States tends to have a total alkalinity below 50 PPM, while in the southeastern United States, the average total alkalinity is less than 30 PPM. In the southwestern United States, the water in the aquifer is mostly bedded in limestone or is derived from evaporation, and so the water has a very high total alkalinity of over 180 PPM.

A high total alkalinity—100 PPM and above—will keep your pH stable for a long period of time. A low total alkalinity—50 PPM or under—will need to be remedied or you may have to cope with a sagging pH or sudden drop in pH. This will be discussed in more

detail shortly. It is also possible to have a total alkalinity that is too high. A total alkalinity higher than 300 PPM may cause gill damage.

Not only do carbonate molecules occur in varying amounts in the environment, but they are also an exhaustible resource. When the carbonates are exhausted, the effect is a sudden drop in pH, which can and does kill fish.

A pH "crash" is a quick way to rid your tanks of all those messy fish. Here's how the scenario often unfolds in the hobbyist's tank. The water was changed two weeks ago, and at that time a satisfactory amount of carbonates existed in the system. The fish are fed daily, and the filter reduces their nitrogenous wastes. The hydrogen ions are bound up by the carbonates and all is well. The hobbyist is lulled into a false sense of security because the pH has been stable for weeks. Why check it now? Then the carbonates are finally exhausted, and overnight the fishes' carbon dioxide production, the algae's carbon dioxide production, and the reduction of the ammonia in the filter crashes the pH to 5.5 and the collection is all but lost.

I advise all hobbyists with water of low total alkalinity to use a good commercial buffer that will keep the pH at near neutral and the total alkalinity at about 100 PPM on a weekly basis.

GENERAL HARDNESS

General Hardness (GH) is a measure of all minerals, including carbonate molecules. If you subtract the KH (carbonate hardness) from the GH (general hardness), you will have an estimation of the mineral content in the water. Water with a higher mineral content is commonly called hard, while that with a low mineral content is called soft. In nature, minerals such as calcium and magnesium (which come from calcium and magnesium carbonate) have no effect on the pH of a system. As a result, it is possible to have very hard water (water of high mineral content), but have very little carbonate activity—and consequently, a lower pH. As is the case with carbonate hardness, a general hardness of over 300 PPM is harmful to Goldfish.

OXYGEN AND CARBON DIOXIDE LEVELS

Oxygen is soluble in water, but not very well. Dissolved oxygen may range from 0 PPM up to 14 PPM. For keeping fish, concentrations of 8 PPM and above are desirable.

The key to oxygenation is to increase surface contact of air and water. One common misconception is that the air bubbles of an air stone are adding oxygen to the water. They are, but only to the extent that on the way to the surface they push a column of tank water into contact with the air at the water's surface. We can increase oxygenation just as effectively with a submersible water pump by resting the pump on the tank bottom and aiming the output at the surface. In this manner, you can generate tremendous exposure of water to air at the water surface and gas exchange.

Oxygen is very important to the nitrifying bacteria of the filter because oxygen is integral to the production of nitrite from ammonia. (See the discussion of ammonia above.) Warm water carries less dissolved oxygen than cold water, a fact that is significant to the health of both your fish and your filter. As mentioned earlier in this book, keeping Goldfish at high temperatures (above eighty degrees) increases the oxygen demand of the fish and filter bacteria, while at the same time warmer temperatures actually reduce the ability of the water to provide the much-needed oxygen. Cold water, on the other hand, carries a near-saturation value of dissolved oxygen without much circulation or surface agitation at all. Why is this relevant? Because when considering certain water treatments that consume dissolved oxygen—such as potassium permanganate and formalin—you must remember that cold water is better than warm water.

The fact that cold water carries more oxygen also means that when fish are to be shipped or transported from one place to another, whether across oceans or to the local vet, water of a temperature less than seventy degrees is preferable.

In heavily planted aquariums, dissolved oxygen follows a daily cycle. By day, plants engage in photosynthesis and produce considerable amounts of dissolved oxygen. In some cases you can actually see tiny bubbles rising from the leaves. At night, the plants grow and respire. They reverse their metabolism and produce carbon dioxide and take in dissolved oxygen. The minuscule algae are no different from more complex plants in this regard. As a result, a heavily planted tank or a tank with a lot of suspended green algae may have low dissolved oxygen levels at night.

Carbon dioxide is produced by the respiration of both plants and animals. When you exhale, you produce carbon dioxide. Carbon dioxide levels can exist independently from the oxygen concentration in water. For example, water may have large amounts of oxygen and carbon dioxide at the same time.

In water, carbon dioxide readily converts to carbonic acid, which in turn tends to lower the pH. A large number of fish in a small tank with minimal circulation and surface agitation may actually accumulate sufficient carbon dioxide to lower the pH. On the other hand, removal of carbon dioxide by increasing surface exposure and gas exchange will remove the source of carbonic acid and may raise the pH.

Remedies to carbon dioxide accumulation include increasing surface exchange with air stones or pumps. As suggested earlier, raising the dissolved oxygen of the system does not decrease the carbon dioxide level, but increasing surface exchange of air and water is a step toward maximizing both.

Maintenance Schedule

Water quality is not a guess. The hobbyist has complete control over water quality and can measure water quality with simple tests. The most important tests are for ammonia, nitrite, nitrate, and pH, and a test for total alkalinity is also useful. Measure all of these parameters daily in new systems. In mature systems that have been stable for some time, measure ammonia, total alkalinity, nitrite, and nitrate weekly and pH daily.

Regular water changes are an important way to maintain water quality. When water quality is poor, you should perform daily water changes and suspend feeding until the problem is corrected. In mature systems, perform a 10% to 20% water change every week. At a minimum, you could change 20% to 30% every two weeks. Unless your tank is very sparsely stocked, you will notice that if you neglect the above schedule, at best your fish will not flourish, and in the worst case, they will die.

Use of a buffer on a regular basis is your best hedge against a falling total alkalinity and a falling pH. The two parameters are related, as we have seen above. As a routine, the hobbyist with low total alkalinity should apply a buffer according to manufacturer's directions once per week. Test your water—and remember, it may change through the seasons and over time—to determine if the buffer is a wise or necessary addition. As a rule, use a commercially prepared buffer whenever the total alkalinity is below 30 PPM.

Finally, to preserve water quality your filtration system should have regular maintenance. Wring out sponge filters every three weeks under normal loading. Backwash bead filters once per week under normal loading. Open and rinse canister filters once every six weeks. Rinse power and hang-on filter pads every three weeks under normal loading. With undergravel filters, suction-clean half the tank's gravel every ten to fourteen days, alternating the sides weekly.

Careful Observation

Your final obligation in the husbandry of your collection is careful observation. Of course, we all look at our fish—that's why we keep them! But you should examine your fish regularly. You should notice as you walk into the room if any fish in your collection is isolated or lethargic. Count the fish. Are they all there? Do they hang motionless in the water, or are they dancing, as they should be? Is there a white film on the fish, as the pH sails downward out of control? Do you see the early signs of ich? Is that a new red spot? When you feed the Goldfish, you should notice whether every fish eats. Are they maintaining their body condition? Some people keep behavior and water quality journals, and this can be very helpful.

RED-AND-BLACK PEARLSCALE WITH SOME HEADGROWTH.

Chapter 2

Diagnostic and Health Management Techniques

MATTE RED-AND-WHITE RANCHU.

Diagnostic Techniques

The diagnostic techniques presented below can be roughly divided into two categories: those the hobbyist can learn to, and is encouraged to, perform, which includes visual examination, microscopy, and biopsy. On the other hand, most hobbyists must rely on professional veterinary or scientific service for necropsy and the other services best offered by a diagnostics laboratory, the other category covered in this chapter.

THE VISUAL EXAMINATION OF GOLDFISH

At a glance, one might think a visual examination of a Goldfish is simple, but there are subtleties which can provide a great deal of information about your fish's health.

The first thing to observe is how it "sets" in the water. It should be oriented normally both horizontally and vertically. If the fish is tipped forward in the water, or lists to the side, it may be ill.

The fish's eyes should be clear and active. The eyes of a sick fish may appear glassy or clouded. Sunken or distended eyes may both portend bacterial infection. Bulging eyes are often caused by a bacterial infection

resulting in swelling behind the eye. Sunken eyes are most commonly caused by a loss of proteins through damaged body surfaces including skin and gills, with emaciation as the result.

Respiration should be slow and even, not rapid. Try to observe the fish from an angle that allows you to see the gill arches, which should be a healthy, deep red color. Pale or blotchy gill arches are a sign of disease. The condition of the fish's gills may be one of the most important prognostic signs. Fish with pale gills are usually nearing their end.

The fishes' skin should be clear and normal in color. Red patches and sores suggest water-quality problems, parasitic infections, or bacterial infections. All three conditions may exist, so perform careful testing of the water quality before jumping to conclusions.

The fins of the fish also possess many clues. The dorsal fin of the fish (if present) is usually "up" or erect in a healthy specimen and clamped down in a sick fish. Fins that are ragged or torn may be under attack by another fish, but this can also be caused by a bacterial infection. Close examination of the behavior of tank mates can lead to a clearer diagnosis. If the fins are red or the blood vessels in the fins are prominent, poor water quality is often to blame, and careful testing of all water-quality parameters is imperative.

The fish should be plump and well fed. An emaciated fish may be exhibiting signs of chronic parasitism, internal bacterial infection, or poor appetite as a result of water-quality problems.

BASIC MICROSCOPY

Microscopy, or the ability to use a microscope diagnostically, is perhaps the greatest step hobbyists can take in the health care of their Goldfish. To develop proficiency in this area, one must first learn about the parts of the microscope and how they work, and then practice to perfect one's skill.

Please refer to the diagram in order to begin to familiarize yourself with the parts of the microscope. At the top of the microscope, you will see the eyepieces, or oculars. These usually have a built-in magnifying power, most often of five or ten times (5X or 10X).

Under the oculars, you will see a turret, which holds the different optics, or lenses. The optics usually have a more powerful magnification. The smallest is usually a 10X power, and the strongest is often a 40X strength.

When you have the microscope optics turret set on 40X, your combined power is derived from the multiplication of the oculars and the chosen optics. In other words, the ocular (10X) multiplied by the optics (40X) for a combined power of 400X.

The turret directs the optics down at a platform called the stage. The specimens are collected on glass slides and covered with an extremely thin piece of glass or plastic called a cover slip. The specimen, on its slide and under its cover slip, is then placed on the stage.

Beneath the stage, there should be some means of restricting light, commonly called an iris. This may be a dial that you can turn to line up progressively larger holes over the illumination source. It could also be an actual diaphragm such as the ones used in cameras. In this case, a slider will adjust the iris diaphragm from an open to closed position.

The simplest microscopy is performed without staining the specimen. When you do not use stains, you will use the smallest possible iris aperture. Using the microscope in this way is called light/contrast microscopy. As you advance in the use of the microscope, you may want to start using some stains. When you begin to use stains and higher magnifications, you will require more light. To show detail in stained preparations, contrast will become less important.

Under the iris diaphragm, there will be either a mirror or an electric light source. An electric source of illumination is preferable. Microscopes that use mirrors are

tedious to use at best, and they cannot be used in the dark, which is often the best environment in which to use a microscope.

To begin to use a microscope to examine a sample of a fish's body mucous—what we will be examining in most cases—follow these simple steps.

- Turn on the power.
- Close the iris diaphragm or choose the smallest iris aperture in the disk.
- Rotate the turret until the lowest (shortest) optic is in position. This is the optic with the lowest number, since the number refers to its magnifying power.
- Adjust the optic control knob to bring the optic as close as possible to the slide with the specimen on it.
- Begin to look at the slide through the ocular and slowly turn your control knob until the mucus appears. The black circles are bubbles.
- Now that you can see the mucus under the microscope, you might rotate the turret to choose a higher-powered optic. Focus with the control knobs on the sides of the microscope. You will rarely use the highest-powered optics.

There are some caveats to be aware of when using the microscope. First, you should make sure that the microscope is of reasonable quality. Many a hobbyist has lost Goldfish to small parasites such as *Costia* because the microscope did not do a competent job of showing the parasites at 400X.

Hobbyists also make the common mistake of looking for the parasites at this higher power straight away. Always start out at the lowest combined power with the least amount of light.

When using a microscope out of doors, drape a towel over your head. If you do not, you will not be able to see anything under the microscope because the field will be washed out by peripheral light.

As noted above, more advanced microscopy can be performed with the use of stains. Stains are simply chemicals that color specific structures and surfaces of different organisms for closer observation under the microscope. The addition of color helps identify what kind of bacteria might be present, and also reveals certain physical structures that can help differentiate parasitic species. I have not had to use any stains for the clinical work I have been doing over the last several years, and most Goldfish hobbyists won't either. Some, however, will find it interesting to stain the internal structures of organisms that they find under the microscope. Diff-Quik is a basic stain that helps differentiate gram-positive and gram-negative bacteria and will define some structures of parasites. The Ziehl-Neelsen stain helps identify *Mycobacteria*. A full description of staining

PARTS OF A MICROSCOPE

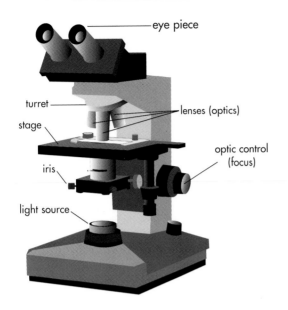

eye piece

turret

lenses (optics)

stage

optic control (focus)

iris

light source

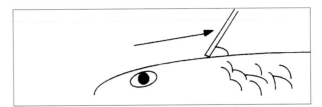

PERFORMING A MUCUS SCRAPE, SHOWING PROPER ANGLE OF COVER SLIP.

technique is beyond the scope of this book and, again, not necessary for the hobbyist.

BIOPSY OF GOLDFISH

A biopsy is the removal of tissue, cells, or fluids from a living organism for examination. This is an extremely useful—even indispensable—technique for diagnosing Goldfish. The equipment needed for carrying out a biopsy of your Goldfish is relatively simple: a box of glass microscope slides and a box of cover slips. Plastic cover slips are preferable because they do not break under stress.

The two major areas for biopsy are the surface of the fish and the gills. Let's start with a surface biopsy. The best places on the surface of the fish to find parasites are generally on the ventral surfaces (underside) of the fish and especially the area on the side of the body just behind the gill covers (opercula). Reach into the tank and gently catch the fish. Hold it with its belly up against the side of the tank, just a little above the water line, so that if it escapes your grasp it returns to the

safety of the tank. Be careful not to rub the fish all over with your hands in the process of apprehending it. If you wipe away most of the surface mucus in the capture process you will have little to look at.

Use the plastic cover slip to scrape some mucus from the ventral surface of the fish. The mucus drop should adhere to the cover slip. Then place a drop of aquarium water on the slide and place the cover slip with its drop of mucus onto the drop of water. A seal will form between the cover slip and the slide. This is your specimen or preparation.

After examining the mucous sample under the microscope, you should collect a gill biopsy. Once again, capture and hold the fish in the left hand (the reverse for left-handers) on its back. Insert the left thumb under the gill cover and raise the cover up to expose the gill. Insert the plastic cover slip under the gill cover and lay it on the red gill arch within. With mild downward force, scrape the edge of the cover slip across the surface of the gill arch, recovering a small blob of reddish mucus. Place this on a slide, on top of a drop of water, which suspends the mucus and the parasites within it for easy viewing under the microscope.

A gill biopsy can also be performed by snipping off a piece of gill tissue, with or without sedating the fish, with a pair of iris tenotomy scissors. The piece of gill tissue is compressed under a cover slip on the slide and examined. There may be considerable bleeding from the fish. I originated the gill-scrape method described above early in my veterinary practice on fish in response to hobbyist

THE AREAS HIGHLIGHTED IN BLUE ARE PRIME SITES FOR SURFACE BIOPSY.

DIAGNOSTIC AND HEALTH MANAGEMENT

concerns about such bleeding. I have had excellent results with the gill-scrape method and I highly recommend it. I believe the results of both gill biopsy techniques are equivalent diagnostically, and the scraping technique is less traumatic to the fish—and the hobbyist.

Still, we must remember that this procedure is stressful. Indeed, in smaller fish—for example, fish under three inches in length—some damage may easily be done to the operculum or to the gill arch in the biopsy procedure. For retailers, this is a satisfactory risk for the diagnosis of a large group of fish, but the hobbyist diagnosing a single fish should use proper judgment and consider the risk of performing a gill biopsy on a smaller fish. I have done gill biopsies on small fish only an inch in length without killing them, but the possibility of fatally harming a small fish should be noted and calculated into the decision.

Nevertheless, gill biopsy is imperative in the investigation of any Goldfish disorder. The gill is a favorite territory for *Costia*, among other parasites. Many times a parasite may be found on the gills without ever making an appearance on the skin of the fish, and without a viable gill biopsy, the problem goes undiagnosed. I cannot tell you how many times I have heard "My fish have no parasites" from good, experienced hobbyists, only to discover that they did not biopsy their fishes' gills.

Any parasite you see under the microscope is a potential threat to the Goldfish, but some situations are more threatening than others. When you see a lot of parasites under the microscope—that is, ten or more per low-power field—and the fish appears to be sick, you may assume that the parasite is the cause of the sickness and select a treatment protocol to eliminate the parasite. On the other hand, sometimes you will find a parasite when you are doing a routine biopsy on a Goldfish, though the fish and others in its environment do not appear to be sick. When this happens, you should pause and ask yourself if now is the best time to treat. Sometimes it isn't. If under these circumstances you do decide to treat, choose a treatment that will not make otherwise healthy fish unhealthy. Sometimes you find something under the microscope that is not in the classic textbooks of fish disease. Chances are it's a stray, non-pathogenic organism. Strive to learn the real killers among parasites, and when you encounter something unfamiliar or uncommon, try not to overreact.

Keep your specimens fresh. The parasite *Chilodonella*, for example, is extremely fragile under biopsy conditions and will die very shortly after collection. *Costia* is another parasite that perishes relatively quickly, and it is so small that diagnosis is almost dependent upon seeing the organisms in motion at lower powers.

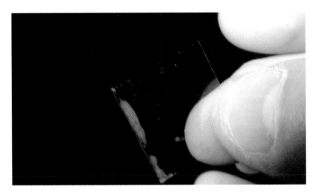

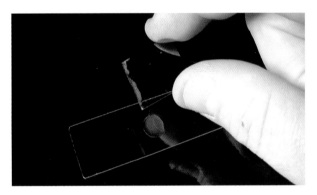

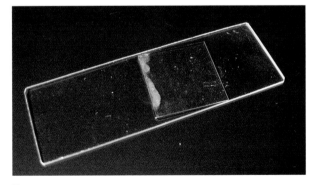

FOUR STEPS IN PERFORMING A GILL BIOPSY, FROM TOP TO BOTTOM: OPENING THE GILL COVER FOR INSERTION OF COVER SLIP; GILL TISSUE ON THE COVER SLIP; APPLYING THE COVER SLIP TO THE SLIDE, ON WHICH A DROP OF TANK WATER HAS BEEN PLACED; THE GILL TISSUE CAPTURED BETWEEN COVER SLIP AND SLIDE AND READY TO OBSERVE UNDER THE MICROSCOPE.

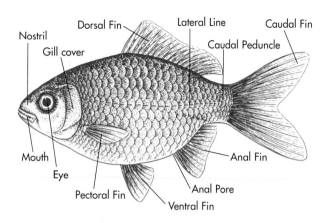

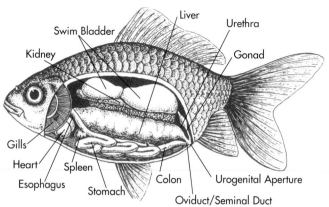

NECROPSY OF GOLDFISH

A necropsy is a postmortem examination. It is an extremely useful diagnostic procedure, especially for those with large collections, but it has its limits for the hobbyist with just a few fish. First of all, to be useful a necropsy must be performed very soon, if not immediately, after death. Though the hobbyist may wish to attempt a necropsy, training and experience are absolutely necessary if reliable, useful results are to be obtained. As a result, you will probably have to rely upon a diagnostics laboratory to carry out the necropsy, and the specimen (the ailing fish) must arrive at the lab alive.

The following section deals with diagnostic labs and the services they perform; here I will outline some of the questions you can expect a necropsy to answer, which will help you evaluate whether you want to sacrifice your specimen to have one performed.

A necropsy is basically a "stem-to-stern" examination of the internal parts of the Goldfish cadaver to try to learn what killed the fish. The standard procedure consists of a series of incisions and a list of organs that are identified and examined by the pathologist. The necropsy seeks to answer the following questions, among others.

Was the fish eating about the time of death? If the gall bladder is very large, and there is no food in the proximal small intestine, then you may surmise the fish had not eaten in a time frame adjacent to its demise.

Was the fish well nourished at the time of death? If the body cavity has very little fat, this may mean that the fish was undernourished. A primary disorder such as intestinal parasites can cause malnourishment, as can tuberculosis, which causes wasting.

Does the fish have intestinal parasites? When you open the intestines to observe the contents, you may be able to examine the contents under a microscope and find eggs of several parasites of Goldfish.

What was the quality of the fish's nutrition? The condition called "fatty liver" is often found in fish that have

been fed large amounts of a refined diet with a narrow amino-acid profile. Catfish chows and other cheaply formulated diets are also common causes of fatty liver in pond Goldfish.

Did the fish die of some kind of tumor? Hard tumors may be found in numerous tissues of the Goldfish. Cancer is not uncommon in larger, older Goldfish. The lifetime barrage of chemicals to which we expose our fish could be contributing to a high incidence of cancers in ornamental fish.

Was the fish egg-impacted? If the belly is full of roe and there is a conspicuous absence of fat in the abdomen with these eggs, the fish may have perished from egg impaction.

Did the fish have cystic kidneys? Cystic kidneys will be found arising from between the air sacs, and appear as large, fluid-filled sacs ranging in color from yellow to amber. They are usually quite large at the fish's death and may be hard until they are incised.

Did the fish die of a bacterial infection? Fish that have died of bacterial infection can be diagnosed on necropsy (of fresh specimens only!) by the detection of the following three clinical appearances: (1) gross abscess in the abdomen replete with pus and necrosis; (2) gills that feature necrotic and discolored sections within the arches; and (3) sometimes an acute mortality from *Aeromonas salmonicida* can cause the internal organs to almost liquefy and the air sacs appear as though a red dye bomb exploded in the air sac.

Was there an air-sac problem? The air sacs are normally pearly white and located in the uppermost vault or recess of the abdominal cavity. Any other appearance may represent a problem.

DIAGNOSTIC LAB SERVICES

A diagnostic laboratory is a scientific lab set up by a land-grant or extension-service college. Almost every state has an extension service, usually based in a taxpayer-sup-

TUMOR.

ported college or institution. Almost every extension service is supported by a diagnostic lab that handles their samples. Increasingly, their work with food and sport fish has broadened to include ornamental fish specimens sent in by veterinarians and hobbyists alike.

Having the help of a competent microbiologist at the diagnostics laboratory is immensely useful in tracking down a fish killer. A microbiologist can collect a bacteriological sample from the internal tissues of a fresh specimen and determine what kind of bacteria was involved and what kind of antimicrobials the bacteria are sensitive to. This can be of great utility if you've already started to treat the fish and the results are not encouraging. When the lab work finally arrives, it usually contains data that can steer you in the right direction. Be advised, however, that if you were going to treat your fish based on lab work and microbiology, you will have to wait up to a week, and by that time you might not have any fish to treat! There are some veterinarians who will not treat until they have received lab results, but most hobbyists are better advised to begin treatment based on their own diagnostic skills while waiting for lab results, and then redirect treatment if the results so indicate.

You may have to coordinate with your local extension agent to submit samples to the diagnostic laboratory. It is also possible that your local veterinarian may be able to submit samples to the local diagnostic lab via overnight parcels, but the fees assessed by veterinarians tend to be many times the actual cost of the submission.

To find your diagnostic laboratory, first check your local government listings for "Extension Services," contact them, and ask where the nearest, most accessible diagnostic laboratory is. Next, call the lab and ask about the methods for and restrictions on sample submission. You may have to set up an account with a business name, which can usually be done. (Many nurseries and pet shops are already taking advantage of this resource.) Diagnostic labs are usually willing to make exceptions for fish and allow hobbyists to submit them directly if their veterinarian won't take them.

When you submit a live (but sick) Goldfish to such a laboratory, you will usually request the following services: gross examination, surface biopsy, necropsy, tissue histopathology, culture and sensitivity, and, if any lesions consistent with viruses are found, an electron microscopy (usually at a surcharge).

Make sure to clarify everything before you send a fish. Make sure a pathologist knows the sample is coming and insure that they have your contact information in triplicate to make sure they can get your results to you.

The pathologist at the diagnostics lab must collect sterile (aseptic) samples from the internal surfaces of the fish, usually the kidney, and the best results are taken from fish which are alive when received by the pathologist. Fish that have been dead for some time are usually suffused with incidental (saprophytic) bacteria, which are not useful diagnostically. To receive useful results from a pathologist, the fish should be sent to arrive alive. This means you will have to ship the fish in a bag with water and pure oxygen, and pack the bag to protect it from extreme temperatures. In the summer, pack the fish with ice or "cold packs" and, if possible, insulate the shipping box with Styrofoam sheets. Heavily insulate the box in winter to avoid freezing. The goal is to have the fish arrive alive.

If sending a live fish is impossible, select a fish that was symptomatic and has been dead for less than thirty minutes. Roll the fish in a wet plastic bag and place it in a heavily insulated cooler on a bed of ice. Tape up the cooler and send it via expedited delivery to the laboratory.

Do not waste your time or the efforts of the pathologist by sending long-dead fish. If the cadavers have taken on that milky-skinned look, with cloudy pupils and a foul odor, laboratory diagnostics can provide little or no useful information.

The results you receive from the laboratory will

AIR SACS.

detail the names of the bacteria that were cultured from your specimens. Then, the bacteria will be grown on specific media, which are freckled with tiny disks containing different antibiotics. When the bacteria are inhibited from growing near a disk, the bacteria are called "sensitive" to the antibiotic on the disk. These are the antibiotics you would then reach for in the treatment of a bacterial ailment of the Goldfish in the collection. This process is called a culture and sensitivity test, and can be very useful in indicating precisely which antibiotics will be effective.

Health Management Techniques

The three health management techniques discussed below each have a different focus. Injection is an important treatment method for combating disease, while anesthesia is a technique that facilitates invasive procedures, and quarantine is mainly a prophylactic, or preventative, technique to prevent infection.

INJECTION

Injection is probably the single greatest medical advance in the management of Goldfish bacterial diseases. The benefits are numerous, but most notably, you can control the dose, the dose cannot be expelled, absorption (especially from the peritoneum, explained below) is efficient, and fish do not have to be eating.

First, however, it must be said that there are times not to inject. Don't inject if the fish is so near death that it is having trouble remaining upright. Don't inject if the fish appears unduly stressed by capture. Delay injection until is has recovered from that stress, because the process of injection will simply compound the stress and may push the fish over the edge. Always remember that injection contributes to stress, and weigh that factor against the possible benefit of injection.

Another reason not to inject a fish is if you lack the ability or emotional steadiness to do so. If this describes you, there's no need to feel humiliated. Many hobbyists do not choose to inject fish. With trepidation comes a shaky hand, and with a shaky hand may come injury to you or to the fish. There are an increasing number of competent veterinary specialists, advanced hobbyists, and field biologists who will help you if you seek them out.

If you do choose to inject Goldfish, you will need a 1 cc tuberculin syringe, a 25-gauge needle, and an injectable therapeutant such as an antibiotic or Vitamin C. A 25-gauge needle is quite thin, scarcely as thick as a common staple straightened out. As the number of the gauge goes down, the needle gets larger. For example, a

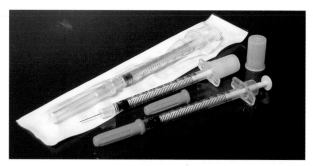

SYRINGES FOR INJECTING GOLDFISH.

INTRAPERITONEAL INJECTION UNDER THE VENTRAL FIN.

INTRAMUSCULAR INJECTION BENEATH THE DORSAL FIN.

INTRAMUSCULAR INJECTION AT THE BOTTOM OF THE CAUDAL PEDUNCLE.

14-gauge needle is more like a drinking straw, and in avian medicine there are 35-gauge needles, which are scarcely as thick as a hair (and bend just as easily). If you are injecting very small fish, these fine needles are probably called for, though they are harder to handle.

The syringe is called a tuberculin syringe because it was at one time used for administering tuberculin antigen. Nowadays, the name simply refers to a small syringe with a 1-milliliter volume. Tuberculin syringes are commonly used for the administration of insulin to diabetics.

It is easier to inject a fish than one might expect. There are several commonly used routes of injection. For our purposes, we can divide them into intraperitoneal and intramuscular injections. Intraperitoneal injections are delivered into the belly around the internal organs. Absorption is excellent via this route. Hobbyists worry that the fish might suffer some damage to internal organs if the fish moves. This is a very rare outcome. There are two points for intraperitoneal injection. The first is the site adjacent to the anus between the ventral fins and off the midline. Another intraperitoneal injection site is under the ventral fin. There is a spot right under the fin where the scales and skin are thin and the needle slides right in.

You can also inject into the muscle. The preferred intramuscular site is out of sight under the caudal peduncle, in the muscles of the tail. This site tends to be preferred because defects in the skin caused by intramuscular injections here don't show as much as they do in the other intramuscular injection site, the muscles of the back under the dorsal fin. Ornamental fish take their injections in the back very well, but many hobbyists are concerned, rightfully, about a mark that might be left and opt for methods less visible.

I recommend injection via the intraperitoneal route, adjacent to the ventral fin, as shown in the photo on the opposite page.

Apprehend the fish with your hands or a net, roll it onto its back, keeping it in the water, and insert the needle under the skin at the desired point at an angle of about 30 to 45 degrees to the skin, with the needle aimed forward, toward the fish's mouth. The needle should go in with gentle pressure. Push the plunger of the syringe gently, and then withdraw the needle.

When injecting, it is all but impossible to avoid piercing a scale. Any place you decide to insert the needle, you will actually be penetrating from two to four layers of scales. The point between two scales, for example, will often feature the "middle" of another scale over and under the apparent meeting of the two scales that are side by side. Some scales may be removed with each injection. This is sometimes preventable (in larger fish)

if you place your fingernail on the skin adjacent to the needle shaft as you pull the needle from the skin. You're effectively holding the pierced scale on the fish, as the needle exits. I've never found it worthwhile to do with my own fish, but I have been asked to do this on others' champion fish.

Goldfish are surprisingly easy to handle for injection. Very large Goldfish may be injected through the fish net, or through a plastic bag.

Many hobbyists, once they master the technique of injection, are too ready to use it. Some of the cases that merit injections are obvious fin rot, body sores, red belly, or dropsy, as well as recent imports that lie on the tank bottom.[2] On the other hand, a fish with a pink smudge on the body, but which is otherwise behaving normally; a fish appearing ill in bad water conditions, but without sores or lesions; and a fish with a ragged edge to one fin, but which is otherwise behaving normally probably do not need to be injected. Fish that are gasping at the surface should not be injected before checking the pH and ruling out poor water quality.

In many instances, such as those indicated above, an injection can be a life-saving step, but before undertaking injections, please realize that injections subject the fish to the stress of handling. Make sure that before you inject a fish, you have tested all water-quality parameters, including pH and levels of ammonia, nitrite, and nitrate. If all is well with the water and the symptoms are worsening or are obviously bacterial, you should proceed to perform or have the necessary injections performed by a veterinarian. The number of injections and intervals between injections differ, of course, depending upon the disease and the drug injected. See the Formulary for details.

ANESTHESIA

Anesthesia is useful in cases when you need the fish to remain still during treatment, such as dislodging a foreign object from the mouth or suturing a pectoral fin, and of course it is indispensable in surgery, as in removing headgrowth that obstructs vision or performing a quartz-implant coeleotomy. While it's true that fish have no spinothalamic tract and therefore are anatomically prevented from feeling severe, deep pain, anesthesia will also prevent the stress of handling and any discomfort during a procedure, in addition to keeping the fish still and allowing the veterinarian to do the job.

Oil of cloves is a good anesthetic that is readily available in several forms from health stores. When anes-

---

2. Though at this time dropsy is statistically incurable, injection probably offers the only chance of recovery, however small that chance may be.

thetizing a fish, start by preparing three different vessels of water. The first will have 5 drops of oil of cloves per gallon of water. The second will have 2.5 drops of oil of cloves per gallon. The last will have only clean water, without any oil of cloves.

Start by measuring vessels one and two so you know how many drops of oil of cloves to dose them with. Before adding it to the vessels, it's best to emulsify the oil of cloves—that is, mix it very well with water—so it will be more evenly distributed throughout the vessels. To do this, place the proper number of drops in a small jar half-filled with water, cap it, and shake it vigorously, then pour the emulsified mixture into the vessel. Do the same for the second vessel, which has half the dosage. Remember, the third vessel has no oil of cloves.

Place the fish into the first vessel, and within five to fifteen minutes (depending on temperature and other factors, such as the size of the fish) it will become lethargic and roll over. When it is substantially motionless, but still breathing, you may proceed with your procedure. Do not wait until the fish is completely motionless or has stopped breathing, or you will euthanize, not anesthetize, the fish.

As you proceed with treatment, watch the fish carefully and move it from vessel to vessel to keep it at the proper level of sedation—breathing regularly but not flopping actively about. In most cases I start with the fish in the 5 drops per gallon induction water, move it to the clear water for a few minutes after it is fully sedated, and then to the half-strength (2.5 drops per gallon) water until the surgery is completed. This can be sustained for some time. The longest fish surgery I have performed to date lasted seventy minutes.

There are several precautions to observe when using oil of cloves. First, if you have any doubts about this procedure, don't attempt it; send your fish to a competent veterinarian for treatment. Second, it is important to keep track of the depth of the fish's sedation at all times. It is easy to forget this while concentrating on the procedure or surgery you're performing, but it can be fatal. Finally, handle the oil of cloves with the respect it deserves.

Recovery from anesthesia induced by oil of cloves usually takes over fifteen minutes. During recovery, the fish should be in clean aquarium water and should be "walked" or held upright for best results. It is stressful to the fish to float upside down helplessly, particularly if it

has just had a surgical procedure. You can carefully anchor a fish between a sponge filter and the side of the tank until it awakens.

Veterinarians may use other agents for anesthesia, but these are usually controlled and sometimes quite dangerous substances unsuitable for use by hobbyists.

QUARANTINE

Quarantine is perhaps the most important technique I will describe. You should become a master of quarantine. This will require a complete understanding of what you're doing, why you're doing it, and what to look for while you're doing it. Let's talk about what quarantine is.

Quarantine is simply a well-thought-out "waiting room" for your aquarium. It prescreens any fish that might be carrying an infectious agent from entering your main collection.

Anyone with a penchant for purchasing new fish will need a quarantine aquarium. The equipment needed for a quarantine aquarium depends upon the size and number of fish you want to hold. The larger the better. I will repeat that for emphasis: The larger the aquarium is, the better.

The quarantine tank must be cycled before the first fish is put in there. You can start this cycle in your quarantine tank by keeping it a little warmer than usual, about eighty degrees; feeding regular fish food to the system despite the lack of fish; and most important, wringing out an established filter sponge or other active filter material from an established tank into the system. Your filtration system will assimilate the material squeezed from the active filter and make use of the bacteria you've inoculated into the system for a jump-start of a new bacterial colony.

The quarantine aquarium needs to have above-average aeration and water circulation. On the other hand, the fish must also be able to relax and rest, so there should be specially engineered dead spots where the current does not interfere with sleep and convalescent processes. Fish will thrive better in tanks with considerable algae on the sides than they will in sterile tanks.

There is room for debate about whether your quarantine tank should include a 0.3% salt level. It can be argued that the addition of salt is an undue stress and detriment to appetite during the crucial quarantine period. On the other hand, if you do not have a microscope and therefore cannot rule out the presence of parasites, I recommend maintaining a 0.3% salt concentration in the quarantine tank to reduce or eliminate any ciliated protozoan population.

There are also several preemptive treatments you can use to prevent the development of illness during quarantine. Your quarantine tank can be treated with a 0.3% salt solution, and then a dose of Program or Dimilin. Close observation should provide early warning of any problems, and a prophylactic course of Fluke Tabs, using the four-day cycle described in the Formulary, could be employed. As described in the Formulary, these treatments are generally benign, and they probably have a place in the preemptive treatment of incoming Goldfish.

I strenuously recommend that fish be encouraged to eat anything they will accept while in quarantine, not just what you think they should eat. For example, I feed my quarantined Goldfish a mixture of tropical fish flake food and crushed freeze-dried krill. Of course this diet is very high in protein and cannot be recommended for the long term, but it is eagerly accepted and a full belly tends not to be a sick one.

Others suggest feeding a medicated food in quarantine, and if the fish will accept it there is no problem with this approach. One such food is MediGold, which contains four antibiotics—sulfadimethoxine, ormetropin sulfa, oxolinic acid, and kannamycin—and is well accepted by Goldfish.

Observation of fish in quarantine is more than half the battle. You must observe and measure water quality, you must observe appetite and activity level, and you must observe for the appearance of any signs of disease.

Water quality should be tested in quarantine on a daily basis. The top three tests are of pH and ammonia and nitrite levels. A nitrate test is not a priority until the system is established, or if it lacks algal growth. Bad water quality in quarantine is certainly worse for the incoming fish than no quarantine at all.

If fish become sick in quarantine, and it's not because of water quality, quarantine is working: you are saving your precious collection from infection. If you have a microscope, use it to biopsy and diagnose the sick fish and decide on a specific treatment. If you don't, you may need to try the much less desirable shotgun approach to therapy, proceeding as follows:

1. Test pH and levels of ammonia, nitrite, and, in older quarantine systems, nitrate, and correct as needed.

2. Remove a fish or two from quarantine and examine them extremely closely for signs of attack by anchor worm. Look at the gills and see that they are red and meaty. If there is any discoloration, streaking, white patches, or necrosis, or if the gills are pale, please consider all possibilities given in the section on bacterial gill disease.

3. In the specific absence of all disorders mentioned in (2) above, add salt to make a 0.3% solution and watch for improvement.

4. If the fish have not improved within twelve to twenty-four hours, consider the application of a single dose of Droncit or a single treatment with Fluke Tabs (see Formulary).

5. Twenty-four hours after the treatment for flukes, do a 50% water change and replace salt to maintain a 0.3% concentration.

6. The fish should be better at this point unless one of the above suggestions actually revealed the problem.

7. If not, repeat the fluke treatment four days after the first treatment. Do a 50% water change twenty-four hours later.

Quarantine should last for at least a week, with regular water tests, examinations of fish and their gills, and observation of appetite and activity levels. A two-week quarantine is better if you have sufficient room for the fish to be comfortable.

Chapter 3

Pathogenic

Threats to

Goldfish

Health

CALICO RANCHUS.

Goldfish are vulnerable to many health problems, of which perhaps the most prevalent and serious are the pathogens. For the purposes of this text, the pathogens include parasites, bacteria, fungus, and viruses. I will treat each of these in turn in this section, describing the symptoms, the microscopic appearance of the pathogen, and treatment. For detailed therapy instructions, however, I refer the reader to the Formulary, which has the most current and preferred methods of treatment.

Parasites

Parasitic infections are extremely common, and as a group present the most persuasive argument for quarantine. Indeed, it is safe to assume that any new fish you buy carries some sort of parasite. We will consider three main categories of parasites, ciliated protozoans, monogenetic trematodes, and crustaceans, in that order.

We will begin our discussion of parasitic infections with the ciliated protozoans. These parasites are microscopic and they feature cilia (tiny "hairs") as their means of getting around on the fish or in the water.

Ciliated protozoans are undoubtedly the most damaging and also the most common group of Goldfish parasites we will discuss.

CHILODONELLA

Chilodonella species is a ciliated protozoan parasite of extreme importance. *Chilodonella* is very prevalent and was at one time the most common killer of fish in spring. It is easily transmitted in water and by non-quarantine fish. *Chilodonella* primarily attacks the respiratory system. Affected fish isolate themselves, clamp their fins, and begin to decline. Excess slime and spider-web hemorrhages may appear on the skin. Finally, in the last stages of the infestation, the fish begin to gasp at the surface.

Chilodonella can be observed in a body scrape of mucus observed under the microscope. It will appear as heart- or onion-shaped organisms with a granular filling (the cytoplasm of the cell) and a pharyngeal basket which appears to the untrained eye to be a clear bubble at the front end of the organism. *Chilodonella* may swim in a straight line, but they more commonly swim in tight circles. *Chilodonella* does not survive for very long in slide

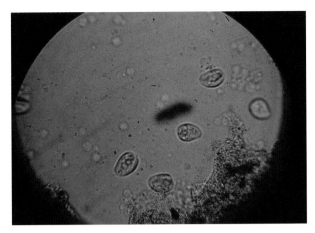
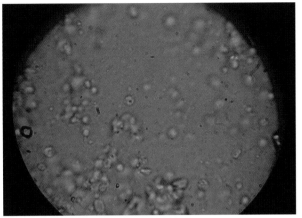

CHILODONELLA. RIGHT: COSTIA, PHOTO AND DIAGRAM.

preparations, so you must view the slide within five to seven minutes of collection of the mucus sample. Once the organisms die, they lose their characteristic internal structures and appear as circular, granular balls that can be easily mistaken for motionless *Ichthyophthirius* organisms.

The most effective remedy for *Chilodonella* is salt. A 0.3% concentration is effective in all cases; indeed, I have never seen a resistant case. See the Formulary for the dosing regimen.

When salt treatments are not practical because the plant material in the system is more important than the fish, *Chilodonella* may also be controlled rapidly with formalin at 25 to 50 PPM and with potassium permanganate at 2 to 4 PPM. See the Formulary for the most current, preferred methods of using these compounds.

COSTIA

Costia necatrix (some older texts refer to this organism as *Ichthyobodo necatrix*) is one of the most serious pathogens of Goldfish. *Costia* is very prevalent. Outbreaks of *Costia* occur most commonly in spring, especially in fish kept outdoors. The organism is very tiny and defies amateur microscopy. Its effect on the gills is profound and an outbreak usually causes many losses unless the hobbyist identifies the cause quickly and proceeds with treatment just as swiftly.

Fish infected with *Costia* develop slimy patches about the head and gill covers. Some fish die suddenly without any external symptoms. In other cases, the fish gasp desperately for oxygen as the organism destroys their gills.

Costia is extremely minuscule and will evade detection at magnifying powers less than 300X. Under microscopes of that power and higher, you will see a translucent, colorless, comma-shaped organism that is rapidly

motile (they swim like crazy) in a corkscrew fashion. In most cases, a biopsy of the gill or one of the white, mucus-laden areas of the fish will reveal swarms of thousands or millions of individuals.

Costia is usually a quick killer, but it can also be carried through the summer by healthy fish that are somehow able to carry the parasite without expiring. Costia can resist drying, which means that nets and other equipment that were previously in contact with infected fish can carry the pathogen even if they are now dry.

The most commendable remedy for *Costia necatrix* is salt. A concentration of 0.3% is usually effective, but there is a new strain of *Costia* that may be resistant to this salt level and even survives a salinity concentration of 0.6% or higher (see the Formulary). In these cases, we must resort to formalin. For the treatment of *Costia*, use formalin at 25 to 30 PPM for two hours, followed by a water change ranging from 50% to 95%. This is repeated daily for four to five treatments. Please refer carefully to the section in the Formulary on formalin.

EPISTYLIS

Epistylis is a relatively uncommon parasite of Goldfish. It appears as a tuft of whitish fluff extending out from under a scale or wound on the Goldfish. To the naked eye it appears to be a fungal infection but looks radically different under the microscope. Usually, fish with *Epistylis* are rather hale considering they are parasitized. *Epistylis* does not occur in clean tanks or environments that have a low organic load. It is likely to appear on common pond fish in unfiltered ponds and lakes. I have not recovered *Epistylis* from any high-quality Goldfish kept in aquariums. I have cleared the few cases I have seen in ponds with massive water changes, removal of the organic load in the system, and the application of 0.3% salt solution, as described in the Formulary.

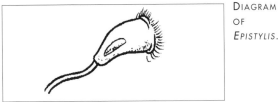

DIAGRAM OF EPISTYLIS.

The key to the successful treatment of *Epistylis* is proper diagnosis. Since it is not a fungus, it cannot be cured by antifungal remedies, which will leave the pathogen unaffected as the fish succumb to it.

HEXAMITA

Hexamita is a not actually a ciliated protozoan, but I have included it with this group for convenience. It is a tiny, flagellated protozoan parasite that was at one time associated with "hole-in-the-head" lesions in Cichlids and Discus. Later research suggested that this was a condition caused by several factors, including inadequate nutrition, inadequate lighting, and poor water quality, and the threat of

FRAYED FINS CAUSED BY *HEXAMITA*.

Hexamita was downgraded. Given the cases of *Hexamita* I have diagnosed in recent years, however, I am filled with a new respect for this parasite as a serious threat to Goldfish health.

A fish suffering from attack by *Hexamita* will be lethargic, followed by significant erosion of the fins and skin. The body may become entirely milky and the protective slime coat may come off in strands. The fins begin to look as though the tissue between the rays is being eaten away.

Microscopically one will observe millions of tiny microorganisms that are far smaller than even *Costia*. To identify these pathogens requires a microscope of at least 400X magnification. Indeed, to see the flagella would require a 1000X magnifying power.

Though in my opinion *Hexamita* is not common, it may be a chronic, resident threat to aquaria. Flagyl (metronidazole) is the treatment of choice. See the Formulary for treatment.

ICHTHYOPHTHIRIUS

Ichthyophthirius multifilis is commonly known as "ich" or "white spot." Ich is one of the most common parasites of aquarium fish, and no other pathogen is even a close second place in terms of prevalence. Ich usually appears as a dusting of fine, white spots all over the body of the

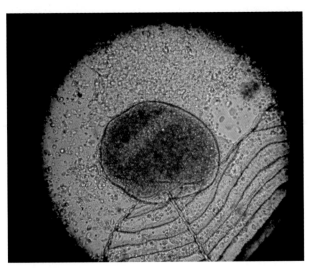

ICHTHIOPHTHIRIUS, OR "ICH."

victim, hence the name "white spot." Ich is not always characterized by the ubiquitous spots, however; I see many affected fish without them. A fish may be breathing its last, its gills absolutely encrusted with ich organisms, but not have a single white spot.

The white spot you see on a Goldfish with ich is actually an immune response in the skin stretched over the organism underneath. We call this organism "sub-epithelial," or "under the skin." In some cases, dependent upon temperature, immune status, and other variables, there may be no immune response in the skin, though you can recover an abundant number of ich organisms from a biopsy of the fish.

Goldfish can also carry ich in small numbers without showing signs of disease or the characteristic white spot. At low levels of infestation, there seems to be a détente between the body's immune system and the organism. Research has also shown that a competent immune response can eliminate ich from the body completely. Efforts are underway to develop a vaccine against the ich organisms to stimulate immunity in Catfish and other economically important species.

Most cases of ich show up within a few days after

the hobbyist has added new fish to their collection without quarantine. Affected fish will isolate themselves and develop symptoms of lethargy, clamped fins, and in many instances, a peppering of white spots from head to tail. In other cases, the fish will develop difficulty breathing, and a reddish color suffuses the skin. This symptom is particularly common in colder water.

The ich organism is easily identifiable in a mucus scrape under the microscope. At even 100X combined power, you will see the free-swimming "swarmers" or the large, sub-epithelial organisms. The free-swimming swarmers appear as highly active, teardrop-shaped organisms with a green or tan granular interior. The sub-epithelial organism is large, round, and covered with very fine cilia, which rotate the organism on its axis. The sub-epithelial organism is usually not translucent, but you can see the horseshoe-shaped nucleus inside.

The life cycle of ich is the key to its control. The organism enters the system as a free-swimming "swarmer" in contaminated water, or it may come in on a fish in the sub-epithelial form. The organism under the skin will swell and develop into a packet that erupts and falls to the bottom of the aquarium. There, it swells and then erupts again, liberating thousands of free-swimming swarmers that swim up into the water in search of a new host. They penetrate the skin of a fish and the cycle begins again. The speed with which the organism proceeds through its life cycle is dependent upon the water temperature. The organism may remain under the skin for over a week if the temperatures are under sixty degrees. The ich organism is impervious to any water-borne treatment while it is under the skin of the fish. Our window of opportunity to kill this pathogen is during its free-swimming phase. The most efficacious treatment in this application is salt at a concentration of 0.3%.

When treating ich with salt, first remove all live plants from the aquarium, since the salt will harm or kill them. Before the treatment, perform a partial water change and ensure that all water-quality parameters—ammonia, nitrite, nitrate, and pH—are optimal. Once your environment is perfect, add salt at the rate of 1 teaspoon per gallon of water, every twelve hours for three applications. For example, if you add the first dosage of salt at twelve noon, repeat again at twelve midnight and once more at twelve noon on the following day. Use only non-iodized salt that does not contain YPS (yellow prussiate of soda). Keep the salt in the system for fourteen days, and remove it at the conclusion of the treatment by a substantial water change.

Depending upon the temperature of the aquarium, the ich spots may actually worsen for one day. In some

THE SPOTS CAUSED BY ICH.

cases, a few ich spots will suddenly multiply into "millions" as the skin of the Goldfish responds to the salt doses. This is normal. In twenty-four or thirty-six hours you will notice a decline in the number of ich organisms, and finally, after four to five days, the crisis should be over.

A word of caution: ich is often what is called a "sentinel disorder": an epidemic of ich is commonly a warning of poor water quality. During any parasitic outbreak, you should check your water-quality parameters frequently and correct any problems you discover.

When the presence of plants is a serious consideration and prevents the use of salt, the hobbyist is faced with a dilemma. The most effective anti-ich medications other than salt are also the most damaging to the plants and to the filter. Two of the most commonly recommended are formalin and copper. I do not recommend the use of compounds containing formalin for the clearance of ich because the formalin is a considerable stressor to Goldfish; it may burn their fins very badly, and it does not remain in the water for very long. Copper is devastating to the plants and also harms the biological filter. See the Formulary for uses of copper and formalin as treatments.

A medicated food available from Tetra Products contains malachite green. Research has found that the oral administration of malachite green eradicates the sub-epidermal form of ich, but it takes a rather long time, and not all sick fish will eat. Still, it offers a method of control that has little if any environmental impact.

OODINIUM

Oodinium, a ciliated protozoan, is the causative agent in "Gold Dust" or "Velvet" disease. This sessile organism makes affected Goldfish appear to be covered with a velvety gold dust. Oodinium can be easily observed at a combined magnification of 100X. It appears as a pear-shaped or pentagonal organism. It does not move across the field; Oodinium is normally attached to the fish via a fine, needle-like rhizome that penetrates deeply into the skin. Like "ich," the *Oodinium* organism eventually ruptures, releasing new "swarmers" into the water to perpetuate the attack. In many scrapes of *Oodinium* you will see the pear-shaped tops of the organisms and also the pear-shaped tops with their stiletto intact. Salt is rarely effective in treating *Oodinium*, but formalin and copper are, and copper is the preferred treatment (See the Formulary). *Oodinium* was at one time a much more common diagnosis than it is today. In the past any parasite that caused excessive mucus production was identified as *Oodinium*, but modern microscopy has shown this to be untrue. I have very rarely encountered *Oodinium* in Goldfish. It is more common in freshwater aquariums or recently purchased Goldfish, and it is a greater problem for the wholesaler who receives fish directly from the breeder ponds. The problem has usually been brought under control with copper treatments before any infected fish reach the retailer or consumer level. Untreated, however, *Oodinium* is a devastating disease.

TRICHODINA

Trichodina is another common pathogen of Goldfish. It is highly prevalent and can be recovered from at least some fish in any retail pet store in the nation unless all systems are salted to a concentration of 0.3%. *Trichodina* is a unique pathogen in several ways. First, *Trichodina* is a problem in tanks that are rich in organic debris and detritus. Researchers have found that in some instances, *Trichodina* will disappear when fish are maintained in very clean tanks. *Trichodina* is also unique in its ability to remain pathogenic at very low temperatures—even as low as the mid-thirties. *Trichodina* has another unique characteristic: it is also occasionally resistant to salt at a a concentration of 0.3%. The salt-resistant varieties of *Trichodina* originate principally in Goldfish from Japan; I have not encountered salt-resistant *Trichodina* in Chinese imports. This does not imply that the Chinese imports do not have this salt-resistant mutation, and no such assumption should be made on that score. Though salt is effective in most cases, when it fails the results can be serious. In most instances of salt resistance, double and triple salt concentrations effectively eliminate the pathogen. Otherwise healthy fish will survive salt concentrations up to 0.9%, or 3 tablespoons of salt per gallon. (See the Formulary for further information on this treatment.)

Fish infested with *Trichodina* will appear to have irritated skin. The victim will conspicuously flash and scratch against objects. Eventually, the damage to the skin may result in sores or ulcers. It is important to remember, however, that *Trichodina* is not the only organism that causes flashing.

Trichodina is easily seen at relatively low magnification—a combined power of 100X to 200X is sufficient. Under the microscope, it appears as a flat, saucer-shaped organism. On closer examination, the organism is fringed on the outside margin by thousands of tiny "hairs," or cilia. Inside the saucer, there are varying numbers of teeth, or "denticles." The many subspecies of *Trichodina* are differentiated by the numbers of rings and denticles present, though this makes no difference in treatment.

Remedies for *Trichodina* are many. My first choice is salt at a 0.3% concentration because it is sparing to both fish and filter bacteria. When salt is impractical because of the presence of plants, the hobbyist can use formalin or potassium permanganate according to the methods described in the Formulary.

FLUKES

Monogenetic trematodes are a separate class of parasites from ciliated protozoans. "Monogenetic" means that they do not have an intermediate life cycle that takes place off the fish, as do the digenetic trematodes (which are not a serious Goldfish pathogen).

The common monogenetic trematodes that parasitize Goldfish are of the genus *Dactylogyrus* and *Gyrodactylus*. *Dactylogyrus* species are commonly called gill flukes, and *Gyrodactylus* species are commonly known as body flukes. They are more precisely differentiated by their mode of reproduction and the presence of eyespots. The gill fluke *Dactylogyrus* lays eggs and lives in the dark, which has led it to develop eyespots that allow it to see. The body fluke, *Gyrodactylus*, lives on the fishes' skin, bears live young, and has no eyespots. Despite their common names,

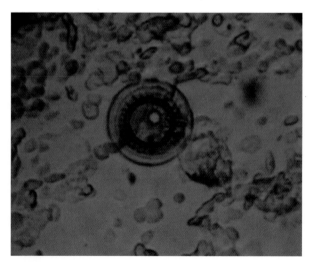

TRICHODINIA.

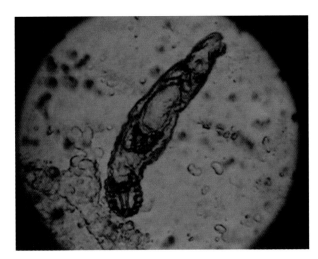

FLUKE.

body flukes and gill flukes can almost always be found together and are often both distributed evenly over the body. In almost a decade of light/contrast microscopy and surface biopsies, I don't recall a single occasion when I noticed gill flukes exclusively on the gills or body flukes restricted to the body.

Flukes are extremely prevalent. They are one of the most common Goldfish pathogens recovered from sick and healthy fish in clinical practice. The fluke derives its nutrition from the slime coat of the fish. It does not suck blood or bite chunks of tissue from the fish, but will ingest nutritive mucus via its anterior (rear) end. Fish that are under attack by flukes will develop an excessive slime, isolate themselves, and clamp their fins. They may also show excessive scratching and flashing behavior. Eventually, the fish may develop sores or ulcers on their bodies as a result of the scratching behavior. Flukes are also known to carry hazardous bacterial fish pathogens on the two hook-shaped haptens at their back end. These bacteria are deeply inoculated into the skin by the haptens. I maintain that so-called "ulcer disease" is more commonly transmitted by flukes than by any other vector. In fact, it is probably safe to assume that any fish that feature bacterial ulcers on the body are or have been parasitized by flukes.

Flukes can also do considerable damage to the gills of fish. With their hold-fast haptens deeply embedded in the gills of the fish, they can trigger bacterial gill disease through three mechanisms: (1) direct trauma in the form of chronic bleeding; (2) indirect stress, which precipitates a bacterial gill disease outbreak; and (3) direct inoculation of the bacterial pathogen into the gill tissue.

Flukes are extremely easy to identify under the microscope; their appearance is highly characteristic and unmistakable. They are the largest pathogen for which you need employ a microscope. They are easily wit-

nessed at a combined power as low as 40X. The fluke is a tubular parasite with suction cups on one end and a gripping end which features a ring of small hooks which fan out around a pair of vicious-looking hooks. These are the haptens. Inside the body of the fluke one will observe either an oval egg (in the case of *Dactylogyrus*) or a complete miniature of the mother (in the case of *Gyrodactylus*). In the early research done on trematodes of this type, scientists were amazed to dissect as many as four generations of embryos from within one adult fluke.

In my opinion, flukes are the most compelling argument for owning a microscope. Without a microscopic examination, you could use salt as a blanket treatment and effectively treat at least seven common pathogens. If you also treated with Dimilin or Program, there is only one parasite that would be left behind: the fluke. Since all the methods of treating flukes involve either significant expense or risks to your fish, it is worthwhile to confirm their presence microscopically before initiating treatment.

There are several ways in which the fluke life cycle affects how we treat them. The mother fluke often contains several future generations of larvae or durable eggs in her body. Though we kill the mother with a waterborne treatment, her body will remain at the aquarium bottom until the egg or larvae emerge from the remains of the mother and seek out a new host. This is the reason a repeat treatment is necessary: we must kill not only the first but also the second generation of flukes. I recommend a repeat treatment approximately four days after the first one.

During the first treatment, disconnect your biological filter. Common sense might suggest that you should sterilize the filter to get rid of any parasites hiding in it (thus killing your nitrifying bacteria), but this is not necessary, since you will be doing a repeat treatment. After the first treatment, you can resume biological filtration with your potentially infected filter. Any flukes in the filter will move out into the aquarium and search of fish hosts, because if they do not they will die of starvation. During your second treatment, disconnect the filter again. The only parasites that might possibly remain in the filter at this time are senescent adults, because there has been no time for larvae to reemerge and take up residence in your filter. Nevertheless, I recommend a third treatment just in case. Understanding the life cycle of the fluke is important in the determination of your treatment regimen.

Recent research on flukes has revealed an interesting—and reassuring—result: a closed population of fish cannot support flukes indefinitely.[3] The fish seemed to develop specific surface immunity that eliminates the

3. Scott, M.E. and R.M. Anderson, *Parasitology*, 89 (Pt 1):159–94 1984 Aug.

flukes gradually. Only by introducing immunologically naive fish to the group can a viable, expanding population of flukes be maintained. The significance of this study is that if you close your Goldfish collection and resist the urge to bring in potentially infected fish, you could avoid sustaining a fluke population and any future fluke infestations.

Remedies for flukes include potassium permanganate, Droncit, Fluke Tabs, formalin, and HealthGuard (a product containing formalin). Copper, chloramine T, and acriflavine have also been used with success.

When treating flukes, be sure to repeat treatment at an appropriate interval to intercept any surviving larvae after the initial treatment of the adult flukes. Once again, my recommendation is treatment at four-day intervals when the water temperature is from seventy to seventy-eight degrees. Be sure that you've considered all pertinent environmental factors and consequences when choosing your chemical treatment. Be sure, too, that you really need to use them, since many treatments for flukes are potentially dangerous to your fish. Be extra careful to measure carefully and correctly.

ARGULUS (FISH LICE)

The fish louse, *Argulus*, is the first of the crustacean parasites that afflict Goldfish. With a gilled respiratory system, *Argulus* looks like a small, one-eighth-inch, green flying saucer that scuttles through the water in search of prey. When it encounters a host fish, it can grab on to the fish with suction cups and then insert a razor-sharp stiletto through the skin for a nutritious meal of blood.

Argulus is visible to the naked eye. It appears as green dots that move about the fish or from fish to fish. In most instances, the fish are flashing and scratching themselves, and they may even jump out of the aquarium to evade their attackers. In advanced cases, scores of *Argulus*

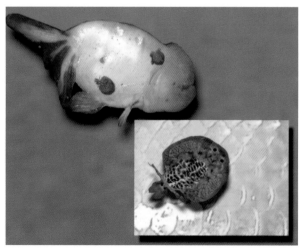

ARGULUS, OR FISH LICE.

attacking the fish may cause red lesions on the skin.

Argulus is highly resistant to organophosphates and to formalin, and the doses required to kill the parasite will probably kill your fish first. Dimilin (diflubenzuron) or Program (lufenuron) are effective. They are discussed in detail in the Formulary.

ERGASILUS

Ergasilus is also known as the "gill maggot," and for good reason: it looks like a maggot attached to the gills. This crustacean parasite also strongly resembles an immature copepod, and hangs in the gill tissue with hooks. Fish can have so many of these attackers that the gill arch is not visible. *Ergasilus* is as sensitive to Dimilin and Program as any other crustacean, and they are the recommended treatments.

Ergasilus is rarely encountered in North America, and to date I have never seen a case.

INTESTINAL WORMS

Intestinal parasites such as tapeworm, *Anasakis*, and *Capillaria* are uncommon pathogens of Goldfish but are found from time to time. They cause disease primarily by taking up valuable space in the intestine and by damage done directly to the intestinal lining by their attachment.

Diagnose intestinal parasites by collecting a fresh specimen of solid waste from the fish, preferably at the moment it is deposited. Pipette the sample onto a slide and squash it under a cover slip. Examine at a combined power of 40X and then 100X to observe the presence of the eggs of any intestinal invader. If they are found, treat with Tramisole (levamisole) or Droncit (praziquantel) as described in the Formulary.

LERNEA ELEGANS (ANCHOR WORM)

Anchor worm is not a year-round concern in hobbyist collections but is a seasonal threat. Unlike other parasites, anchor worms are not triggered by stress. They tend to be explosively contagious and can infect healthy fish even if they are not crowded or stressed.

Anchor worm appears in Goldfish initially as a "harpoon" sticking to the side of the fish. The protruding, worm-shaped female elongates and develops a Y-shaped bifurcation at the end. The worm is not active and does not move on or around the fish. It may be yellow, white, tan, or even dark green. The area where the head of the worm is lodged under the scale is red and may bleed. Secondary bacterial infections caused by the wound may be life threatening.

The female worm protruding from under the scale may reach almost three-eighths of an inch in length. The arms of the Y are actually the paired egg cases of

LERNEA, OR ANCHOR WORM.

this parasite. These eggs will eventually hatch and start the cycle of infestation all over again. The microscopic larvae of the anchor worm attack the fish with the same voracity as the adults, causing flashing and scratching long before the first adult worm can be seen. A male and female subadult will breed, the male spiraling off to die while the female lodges under a scale and begins to develop. By the time you see the first adult worm, considerable damage has been done to the skin and gills of the victim by the microscopic larval forms.

Lernea is more commonly encountered in the fall of the year. The most serious mortalities are encountered at the hatchery and grower operations. The problem is usually diagnosed and treated (or the afflicted fish have died) by the time the surviving fish reach their retail destinations.

Lernea elegans can be removed with forceps, and the wound treated with topical disinfectants such as mercurochrome or tincture of iodine. Until recently, I used Dimilin (diflubenzuron). Since 1998 I have used a sister compound to Dimilin called Program, which is actually lufenuron. See the Formulary for a more detailed discussion.

Organophosphates were at one time touted as the treatment of choice in the management of *Lernea*, but they can be harmful to fish and to humans, and with the newer remedies available, we can avoid their use.

Bacterial Infections

Bacterial pathogens of Goldfish are numerous. First, let's discuss what bacteria are. Bacteria are among the smallest microorganisms that are capable of independent life. Viruses, which are considerably smaller, are strands of renegade DNA and have to utilize the physical resources of other cells in which they live for their existence. Bacteria can live in or on cells and derive their nutrition from the media in which they live. Bacteria can spread from fish to fish with or without a physical vector or carrier. Some bacterial infections of fish, such as tuberculosis (*Mycobacterium tuberculosis piscium*), can even infect humans through open wounds.

Among the most common bacteria in Goldfish are *Aeromonas salmonicida*, *Pseudomonas fluorescens*, and *Flexobacter columnaris*.

Bacteria such as *Aeromonas* and *Pseudomonas* thrive on nitrogen, whether in fish tissues or from materials in the water. In a cubic centimeter of ordinary water inhabited by fish there may be more than ten million suspended bacteria, many of which are pathogens for fish. Yet, as long as the fish have no wounds or abrasions, an absence of parasites, little or no stress, good water quality, and good nutrition, the bacteria do not enter the fish. Take away any one of those favorable conditions, however, and a bacterial infection may occur.

Bacterial counts can skyrocket under circumstances where mulm and other detritus (dead fish, uneaten food) are allowed to accumulate in a system, reaching a point where the water becomes turbid with their sheer numbers. In cases when nitrogen-using bacteria (such as *Pseudomonas* and *Aeromonas*) have propagated due to the accumulation of nitrogenous byproducts and mulm, it is even more likely that some of these may eventually gain access to the fish and begin utilizing their tissues as a nitrogen source. In other words, when the filter becomes dirty and clogged with organic matter, pathogenic bacteria flourish within it, lying in wait for our fish to get stressed or be perforated by some parasite.

Bacteria kill fish primarily with four, often distinct, clinical pictures. The first is septicemia. Upon access to the fish's internal system, bacteria may disable the function of a vital organ—for example, the kidney. Such a fish would appear normal to the eye, but may die suddenly; or it may swell and die with almost equal speed. These types of losses—that is, losses without sores or rotten mouths—are often overlooked as bacterial infections, and so the owner does not take steps to eliminate the bacterial infection. Only autopsy will demonstrate the damaged internal organs and confirm the diagnosis.

A second manifestation of bacterial infection is furunculosis, or ulceration. Bacteria may create ever-expanding ulcers on the skin, fins, or mouth that allow for massive disruption in water and electrolyte balance. Subsequently, osmotic shock may result in the death of the fish. Most hobbyists can make this diagnosis because they can see the ravages of the bacterial activity, and thus they can take appropriate action. Fish with ulcers can easily worsen and progress to septicemia. Ulcers can perforate and kill the fish, or they may create such massive fluid-balance disorders that the fish perishes. Also, the bacteria may eventually leave the skin and spread to and destroy an internal organ.

So-called "toxic shock" is a third manifestation of bacterial infection. Certain bacteria (*Aeromonas* species) can produce toxins that circulate through the fish's bloodstream, causing hemorrhage, liquefaction of internal organs, and death. Such toxins have been

experimentally isolated, and when injected into fish, cause illness and death. This is another type of bacterial infection that causes death without external symptoms, making proper diagnosis difficult without performing a necropsy.

A fourth manifestation of bacterial infection is called bacterial gill disease. *Aeromonas* and its cousin *Pseudomonas* (as well as a myriad other bacteria including *Flexobacter*) can infect the gill arches, causing discrete and eventually large areas of tissue to die, making the gills looks blotchy with white streaks, and necrotic

BACTERIAL PATHOGENS AND NOTES

Aeromonas hydrophila complex (*punctata*)	Bacterial hemorrhagic septicemia, spring viremia of Carp, Carp erythrodermatitis, swim bladder disease, ulcer disease	Skin hemorrhages, pop eye, bloaters, pinecone disease, ulcers	Numerous strains of *Aeromonas* exist, making development of a vaccine very difficult to impossible
Aeromonas salmonicida	Ulcer disease in Goldfish	Infected fins, ulcers	In truth, most of what you'll culture is *Aeromonas hydrophila*
Edwardsiella sp.. (*E. ictaluri*: catfish) (*E. tarda*: others)	Septicemia, "hole in the head"	Gastroenteritis, septicemia, hole in the head, corkscrew swimming	A Channel Catfish disease
Flexibacter columnaris	Cottonmouth disease, cotton-wool disease, fin and tail rot	Skin lesions, swollen gills, fin and mouth erosions, ulcers, [microscopically: "haystack bacteria"]	People always think this is a fungus, because it looks "tufty." Rapidly fatal if in the gills, which look "bleached"
Pseudomonas (*flourescens*)	*Pseudomonas* septicemia	Septicemia, hemorrhagic septicemia, Ulcers	Not as common in our Goldfish as *Aeromonas*
Streptococcus ssp.		Skin hemorrhages, pop eye, bloaters, pinecone disease, ulcers, corkscrew swimming	Perhaps more common than originally thought. Responds to many of same treatments as *Aeromonas*
Mycobacterium fortuitum	Tuberculosis	Granulomatous lesions in internal organs, non healing ulcers, pop eye, wasting, fading color, and "broken back"	Brought out of control by stress. Spread by cannibalism. Can be transmitted to humans. Functionally untreatable

areas. The damage to the gill tissue kills the fish, usually within seventy-two hours of the first clinical symptoms of illness.

No single bacterial pathogen is always the cause of bacterial gill disease. The fish usually die "suddenly," but careful examination of other Goldfish in the collection often demonstrates fish affected with varying stages of gill damage. Fish detected early on can be saved with injections of the appropriate antibiotics.

Bacterial infections can be expected in any fish or group of fish which has suffered the stress of shipping, fasting, wintertime temperatures, chilling, overheating, crowding, parasitism, trauma during breeding or handling, or poor sanitation or nutrition.

All of these problems must be corrected if you are to have any luck recovering fish from bacterial infections.

A good first step in managing bacterial infection in a tank is to divide the collection into smaller numbers to reduce the stressful effects of crowding. This also makes it easier to maintain perfect water quality and low bacterial counts in the water. Then the more pathogen-specific therapies can be undertaken.

Let's review the many forms that bacterial infections can take and how we can eradicate them.

BACTERIAL GILL DISEASE

Whenever a Goldfish starts behaving abnormally, examine its gills. Check all (or a sample) of the fish in the system, and look for obvious discoloration, white patches, streaks, or decomposing areas in the gill arches. The gills of fish that have died from bacterial gill disease are red, with patches of rotten tissue. Sometimes there will be streaks through the gill tissue, not around the arch. If you find these symptoms, start by checking your water quality. Your fish may be suffering from what I call "environmental gill disease"—that is, poor water quality. Test for pH and levels of ammonia, nitrite, and nitrate, and correct any less than ideal conditions. The two most common causes of bacterial gill disease are low dissolved oxygen and overcrowding. These two conditions are more likely to cause bacterial gill disease than any particular bacteria.

If and only if the water quality is good, you should probably interpret the poor gill condition as a bacterial infection, and make the further assumption that a parasite has caused this condition. Examine, diagnose, and treat the parasite with a non-stressful regimen. Salt is a good example of a medication that will curb many parasites without stressing the fish unacceptably; if the parasite is flukes, use Droncit, which does not stress the fish.

Next, treat for the gill disease with antibiotic injec-

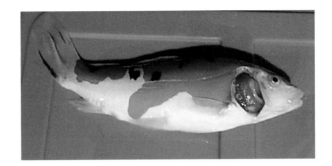

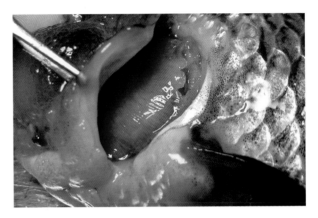

NECROSCOPY OF A KOI WITH BACTERIAL GILL DISEASE.

tions or water treatments (such as furazone green), separately or together. Chloramine T may be effective in the treatment of this condition and can be recommended for larger groups of fish or where injection is impractical. Chloramine T may also be used as a valuable adjunct to injection. See the Formulary for its use.

BODY SORES

Body sores are large red sores that may start as a red patch of scales. The scales can peel off revealing a hole that exposes muscle and flesh.

Swab body sores with hydrogen peroxide or potassium permanganate as described in the Formulary. Salt the tank to a concentration of 0.3% to reduce the osmotic pressure on the sores and stimulate the slime coat. Inject these fish with an antibiotic such as Azactam,

Amikacin, or a combination of the two at full dose, and make sure the water quality remains perfect, with zero nitrates.

It is important to be able to recognize healing sores. Some hobbyists expect a wound to heal immediately

after an injection, but in fact this takes weeks. The perceived failure of the wound to close in a day or two can result in over treatment and the death of the fish. A healing wound typically progresses through a series of recognizable stages. On the day the wound is diagnosed, it is "steak" red and bloody. Skin tags and strands hang from wound edges. This is the time to scrub the wound with hydrogen peroxide or potassium permanganate on a cotton ball, begin injection therapy, and place the fish in a 0.3% salt solution.

With any success, by the second day the wound is maroon or almost blue-red. The edges of the wound are cleaner and look whiter. Leave the wound alone and give the fish its second injection. Encourage the fish to eat some richly nutritious food such as krill. On the third day, the wound is basically the same except it is a bit smaller and the edges are characteristically white and smooth. By the fourth day, the wound is a dark pink. Give the third injection. On the sixth day of treatment, the edge of the wound edge is definitely white and closing in on the center, which is a dark to medium pink. Because the healing progresses, only three injections are given. More would be called for if results are not forthcoming. Remember, "not worse" is sometimes all you want over a twenty-four-hour period. On day eight, the wound is pale pink and ringed by smooth white scar tissue.

FIN ROT
The fins of a fish with fin rot begin to look milky or cloudy, and then the tips whiten and rot off. In treating fin rot, we must be careful to avoid the use of highly caustic medications such as potassium permanganate or formalin. The "burns" caused by these caustic chemicals will only further harm the fish. Perfect water quality, a 0.3% salt solution, and nutritious food will

usually check this condition. If the fin rot is advanced and the fish is near death, treatment with furazone green and injections of Baytril or chloramphenicol may help. Refer to the Formulary for dosage regimens.

MOUTH ROT
Mouth rot is often initiated by a parasitic attack, so check for parasites first. Bacterially caused mouth rot occurs when fish in overcrowded tanks rub their noses against the sides of the aquarium or objects in the tank. The mouth appears reddish, as if the fish were wearing lipstick. Soon the lips begin to separate from the fish and strands of tissue begin to detach. Eventually the mouth may collapse on itself, leaving only a jagged hole as the oral cavity.

The first step when mouth rot appears is to carefully check water quality. A good first step is to swab oral lesions with hydrogen peroxide, using a cotton ball. Injection with Baytril or another suitable antimicrobial and removal of the affected fish to more spacious facilities will often save it.

POP EYE
The fish's eye (or eyes) protrude from the socket. Initially, they may bulge only slightly, later appearing completely popped out on what appear to be fleshy bags of water. The protruding eye is often picked off by a tank mate or caught on tank décor. Pop Eye is usually a sign of grave bacterial or tuberculosis infection behind the eye. Sometimes it can be caused by trauma. In any case, perfect water quality (including zero nitrates) and an injection of Baytril may be warranted. Most water treatments will not reach the affected area behind the eye and will only compromise the beneficial filter bacteria. A 0.3% salt solution will help reduce the osmotic pressure on the fish and may help the eyes return to normal.

RAISED SCALES
The appearance of areas of raised scales can be a precursor to bacterial infection and body sores. It is also a sign in many cases of a localized infection of *Costia*. The first step is to check all water parameters. If they are perfect, then a salt solution of 0.3% to 0.6% may correct this sign, but swabbing the area with hydrogen peroxide is also a useful adjunct. If the scales in the raised area began to shed, revealing sores, inject the fish with Baytril according to the Formulary.

RED BELLY
This refers to abdominal swelling with a redness showing through the skin. By the time this condition can be

detected, cure is impossible. Any fish exposed to the sick fish should be injected with an antibiotic such as Azactam, Amikacin, or a combination of the two at full dose (see the Formulary). Add salt to the aquarium water to make a 0.3% concentration.

This condition, like all bacterial infections, has probably been triggered by parasites. Perform a microscopic biopsy and treat any parasites you find.

RED BLOTCHES

These are a precursor to red body sores and should be treated as sores. First check the water-quality and correct it as necessary. Add salt to the aquarium water to make a 0.3% concentration. You should examine carefully for flukes and other parasites and treat them if diagnosed.

SUDDEN DEATH

A single sudden death in a large group of fish can be a sign of a chronic water-quality problem. Perform the full battery of water tests before jumping to any conclusions. A careful necropsy may show signs of bacterial infection. Examine the swim bladder and the gills in particular. In the gills you would see clear evidence of bacterial infection with the appearance of jagged or "moth-eaten" holes in the red gill tissue. Sometimes bacterial infections in the gills appear simply as white streaks through the gill filaments. If you see lesions like these in the gill tissue, perform antimicrobial therapies at once, because other fish in the same tank have been exposed to both the pathogen and the predisposing stressors that contributed to the death of the first fish. Bacterial infections in the swim bladder may appear as bright red blotches (hemorrhages) in the air-sac wall. The air sac appears as if a red dye bomb exploded inside. This is a classic sign of bacterial infection and when death is very rapid, it is sometimes your only forensic clue.

Fungal Infections

Fungal infections are relatively common in Goldfish. They are only seen in fish that are immune compromised or which have areas of tissues that have been damaged and left exposed to fungal invasion. Fungal infections usually appear as small to large tufts of white cottony material on the skin and fins of affected fish, but visual appearance is an unreliable means of diagnosing fungus because the naked eye cannot distinguish between *Columnaris* bacterial infections, *Epistylis* parasitic infections, and fungal infections. For accurate diagnosis, a microscope is required.

There are several fungal organisms that infect

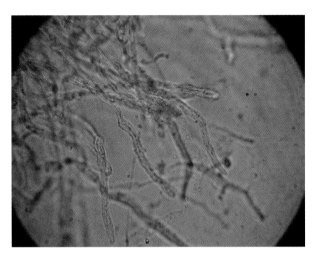

COLUMNARIS UNDER THE MICROSCOPE.

Goldfish. The most common fungal pathogen of the skin is *Saprolegnia*. Under the microscope it has a very characteristic appearance, resembling clumps of hundreds of coarse strands of hair. *Branchiomyces* is an aggressive gill fungus that kills fish by destroying their gill tissue.

BRANCHIOMYCES

Branchiomyces species compromises the blood supply to gill tissue and the affected areas die and slough off leaving gaping holes in the gill arches. The fungus relies on high organic loads, high nitrate levels, crowding, and heat to spread and kill fish.

Fish afflicted with *Branchiomyces* will linger at the surface and die in three days, sometimes one by one, starting with the smallest fish. When you examine the fish, you will notice the gills are eroded and there are large, easily visible areas of dead tissue in the gills. Using special stains, star-shaped fungal elements are visible under the microscope, but treatment is so simple that ordinary visual examination is sufficient.

Cool water will slow the fungal infection down and save fish lives. *Branchiomyces* requires warm water to thrive and is most common when fish are crowded, there are high organic loads, and the water is warm. Cool water carries more oxygen and slows down the metabolism of the fish. Increasing aeration without increasing current (which will force the fish to be more active and therefore speed up their metabolism to require more oxygen) may be life saving.

Formalin is very effective in treating *Branchiomyces* (see the Formulary).

SAPROLEGNIA

Saprolegnia species and similar external fungal infections occur under two circumstances. When Goldfish are poorly handled, chilled, and stressed, they can

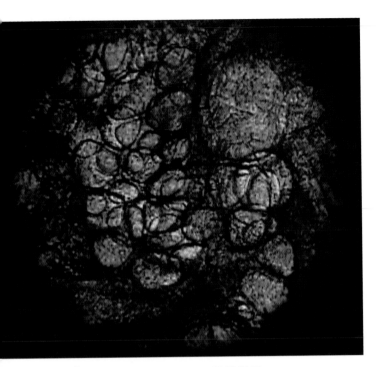

LYMPHOCYSTIS UNDER THE MICROSCOPE.

develop large areas of fungal growth, causing inactivity, loss of appetite, weak swimming motions, and overall lethargy. This kind of fungal attack is seen only in fish that have suffered such poor treatment that their immune system is depressed or completely annihilated. The fish isolate themselves and eventually die. Fish with fungal lesions that are also lethargic or obviously sick should be treated with methylene blue or potassium permanganate at 2 PPM. Use methylene blue as an eight-hour bath followed by a partial water change daily until the lesions subside. If you treat with potassium permanganate at 2 PPM, treat every third day, making sure to eliminate any potassium permanganate remaining in the water after each treatment with hydrogen peroxide (as described in the entry on potassium permanganate in the Formulary). No more than two or three treatments following this regimen should be necessary.

Relatively harmless fungal lesions can also develop at the site of a previous trauma. In these cases the fish is decidedly energetic, eating, and the lesions are restricted to those areas that were previously damaged. These fish may benefit from direct topical application of methylene blue, malachite green, or potassium permanganate paste. Repeated water treatments are not needed because this second manifestation of fungal attack will subside on its own.

Remedies for fungal infections depend upon the degree of fungal spread. If the fish has minor fungal lesions but is eating and acting normally, it may benefit most by minimal handling, impeccable water quality, and better nutrition. Fish with fungal lesions that are also letharigic and inactive will do well in warmer water—about seventy-eight degrees—offered enticing foods such as crushed freeze-dried krill, and treatment with furazone green, methylene blue, or malachite green. See the Formulary for proper dosages and regimens.

Viral Pathogens

Viral infections in Goldfish have recently taken a turn for the worse. At one time, the most serious virus affecting Goldfish was the lymphocystis virus, which causes skin tumors. In most instances, these lesions disappear when treated with acriflavine or, given enough time, go away on their own. Carp pox behaved in much the same way. More recently, researchers have proven that there is an infectious hematopoeitic necrosis (IHN) virus in Goldfish. This virus will no doubt be seen increasingly as more and more ornamental fish are shipped around the world.

IHN VIRUS

The IHN virus is well known in several species of fish but has only been reported in Goldfish on a few occasions. In all instances, the symptoms were similar: the fish became listless and died, and even before their death, dissection revealed softening and necrosis in the spleen, kidney, pancreas, and intestine. Almost all infected fish died. This disease is diagnosed based on the absence of other pathologies and the presence of the herpes virus associated with lesions. The virus can only be identified through electron microscopy.

At present there is no effective treatment.

LYMPHOCYSTIS VIRUS

Lymphocystis virus appears as a white, crusty dermatosis on the skin. The viral eruptions usually originate at the edge of the fins, but almost as often on the skin. The virus infects the epidermal cells and causes them to swell. Under the microscope we see huge, frothy looking cells with a tan or amber color. This is a diagnostic feature distinguishing lymphocystis from carp pox, which also causes warty eruptions in the skin but which does not cause the cells in these eruptions to become huge or oddly shaped.

Lymphocystis is weakly transmissible, and it is not common to witness epidemics of lymphocystis. It can be transmitted by direct contact of the virus or virus-infected cells with wounds, and ingestion of virus particles or particles of infected cells from lesions will also transmit the condition.

Lymphocystis can be treated with acriflavine baths. Place the fish in a bath prepared according to the manufacturer's instructions or those provided in the Formulary and leave it there for six to eight hours per day (with adequate aeration). The fish may be returned to the main system between treatments. When you remove the fish from the bath, the lymphocystis lesions will be stained a pale green. Shortly thereafter, they will regress and disappear.

PAPILLOMATOUS LESIONS

Papillomatous lesions, or warts, are often caused by the cyprinid herpes, or carp pox virus. Almost everything that was reported above about the lymphocystis virus is also true for the carp pox virus. It, too, is weakly transmissible and poses no threat to Goldfish life. The most commonly reported therapy for carp pox (once the condition has been clearly distinguished from lymphocystis) is a prolonged bath in water of at least seventy-four and preferably eighty to eighty-two degrees. Reportedly, the recovery rate is improved with a salt solution of 0.3%.

CHOCOLATE BLUE TELESCOPES.

Chapter 4

Environ-

mental

and Other

Threats to

Goldfish

Health

RED-AND-BLACK CELESTIAL POMPOM.

Goldfish health is affected by far more than pathogens. Indeed, their very environment is often the greatest threat to their survival. This is especially true in new, unbalanced systems in which the new load of fish and the relative lack of beneficial bacteria create poor water quality. Perhaps the most important aspect of Goldfish care is the management of water quality.

Ammonia Poisoning

Ammonia is directly caustic to fish surfaces, fins, and gills. Redness in the skin, excess mucus production, depressed appetite, clamped fins, and lethargy are all seen in fish living in ammonia-rich waters. These symptoms may also be indications of other kinds of water-quality deterioration or of parasitism, however, so accurate water testing with an ammonia test kit is crucial for distinguishing between ammonia poisoning and other illnesses.

Ammonia is a special threat in aquariums that are newly set up and have not yet established a colony of beneficial bacteria. Ammonia accumulation is a main culprit in what is commonly called "New Tank Syndrome" and is one of the leading killers of fish. Once *Nitrosomonas* has proliferated to adequate levels, the ammonia levels decline and the nitrite levels increase. A cycled tank should have zero ammonia levels.

Remove ammonia by large water changes—up to 70%—and correct the situation by making sure you have a functioning biological filter that can handle the biological load of your system. You may have to reduce stocking levels and feeding as well.

Nitrite Poisoning

Nitrite poses a threat to the fish in two ways. First, it directly irritates the skin and gills, contributing to the cumulative effects of stress on the fishes' immune system. Second, nitrite is absorbed through the gills passively and binds with the red blood cells in the fishes' bloodstream, making them unable to carry oxygen. The condition is called met-hemoglobinemia, and it is diagnosed by a brownish colored blood. If the condition is suspected in a large system with expendable fish, a very sick fish can be decapitated and the blood oozing from the large vessel under the spinal column can be observed. Fish that have been killed by high nitrite levels often have widely flared gills upon death.

There are many remedies for nitrite poisoning. The first order of business is to decrease production of this compound by suspending or reducing feedings until the nitrites abate. If there is a lot of debris or mulm in the system, this nitrogen-rich material should also be reduced or removed. Large water changes will also work well to reduce the load of nitrite on the system, but a 10% to 20% water change in a system that is overloaded with ammonia or nitrite is insignificant. I recommend up to a 70% water change.

The best remedy for nitrite intoxication, once the water change has been executed and feeding is reduced, is the application of salt at 0.3%. This is somewhat paradoxical, since salt slows down the activity of *Nitrobacter* bacteria, but the salt also blocks the passive absorption of nitrite across the fishes' gill membranes. While the effect is not permanent, neither is the presence of nitrite, so a 0.3% salt solution is useful to carry fish through a temporary nitrite rise.

Nitrate Poisoning

Nitrate was at one time considered to have no effect on fish health up to levels as high as 300 to 400 PPM, but we now know that this is not true. High nitrates can cause the blood vessels in the fins and skin to dilate, and this makes the skin look streaky and the fins appear to have varicose veins. The fish may also show extreme reluctance to swim about. The most significant effect is on the immune system. Even low-level nitrate accumulations are immune suppressive. Fish in high nitrate levels will be sickly and prone to infections of all kinds, and their appetite is negatively affected. Always check the nitrate level when your fish are suffering from an illness you cannot diagnose. Reducing the nitrate level to below 40 to 50 PPM will often result in the complete recovery of the fish and a return to the typical level of "playful" activity.

A high nitrate level has been suggested as a cause of "flipover" disease, in which the Goldfish flips upside down and cannot right itself permanently. This is discussed in detail in chapter 6.

Nitrates can be a problem in aquariums where plants aren't grown, algae is inhibited, excessively cleaned off, or killed by the application of a herbicide. Without plants or a healthy carpet of algae, nitrates will accumulate and start slowly killing the fish. In my experience, levels over 200 PPM are toxic. Nitrate accumulations can be corrected with regular water changes and by encouraging the growth of a healthy carpet of algae on the tank sides.

Derangements of pH

The signs of a pH derangement will proceed according to the following steps. Initially, as the pH begins to decline, you will notice that when at rest, the fish tend to remain near the surface and their activity levels decline. As the pH drops a little lower, their appetite suffers. Shortly after this, as the pH drops another point and nears 6.0, you'll see a milky skin on the fish. As the pH drops even lower, the fish lose slime in strands as their skin is burned by the increasingly acidic water. The activity level of the fish will be very depressed and they will either descend to the bottom to die or gasp at the surface. A further drop will result in death.

Begin emergency treatment for a tank that has experienced a pH crash by removing all dead fish. Then apply the recommended dose of commercial pH buffer. The accepted truism for decades has been that you should never change the pH of a system by more than one-quarter point per day, but in this case the most successful approach is to raise the pH into the normal range as quickly as possible.

To prevent a pH crash, check your pH and total alkalinity regularly and, if you have total alkalinity below 30 PPM, use a buffer.

Oxygen Deprivation

Fish gasping at the surface of your tank are not necessarily a sign of low dissolved oxygen; the fishes' gills may be partially destroyed by a pH crash, other water quality problems, or parasites. Dissolved oxygen can be tested with chemical tests.

There are numerous remedies for low levels of dissolved oxygen. We can cool the aquarium with a fresh influx of water, and even add ice to the aquarium during a short-term crisis. Shading the water in ponds or removing the aquarium from a window location will reduce the temperature and help keep dissolved oxygen levels up. We can reduce the plants in the system to prevent depression of dissolved levels of oxygen at night. We can increase surface exposure of the water for gas exchange with an air stone or a water pump moving water at the surface. We can decrease feeding amounts and intervals in order to decrease the oxygen demand of fish, which can double for the first few hours after eating. Hydrogen peroxide may also be used to raise dissolved oxygen levels. To do this, prepare a 3% USP solution of hydrogen peroxide in a bottle with a sprayer head.[4] Use this to provide one pump or squirt (about 1.5 milliliters) per gallon of water. Direct the stream below the water's surface and do not repeat for several hours. Hydrogen peroxide takes thirty minutes to work. Do not add more than the prescribed amount or you will burn the fish.

Temperature Extremes

Temperature may be a threat to Goldfish because temperature effects the ability of water to carry dissolved oxygen. Warm water will simultaneously increase the fishes' metabolism and oxygen requirement. As mentioned earlier, warmer water carries less oxygen. Therefore, while more oxygen is needed, less is available.

Temperature is also a threat to Goldfish when they are left outside over the winter in temperate climes. There is considerable debate over the proper temperature at which we should maintain our Goldfish.

4. USP stands for United States Pharmacopeia, an organization that establishes and disseminates medicinal standards.

Venerable tomes insist that Goldfish are a cold-water fish and warn against keeping them in heated tanks, though actually the temperatures at which most tropical fish are kept are ideal for Goldfish. Goldfish will flourish in water occasionally as warm as one hundred two degrees if it is properly aerated. I have customarily kept Goldfish of all varieties in water as warm as ninety during the summer, and I maintain that warmer water is actually better for Goldfish. My fish have shown superior growth and appetite, and the biological filter has performed best at temperatures in the mid to high seventies.

I have long maintained that fancy Goldfish with round bodies do not thrive as well if left outside over winter. I have found that the smaller specimens of these varieties—Ranchu, Ryukin, and Oranda—do fine for the first several winters, while they are still small, but as they grow larger and rounder flip over and die with increasing incidence when exposed to winter temperatures. Hobbyists who keep their fish outdoors with water temperatures near the freezing point may contest this, but, based on my clinical experience, I disagree.

I am aware of many fish that have lived through such winters, as far north as Canada, but I am also aware that the high number of Goldfish that are brought to me for treatment of flipover disorder and other maladies arrive not in the middle of summer but in the late fall and spring of the year. Many times, merely placing the fish in warmed hospital facilities preparatory to surgery obviates the need for surgery altogether.

My point is not that the majority of your fancy Goldfish will fall ill or die if left outdoors, but that there will be a higher incidence of illness among these fish than if they were maintained at balmy temperatures year round.

Some collectors and breeders maintain that it is the rise in temperature from late winter to spring that stimulates the spawning reflex, and there is a grain of truth to this, but the rise need only be a few degrees. I have successfully spawned Ranchus with a rise from sixty-eight degrees (indoors) in midwinter to the high seventies by mid-spring. Increased photoperiod is also an important element, but there is no need for you to drop the temperature of your fish to below fifty degrees, and they will be generally stronger and healthier if you do not do so.

Other Threats to Goldfish Health

Goldfish are certainly prone to diseases and disorders from external, environmental threats, but what happens when a fish is "messed up" all by itself—for example, when a Bubble Eye Goldfish gets its bubble sucked off in the filter intake? In this section, we will discuss some physical abnormalities that arise from non-infectious causes.

BUBBLE EYE DAMAGE

Bubble Eyes are especially prone to having their sacs sucked into a filter intake. While this is disappointing, the sack will usually grow back if water quality is excellent. The first step of treatment is to Bubble-Eye proof the tank. You may have to resort to a sponge or undergravel (NOT reverse flow, however) filter, probably the only types that a Bubble Eye cannot somehow or other hurt itself with.

Bubble Eyes are also subject to infections in which the fluid inside the eye sac becomes infected. The sac may appear red or, later, a cloudy, opaque white. For such fish, impeccable water quality is imperative. The infection usually does not respond to injectable antibiotics, but I nevertheless recommend them, together with perfect water. I have had excellent survival rates with this treatment. Successful treatment is indicated when the general whitish color disappears and seems to shrink down into a tiny white ball, which never entirely disappears.

CAPS AND HEADGROWTH

Orandas and other capped varieties of Goldfish sometimes develop white pustules on their headgrowth. Many people are deeply concerned about this condition, and still more will treat the fish with caustic remedies, compounding the fishes' stress. In most cases such capped fish have extensive headgrowth. The fish will usually be well fed on a variety of foods, and well kept in general. Still, there will be small white tufts of "fluff" nestled deep in the head cap. In some cases, there are as many as four to five little spots of "infection."

A microscopic biopsy of these tufts of white material reveals an abundant number of red and white blood cells. There are no fungal elements and usually no bacteria are detected. This common phenomenon lacks a verifiable explanation, but the current theory is that during the most active phases of the development of the headgrowth, there is probably a deficiency of blood flow to supply the increasing mass of tissue and the crevices in the headgrowth show this strain in the form of a low-grade infection or even avascular necrosis (death of some of the tissue because of deficient blood supply). Goldfish with headgrowth pimples but that are otherwise doing well should be closely observed but not medicated. Of course check to be certain that your water quality is optimal, but do not medicate for this condition.

If you are concerned that the pimples in the head cap are more than just "growing pains," look for lethargy or lack of appetite, fin clamping, or redness spreading under the pimple in the headgrowth. If these symptoms are present, inject an antibiotic intraperitoneally, offer the best, most tempting foods, and supply perfect water quality.

Another peculiar "disorder" of Goldfish is the growth of the cap over the eyes. Some Chinese and Japanese breeders even select intentionally for this extreme headgrowth. In most instances, this does not affect the fish. Blind fish can apprehend food as effectively as their sighted companions. However, it is true that sighted fish are more active and interact more with tank mates.

Headgrowth covering the eyes can be corrected with surgery, and I've had great success and achieved very pleasing cosmetic results. For details see the Surgical Procedures section starting on page 80.

ELECTROCUTION

If you are using any electrical equipment—pumps, heaters, lights—in or around your tank, you may at some time have a short or "leak" that sends an electric current through the tank water. Electrocution may cause a suddenly kinked back in fish. If you discover a fish or two in your system with a suddenly broken back, call an electrician to check your tanks and equipment for shorts, leaks, or ground faults. Obviously, this is a hazard not only to your fish but to you as well.

An "electrocuted" fish will display a characteristic triad of symptoms that are not customarily seen as a result of dietary or genetic deficiencies: (1) it loses the ability to remain upright in some instances; (2) it loses buoyancy; and (3) it may straighten at rest but kinks again when trying to propel itself through the water.

Fish that have been electrocuted can survive if fed with sinking foods that they can eat without swimming to reach. They should also be separated from competi-

tion at feeding time. If the fish survives, it may return to almost 70% of normalcy: while it may swim and eat competitively, its physical agility will be impaired.

For other causes of kinked backs, see "Symptoms and Solutions," chapter 6.

JUMPING OUT

When a Goldfish decides to end it all and makes the leap to the floor, all is not necessarily lost; there are several factors that may dramatically extend its survival until found. The fish will fare better if the ambient temperatures are cool. It will survive longer if it lands on a nonabsorbent surface, and if it carries considerable water with it to the floor, it may last up to an hour. The longest I have been able to verify survival of a fish out of water is approximately twelve hours. The fish in question departed a garden pond on a cool fall night and wriggled down a hillside into a muddy drainage area where it lay, encrusted in moist soil, until morning.

When you find a jumper, do not give up on it unless the skin cracks when flexed; the fish is completely desiccated; the eyes are concave instead of the usual convex appearance; the pupil is gray (which suggests death came and went more than four hours ago); or part of the fish is missing (and your cat appears to be sated). If there is any possibility that the fish is alive, you may attempt the following routine. Immediately place the fish in cool water from the main aquarium. Gently rinse off any debris that is sticking to the fish, but do not rub aggressively or you may tear the skin of smaller fish. Pry the gill covers open and ensure the passage of water over the gill tissue. Though the gill covers have been "glued" shut by the fishes' mucus, you may find, to your amazement, that they have remained quite red and wet.

At this point, replace the now dirty and debris-filled tank water with clean tank water. Aerate the water very well and place the fish in an upright horizontal position

USE DEXAMETHASONE IF:	DO NOT USE DEXAMETHASONE IF:
Gill excursions are rare	Gill excursions are regular and obvious
The fish is stiff	The fish is flexible and upright
The fish has been out of water long enough to become "sticky" dry	The fish was out of the water for only a minute or two
The fish is inverted/lateral and near death	The fish is upright, reasonably reactive
The fish is cold-shocked	The fish is merely cold
The fish was healthy before the shock	The fish had a chronic illness or weight loss

in front of the air stone or source of water circulation. Do not try to blow water into the oral cavity. The goal is to provide the freshest, best-aerated water possible if the fish attempts any respiration. Very valuable fish can be placed in a bag of tank water filled with pure oxygen, but this very effective method is not usually available to the general hobbyist.

An injection of dexamethasone (see the Formulary) has been shown to save a considerable number of jumpers and some consider it mandatory for the success of their recovery. The chart on the facing page provides a guideline for the use of dexamethasone.

If the fish survives, you will probably find that a considerable portion of its fins disintegrates. The time spent out of water will have dehydrated the fins and they will die back to the last points of viable blood flow. No treatment is usually necessary, and the fish will probably be permanently disfigured. If sores develop on the body, it may be due to the dexamethasone, which is strongly immune suppressive. Aggressive antibiotic therapy will probably successfully repel a bacterial attack and salvage the fish.

TRAUMA

Goldfish may receive wounds from other fish, from their own breeding enthusiasm, and from ornamentation in the aquarium. Pond fish may suffer wounds from the beaks and claws of various predators. The first step in the management of wounds is to establish the cause and to eliminate it whenever possible. If another fish is the cause, remove it; if the fish are bumping into sharp rocks or tank decorations, remove them. Next, assess the condition of the fish. If the lesion is deep or exposes muscle, give the fish an antibiotic injection. Do not apply antibiotics to the main system, as they will harm the beneficial bacteria in your biological filter. (This is true of all antibiotics regardless of manufacturers' claims.)

If the lesion is superficial and the fish is otherwise very healthy and will eat, then my recommendation is not to treat the fish or the wound with anything, but watch the wound closely. Healing is always accompanied by a decline in the redness of the lesion. An increase in the redness of the wound is evidence that an antibiotic injection is needed.

The condition of the water is actually as important as the condition of the fish. If your fish suffers a wound in water that is less than optimal in quality, it is unlikely to heal. In fact, without good water, most minor wounds will worsen. If impeccable water quality is maintained, most wounds will heal on their own.

Chapter 5

The

Formulary

RED-AND-WHITE TELESCOPE.

This section provides information for the correct use of medications. If you do not understand this information, do not risk using it. In addition, if you are unwilling to assume sole liability for its use (or misuse), then this section is not for you.

Take the time to learn about the diseases that can afflict your fish and the medications used to treat them. Using medications correctly is the key to safe treatment. A failure to understand the properties and effects of medications and why you are using them is a guarantee that you will harm your fish and your chances of successful treatment. A "shotgun therapy," dosing your fish with a series of medications in the hope that one of them will work, is rarely successful, and if ever used at all should be reserved for inexpensive fish of little sentimental value. Learning the "why" of fish diseases and mastering the

"how" of their diagnosis and treatment is a far better approach to fish medicine.

It is also important to know when to give up. When a fish is inverted and hardly breathing, it should be put down. When the fish has not eaten for three weeks and you can't or won't feed it with a tube, it should be humanely dispatched. When a fish has had three different courses of therapy and continues to lose weight, maybe it's a hopeless case. Some diseases, such as tuberculosis, cannot be diagnosed without sacrificing the fish.

It is inhumane to allow a fish to suffer without hope of cure or recovery, and in such cases the compassionate hobbyist may want to choose euthanasia. When we euthanize a fish we are exercising a special human capacity to recognize and put an end to needless misery. My preference when euthanizing a fish is to place it in a bowl or bag of fresh water, preferably from the main system in which the fish lives. The bag is placed in a darkened freezer, and left alone. Do not alarm the fish by opening the freezer over and over to check on it. Within a few hours, the water will drop in temperature, as will the fish's body temperature, and it will die. This process is widely reported to be painless and not to cause anxiety or stress.

Sometimes, on the other hand, doing nothing is best. I once had a consultation about a fish that had been very healthy but was sucked up to a filter intake. A huge hole was pulled out of the body. Meat was exposed and the fish bled prodigiously. The fish was in terrible condition, but upon questioning the owner, I found that it was being kept in impeccable water conditions, and there were no other fish to disturb it. When the owner asked me what to do, I told him to do nothing.

"Do nothing?" came the incredulous reply.

"Nothing but check your water quality, hold the water temperature in the mid-seventies and maybe salt to 0.3% to reduce the osmotic pressure at the hole," I said.

"All right," said the owner, with a shrug.

Much later, he sent me a photograph of the fish, completely recovered. The owner had taken my advice and done nothing. The fish was alive because it was healthy to begin with and the keeper did nothing to destabilize the fish or its environment.

Some hobbyists tend to do too much, and end up killing the fish. Perhaps a viable treatment performed in the morning has not resulted in dramatically improved condition by nightfall. The overzealous keeper becomes distraught and begins the destructive process of superimposed or successive (shotgun) treatments.

Sometimes when the treatment we've performed does not result in immediate recovery, the best approach is self-control. Many times—and this is what distinguishes a skilled professional—it is as important to recognize a condition of "not worse" as it is to recognize "better." It is also important to be satisfied sometimes with "not worse" and simply give the fish time to heal.

There are a few medications that, though they are available and have been used in the past, or even in some cases today, I strongly recommend not using. Alka Seltzer and quinaldine, for example, have been used as anesthetics, but Alka Seltzer actually suffocates fish in carbon dioxide to anesthetize them, and quinaldine usually causes liver failure and death several weeks after its use.

Various organophosphates (such as neguvon, dipterex, trichloracide, trichlorfon, malathion, fenthion, and masoten) have been used in the past for clearance of crustacean parasites, but these compounds are health and environmental hazards and, with safer treatments such as Program and Dimilin, there is no reason to risk their use.

Gentamycin is an antibiotic that has been used for bacterial diseases in the past, but hobbyists should avoid it unless there are no other alternatives, and if it is used, it should be used as sparingly as possible. It is too toxic and causes terminal nervous system disorders in a high percentage of fish.

Bath Treatments

Bath treatments have been used as a disease treatment since the earliest days of Goldfish culture. They are easy to carry out, and range from the very effective— such as salt for the treatment of ciliated parasites—to unreliable

RED LIONHEAD.

or even useless— such as the use of certain antibiotics or vitamins in baths. One of the biggest limitations with antibacterial bath treatments is that most of them harm the beneficial bacteria in the biological filter. A way to avoid this, which appears in several regimens given below, is to bypass the filter.

By bypassing the filter, you can spare the beneficial nitrifying bacteria from assault by the chemical that you are dosing with. This is impossible if you are employing an undergravel filter, which cannot be "shut off" from the water in the tank, but it works well with external filters.

If you are using a hang-on power filter, you can remove your bio-media to safe haven in a bowl of untreated tank water and keep the filter running. Some of the newer pressurized canister and bead filters have a bypass feature that allows water to continue to flow without diverting it through the bio-media. You can disconnect a standard wet-dry or canister filter from the aquarium and run it attached to a bucket of water or tank without fish. The filter bacteria will live as long as they have oxygen; without it, they will die off rapidly. In most cases, as long as your filter media remain wet in an open container, the bacteria will remain viable for at least twenty-four hours and, fortunately, few treatments last that long.

If you cannot bypass your biological media (as in the case of an undergravel filter) then you should exhaust all alternatives to the treatment first. Water-quality deterioration is probably more harmful than any parasite.

In addition, environmental variables, such as the amount of organic matter in the water, can make precise treatment with baths difficult. Still, they offer an easy, effective method in many cases, and I will attempt to describe some of the most effective and desirable treatments below.

ACRIFLAVINE

Description: Acriflavine is a powerful dye.
Uses: Commonly used for treating ciliated protozoans of several types, fungus infections, lymphocytes, *Oodinium*, and *Hexamita*.
Dosage and Dosing: For short-term baths (up to a few hours) use 5 milligrams per gallon. For treating lymphocytes or for baths longer than a few hours, use 200 milligrams per 10 gallons or follow the manufacturer's instructions.
Precautions: None.

CHLORAMINE T

Description: Chloramine T is an abbreviation for n-chloro-para-toluene sulfonamide, a quaternary ammonium compound that has been around for years, and was at one time most commonly used for bacterial gill

disease. It is available in powder form, and also as a product called BGDX, produced by Argent Labs.
Uses: Chloramine T is primarily used to control bacterial gill disease and flukes.
Dosage and Dosing: In a 1989 study by Dr. G.L. Bullock, researchers treated fish with 6 PPM and 9 PPM and found that the fish in both groups were not adversely affected.[5] At the 6 PPM dose the bacterial gill disease persisted and killed more fish. The research concluded that doses around 10 PPM were preferable to lower doses. When the studies were replicated using 8.5 PPM, bacterial gill disease was controlled in all cases, a second treatment was required if the condition was not diagnosed at an early stage and crowding and low oxygen levels were not simultaneously corrected.

Use chloramine T as a disinfectant control of bacterial gill disease at from 10 to 20 PPM daily, with a 50% to 60% water change at the six- to eight-hour mark after application. Bypass the filter before applying the chloramine T. After the water change, resume filtration until the dosage on the following day. Normally, I repeat this treatment for three days and then stop. Some folks have gone on to perform five and six treatments, but chloramine T dissociates into a powerful acid and chlorine, and this will eventually cause irritation and redness of the skin of treated fish. Knowing when to suspend treatment is one of the keys to success with this compound.

A primary factor influencing dosage of chloramine T is the alkalinity of the system, which is tied to the pH. Researchers found increased tolerance and safety with chloramine T in water that was higher in total alkalinity and pH. These differences are noted in the charts opposite.

In an experiment by Dr. Jill Spangenberg at the University of California at Davis, chloramine T was tested on Goldfish and Koi with flukes.[6] The study used up to 20 PPM for four hours, which was easily tolerated by the fish. The treatments were done at forty-eight-hour intervals and achieved control of adult flukes in two treatments.

Hobbyists and others who treated Goldfish at 10 to 20 PPM have reported good control of adult flukes using this protocol. However, a third treatment is required at the six- to eight-day point. This will intercept and kill any emerging flukes that might be seeking a host. If done too late, these new adults will reproduce and recontaminate the environment with viable eggs and possibly with embryos again.

When treating fish with chloramine T at 20 PPM for

5. Bullock, G. L. and R. L. Herman, "Efficacy Studies with Chloramine T for Control of Bacterial Gill Disease," Fish Health Section/AFS & Eastern Fish Health Workshop, July 17–20, 1989.
6. Spangenberg, Jill V., "Investigation of the Safety and Efficacy of Chloramine-T in the Treatment of External Fluke Infestations."

Day	Amount	Duration	Cautions
One	10 PPM – soft water 15 PPM – hard water Soft = <50 PPM TA Hard = >50 PPM TA	6–8 hours, please observe	Bypass filter. Change 50–60% water and dechlorinate afterwards.
Two	10–15 PPM	6–8 hours, please observe	Bypass filter. Change 50–60% water and dechlorinate afterwards.
Three	10–15 PPM	6–8 hours, please observe	Bypass filter. Change 50–60% water and dechlorinate afterwards. Salt to 0.3% now.
Five or Six	10–15 PPM	6–8 hours, please observe	Bypass filter. Change 50–60% water and dechlorinate afterwards. Reapply lost salt to 0.3%

eight hours every day, I noted some reddening of the skin at the third treatment. I am sure that the best results will be had with the treatment recommendations in the charts.

If you are using Argent's BGDX, follow the manufacturer's instructions.

Precautions: Overuse of chloramine T can cause caustic burns to fish surfaces. If these occur, discontinue the chloramine T regimen and treat your tank with Aquarium Pharmaceuticals Stress Coat.

Chloramine T has profound effects on filtration. If you cannot prevent exposure of your filter media to this compound, do not use it.

COPPER

Description: Ionic copper (free-form copper) is the only form of copper that kills bacteria and parasites. Using pure ionic copper is dangerous because too much ionic copper can also kill fish. Copper is available in several compounds. In each compound, copper is found in different forms. For example, in pure copper sulfate, the copper is in its almost pure, ionic form and is rapidly available to exert its effect on organisms in the environment. In other copper solutions, the copper is bound (chelated) to other molecules that inhibit or slow its availability. This makes these copper solutions safer to use because they make the ionic copper available to the environment at a slower, more controlled rate. Of the copper-containing products available in the trade, I recommend the brand Cupramine, produced by Seachem Labs.

Uses: Copper can be used as an antibacterial agent in the treatment of bacterial gill disease, as well as an antiparasitic compound effective against but not limited

CHLORAMINE T FOR FLUKE ELIMINATION IN ADULT GOLDFISH				
Day	Amount	Length	Caution	Followup
One	10 PPM in soft water 20 PPM in hard water Soft = TA <50 Hard = TA >50	8 hours	Bypass filter	50% water change with dechlorination
Three	Same as Day One	8 hours	Bypass filter	50% water change with dechlorination
Six	Same as Day One	8 hours	Bypass filter	50% water change with dechlorination

CHOCOLATE BUTTERFLY TAIL TELESCOPES.

to *Chilodonella*, *Trichodina*, flukes, and *Oodinium*.
Dosage and Dosing: Follow manufacturer's instructions.
Precautions: As noted earlier, too much copper can
also kill fish. Care must be taken to test daily for copper
levels when using any copper formulation, because it
can be removed from the water by carbon, and by other
inert minerals including the aquarium gravel and ornamentation. The first doses may be bound up by the
environment, but eventually no more copper is
absorbed by the environment, and continued dosing
can cause dangerous accumulations. An ionic copper
test kit and strict attention to manufacturer's instructions are therefore recommended.

DIMILIN

Description: Dimilin 25%W is the trade name for an
insecticide produced by the Uniroyal Corporation of
25% diflubenzuron and 75% inert ingredients. Dimilin is
primarily used against gypsy moths and other insect pests.
Uses: Dimilin proves equally effective against our crustacean foes *Lernea*, *Argulus*, and *Ergasilus*. Dimilin is a
chitin synthesis inhibitor, which acts as a gyrase of the
DNA that produces chitin. Without chitin, a parasite
has no "skin," and it perishes. Dimilin is not effective
against flukes.
Dosage and Dosing: 1 gram of Dimilin 25%W will
treat 1,000 gallons of water. It is impractical and unnec-
essary to work with smaller amounts, and since it is
completely nontoxic to fish at any dose, this same
dosage can be used for home aquariums of all sizes with

no harm to the fish. It's best to add the measured dose to
a jar of water and shake it up vigorously to mix it thoroughly. This emulsion can then be distributed evenly
around the pond for best effect. Dimilin will not
adversely affect your filter, algae, or plants.
Precautions: Dimilin is a restricted-use pesticide and
the Environmental Protection Agency requires users to
be licensed pesticide applicators. It will kill all insects,
arachnids, and crustacea, whether desirable or not.

DRONCIT

Description: Droncit is a pill form of praziquantel available from your local veterinarian, who uses it to clear
tapeworms from dogs.
Uses: In fish medicine, we use Droncit to clear flukes
and worms from our fish.
Dosage and Dosing: Use Droncit as a water treatment
every third or fourth day without a water change to clear
flukes from Goldfish. It is safe and effective. It does not
harm fish, filter, or algae. If the fish harbor any tapeworms, they will be expelled within two to four hours.
One treatment will clear all intestinal worms.

Use 3.5 tablets of the 34-milligram Droncit tablets
for dogs per 10 gallons of water (a 3-PPM dose). This will
be a very expensive treatment in larger aquaria. As mentioned, no water change is needed. Because of the life
cycle of the trematode fluke, the second treatment on
day three or four is very important to kill any larval flukes
that may not have been affected by the first treatment.
Precautions: None.

FLAGYL

Description: Flagyl is a trade name for metronidazole.

Uses: Flagyl is the treatment of choice for the parasite *Hexamita* and *Spironucleus*.

Dosage and Dosing: Move the affected fish to a 10-gallon hospital tank and add 2 250 milligram tablets of Flagyl to the tank every third or fourth day for three treatments.

Precautions: Flagyl does not seriously harm the beneficial bacteria in the biological filter, but in the case of *Hexamita* there is no need to treat the entire system as there is with most other parasites, so a hospital tank is recommended.

FLUKE TABS

Description: Fluke Tabs are made by Aquarium Products. Each 500-milligram tablet contains methyl-5-benzol-benaimidizole-2-carbamate and dimethyl (2,2,2-trichloro-1-hydroxyethyl) phosphonate. Apparently, the relative ratios of the carbamate pesticide to the organophosphate (trichlorfon/fenthion-like compound) are proprietary and do not show up on the label.

Uses: Fluke Tabs are a top choice for treating flukes.

Dosage and Dosing: For best results, remove all carbon from your filtration system and stop ultraviolet sterilization. On the first day of treatment, use 1 tablet per 10 gallons. Do nothing on the second day. On the third day, perform a 50% water change and filter with carbon. On the fourth day repeat the first day's treatment of 1 tablet per 10 gallons. Do nothing again on the fifth day. On the sixth day, repeat the third-day treatment: a 50% water change and filter with carbon.

If desired, you can add an additional three-day cycle, treating up to nine days. Always aerate well while using.

Precautions: The carbamates are toxic to certain fish, most notably Discus and Catfish, which may be affected adversely. Avoid contact with treated water. Fluke Tab treatments should not be continuous, as many types of fish, but especially Goldfish and Koi, may experience an inflammatory dermatitis if the product is left in the water longer than forty-eight hours. This reddening of the skin together with decreased activity is common when Fluke Tabs are dosed daily, which is the rationale for the above regimen of three-day cycles.

FORMALIN

Description: Formalin is basically formaldehyde gas in water at a concentration of 37%. In some cases it is stabilized in solution by the addition of methanol. Methanol is not inherently toxic to fish, but it can have a stressful effect, and I have had fewer deaths among weak fishes with methanol-free formalin.

When formalin degrades it forms a white precipitate called paraformaldehyde. This is incredibly toxic to fish and should not be allowed in the tank. If this white precipitate appears in your formalin, dispose of the entire bottle.

Uses: Formalin is used to treat fungi, some bacterial infections, most of the ciliated protozoans (ich is an exception), and flukes. Formalin is not successful in treating *Argulus* and *Lernea*, and many, frequent doses are required to kill off the elusive ich organism with formalin.

Formalin can also be used to disinfect plants, in a bath of 4 milliliters per gallon for over four hours. Some plants, however, are adversely affected by formalin and the best plant disinfectant is potassium permanganate.

Dosage and Dosing: Dose 2 milliliters per 10 gallons of water (a concentration of 50 PPM) for exactly one hundred twenty minutes, then do a 75% water change with dechlorinated water. If low levels of dissolved oxygen are a concern—for example, in warm water—use 1 milliliter in 10 gallons of water (25 PPM) and closely observe your fish.

Apply this dosage of formalin daily for bacterial infections, *Branchiomyces*, and the ciliated protozoans. Use it every fourth day for flukes.

It bears repeating that you should increase aeration and circulation when using formalin.

If the fish are in poor overall condition, consider that formalin may kill the weakest among them—which may be your favorite fish. Again, if you're worried, use the half dose of 1 milliliter in 10 gallons of water (25 PPM) and closely observe your fish.

Precautions: When using formalin, always increase aeration and circulation and bypass filter media.

In studies of non-agitated water, using purely chemical reactions in vivo and on paper, every 5 PPM of formalin consumed 1 PPM of dissolved oxygen. That means that a standard 50 PPM dose of formalin would consume 10 PPM of oxygen, virtually eliminating all the oxygen from the aquatic environment. This points up the absolute necessity of aeration and higher circulation when treating with formalin. If the fish are gasping at the surface during treatment with formalin application, the treatment should be stopped immediately.

Never use formalin in water over eighty degrees. Warm water carries even less oxygen, and probably no practical amount of aeration will put enough oxygen into the water to prevent stressing the fish. In warm water, formalin seems to cause more trauma to fish than it's worth.

Because formalin is caustic and may burn fins in young or sensitive fish, do not risk using it on long-finned fish like Veiltails unless you have no therapeutic choice.

Formalin should not be used in winter ponds. Formalin has the habit of settling to the bottom in very cold water (thirty-four degrees) because it becomes heavier than water and concentrates in hot spots that may "burn" fish.

Some hobbyists and experienced Goldfish retailers use less than the 25-PPM dose because they report skin and fin damage with even that dose. There may be variables that contribute to these results, but the 25-PPM dose has proved safe in my practice with fancy varieties, and the 50-PPM dose has not harmed the hardier pond varieties such as Comets and Shubunkins.

FURAZONE GREEN

Description: Furazone green is a combination of two or three furan antibiotics, which are characterized by a good spectrum of action against bacterial infections in Goldfish and reasonably good absorption by fish. It is green because the product contains these furans, which are yellow, and a dose of methylene blue, resulting in a shade of green that is nothing short of electric. Furazone green is commonly available at the local pet shop in capsule or powder form.

Uses: Use furazone green to treat any disease that responds to antibiotics, primarily bacterial infections. It is second only to injection in effectiveness.

Dosage and Dosing: Furazone green achieves its greatest results when used as an eight-hour bath according to manufacturer's instructions on a daily basis, using a fresh solution daily.

Bypass the filter because it may disable or impair beneficial bacteria. Both ultraviolet sterilization (and ultraviolet rays in general) and carbon remove or neutralize furazone green.

Precautions: Furazone green will disable your biological filter (though I have been told by certain wholesalers that their systems have become immune to its effects). The furans are also eventually carcinogenic, which is more of a concern for those who use these compounds daily, such as wholesalers and retailers. Please follow manufacturer's instructions carefully when using this compound.

MALACHITE GREEN

Description: Malachite green has been used for decades in treating fish. It is a powerful dye, deeply penetrating and persisting in fish tissues for a great while after use. The malachite green molecule is composed of three copper ions. As the molecule degrades, you are effectively treating the system with copper (see the discussion of copper).

Uses: Malachite green is principally used to eliminate ciliated parasites such as *Trichodina*, *Costia*, and so forth. It can also be used as a topical treatment for fungal infections (see Topical Treatments).

Dosage and Dosing: Malachite is typically dosed daily as needed at a rate of 0.11 PPM (0.11 milligram/L) for an extended period, until the parasites are completely eliminated.

Precautions: It is important that the malachite green you choose does not contain zinc. This is probably already an obsolete recommendation, since the Food and Drug Administration is actively removing malachite green from manufacture and from pet-store shelves regardless of zinc content. They are concerned that it can cause cancer in humans with prolonged exposure, and since it resides in fish tissues for lengthy periods, it is dangerous if used to treat food fish such as Trout and Catfish. It will also stain the silicone sealant in your tanks.

METHYLENE BLUE

Description: Methylene blue is a basic thiazine dye used as a biological stain, an antidote to cyanide poisoning, and an oxidation-reduction indicator. It is widely used as an antifungal remedy in fishkeeping.

Uses: Methylene blue can be used against fungus as a prolonged or continuous bath or a short dip. It is also used for disinfecting nets and Goldfish eggs.

Dosage and Dosing: Use as a prolonged or continuous bath at 3 mg/Liter. As a short dip, use at 50 mg/Liter but dip for only approximately ten seconds. Use at the same concentration for disinfecting nets. For disinfecting eggs, dose the hatching tank until the water is a light "Windex" blue.

Precautions: Methylene blue is well tolerated by Goldfish, and as long as you can still see the fish in the tank you have not overdosed. It does, however, have profound negative effects on filter bacteria, and can stain ornamentation and sealing silicone.

POND HEALTHGUARD

Description: Pond HealthGuard is a product of SeaChem Labs that is a modified version of formalin—a comparable or related aldehyde. Pond HealthGuard offers all the benefits of formalin without most of the side effects. Clinical testing, as well as my own practice, have shown that Pond HealthGuard does less damage to biological filtration and is less caustic or irritating to fish.

Uses: Pond HealthGuard is used to treat flukes.

Dosage and Dosing: Follow the manufacturer's instructions.

Precautions: Provide vigorous aeration, especially in warm water, and dose a second time after four days to kill emerging fluke larvae.

POMPOM TELESCOPE.

POTASSIUM PERMANGANATE

Description: Potassium permanganate is a caustic alkali that is purple when dissolved in water. It is usually found in a powder or granular form, though there are several commercial preparations of it in liquid form of various concentrations.

Uses: Potassium permanganate is effective in treating flukes, fungus infections, bacterial gill disease, bacterial infections of the body and fins, and ciliated protozoan infestations except ich. Potassium permanganate will have no effect on crustacean parasites, although it may decrease the survival of the immature forms of these pathogens. Ich will remain under the skin, safe from the potassium permanganate, and will not be cleared.

Dosage and Dosing: Advanced hobbyists commonly use potassium permanganate as a dip, but I highly discourage this. There are many superb methods of surface disinfection in fish without a potassium permanganate dip, which can and often does burn fins and gills.

When active, potassium permanganate in water is purple. Potassium permanganate naturally dissociates into manganese dioxide, which is brown. In many instances, it settles out or binds to organic materials on the sides of the tank and the fish. The water may remain amber for a while after treatment. If the water is amber in color, the potassium permanganate is inactive.

Several of the dosage regimens below require that the potassium permanganate be deactivated at a certain point. Potassium permanganate can be instantly neutralized by sodium thiosulfate (the active ingredient of most dechlorinators) applied according to the instructions on the product label. Potassium permanganate can also be instantly deactivated and decolorized by hydrogen peroxide in 3% solution. You can treat a tank with potassium permanganate and then deactivate it with hydrogen peroxide in 3% solution, leaving no trace whatsoever of the potassium permanganate. Moreover, there is some evidence (though anecdotal and unsubstantiated) that the metabolites left behind by this reaction are oxidative and antibacterial.

To deactivate potassium permanganate, use 1.5 milliliters (about one-third teaspoon) of hydrogen peroxide in 3% solution per gallon of water. For very large systems, use 1 pint of hydrogen peroxide per 5,000 gallons. A higher dose of potassium permanganate will require correspondingly more hydrogen peroxide, obviously.

Dosing potassium permanganate is complex and requires precise measurements. It can be done in any of several ways. Select the method that fits your situation best, and use caution in following it.

To make a 0.04 percent stock solution of potassium permanganate, add 2 level measuring teaspoons (or 14 grams) of reagent-grade potassium permanganate to 1 gallon of distilled water. Cap the water container and shake to mix thoroughly.

Use this stock solution to dose as follows. If you want to dose 4 PPM, use:

~1 cup (240 ml) per 60 gallons of water
~1/3 cup (80 ml) per 20 gallons of water
~3 tablespoons (45 ml) per 10 gallons of water

Obviously, if you are using the milder 2 PPm dosage, you will cut all of these amounts in half:

~1/2 cup (120 ml) per 60 gallons of water
~1/6 cup (40 ml) per 20 gallons of water
~1 1/2 tablespoons (22.5 ml) per 10 gallons of water

When the water turns from purple to amber, you can reverse the treatment with one long squirt of 3% hydrogen peroxide per gallon of water.

Two regimens are presented here. Done properly, at the correct dose and at the suggested interval, these regimens will have no adverse effect on gill tissues. If overdosed, however, severe damage may result. Use caution and follow instructions closely.

The first dosing regime follows a daily cycle for four to five days as follows and treats a very broad spectrum of conditions.

Day One: Bypass your filter, maintaining high circulation and aeration by other means. Apply 4 PPM of potassium permanganate in the morning. Wait until the color of the aquarium water changes from purple to amber. On Day One, this may occur rather swiftly. When the potassium permanganate is amber, as checked by placing a sample of aquarium water in a white coffee mug, resume filtration. If the Goldfish are gasping near the surface, seem lethargic, or if the water is opaque with potassium permanganate, perform a water change. If you use a dechlorinator to prepare water for the change, do not use more than necessary as some of the dechlorinator may reside in the aquarium water until the following day, which will inactivate the next treatment.

Day Two: Bypass your filter, maintaining high circulation and aeration by other means. Apply 4 PPM of potassium permanganate in the morning. Wait until the color changes from purple to amber. When the potassium permanganate is amber, as checked in a white coffee mug, resume filtration. Perform a water change, as described above, if needed.

Day Three: Bypass your filter, maintaining high circulation and aeration by other means. Apply 4 PPM of potassium permanganate in the morning. Wait until the color changes from purple to amber. When the potassium permanganate is amber, as checked in a white coffee mug, resume filtration. Perform a water change if needed.

MATTE CALICO VEILTAIL.

Day Four: Bypass your filter, maintaining high circulation and aeration by other means. Apply 4 PPM in the morning. Wait until the color changes from purple to amber. When the potassium permanganate is amber, as checked in a white coffee mug, resume filtration. At the conclusion of this treatment, I would highly suggest that you perform a 50% water change or use hydrogen peroxide in a 3% solution to decolorize and inactivate the potassium permanganate in your aquarium water.

Skip three days and do a single cleanup treatment exactly as you'd done on Day Four, with the same removal of any remaining potassium permanganate with hydrogen peroxide in a 3% solution.

That concludes this treatment regimen. It will be extremely effective against flukes because steps one and five intercept adult and immature flukes. It will have eliminated most ciliated protozoans and *Hexamita* because of its daily use. It will clear bacterial gill disease and other body ulcers in most instances because it is applied daily. It is not a substitute for injection of antibiotics in these cases.

The second regimen is intended for use in minor bacterial outbreaks and especially for flukes. We have had good success with this second regimen especially in very cold water when other medications such as formalin and the organophosphates (such as malathion) would be dangerous.

Day One: Bypass your filter, maintaining high circulation and aeration by other means. Apply 4 PPM of potassium permanganate. Wait until the color changes from purple to amber. When the potassium permanganate is amber, as checked in a white coffee mug, decolorize and deactivate with hydrogen peroxide in a 3% solution at the rate of 1.5 milliliters per gallon of water. Resume filtration once you've decolorized the tank.

Day Four: Bypass your filter, maintaining high circulation and aeration by other means. Apply 4 PPM of potassium permanganate. Wait until the color changes from purple to amber. When the potassium permanganate is amber, as checked in a white coffee mug, decolorize and deactivate with hydrogen peroxide in a 3% solution at the rate of 1.5 milliliters per gallon of water. Resume filtration once you've decolorized the tank.

Day Eight: Bypass your filter, maintaining high circulation and aeration by other means. Apply 4 PPM of potassium permanganate. Wait until the color changes from purple to amber. When the potassium permanganate is amber, as checked in a white coffee mug, decolorize and deactivate with hydrogen peroxide in a 3% solution at the rate of 1.5 milliliters per gallon of

water. Resume filtration once you've decolorized the tank.

This regimen is effective in the control of flukes because it intercepts them at each renewal of their life cycle. On Day One you're killing the entire adult population and on Day Four you're intercepting emerging larva and embryos. The third (and possibly a fourth) treatment can be considered overly cautious but is still recommended because in many instances the initial potassium permanganate treatment was bound out by organics and did not kill all the adults.

Precautions: Be careful when handling this compound. Tiny amounts of dust will be distributed around the area and once wet, will result in a purple stain. It will stain your skin brown, and the stains will persist for a long time. Potassium permanganate is hazardous to your eyes, so wear protective eyewear when using it.

Some hobbyists and experienced Goldfish retailers use less than the 4-PPM dose because they report skin, fin, and gill damage with even that dose. There may be variables that contribute to these results, but the 4-PPM dose has proved safe in my practice with both pond and fancy Goldfish varieties. You may achieve very good results with a half-strength treatment of 2 PPM.

PROGRAM

Description: Program is a brand name for lufenuron, which is also sold under other trade names, including Larvadex. Like Dimilin, Program works as a gyrase that interferes with the production of chitin in target organisms. Chitin is the "skin" of most insects and crustaceans, and Program spells death for fleas in dogs who ingest it in the form of Program tablets every month.

Uses: Program is equally effective against *Argulus*, *Lernea*, and *Ergasilus*.

Dosage and Dosing: Dose Program at a rate of 490 milligram (usually 1 tablet) per 1,000 gallons of water. Program is nontoxic to fish and will not harm them at any dosage. You can use one-quarter tablet for a 20-gallon tank, which represents a harmless, at least one hundredfold, overdose. You can also use a smaller Program tablet, if available, extrapolating from the ratio of 490 milligrams to 1000 gallons.

Precautions: The water from a treated tank or pond should not be allowed exit into the aquifer because it may harm indigenous crustacea and insects. Program will be detrimental to the beneficial dragonfly, which has an aquatic larva, and to crayfish.

SALT

Description: Salt is the greatest bath treatment of all time. Salt is both tonic to fish and toxic to parasites. It controls most of the ciliated protozoa and it can also off-set the negative effects of some water-quality problems such as nitrite accumulation.

Salt is available in numerous forms: kosher salt, water softener salts, solar salt, rock salt, sea salt, synthetic reef salt, non-mineralized salt blocks for cows, and table salt. These are all acceptable, though sea salt is rich in carbonates and will raise total alkalinity and pH, which may be undesirable if there is a significant ammonia accumulation. Also note that cow salt blocks are also sold in a mineralized form that is rich in magnesium and other minerals. Do NOT use these; they will kill your fish. Whatever salt you use, make sure the label indicates the salt is 99.97% NaCl and has no trace minerals added. In particular, watch out for salt that contains yellow prussiate of soda, or YPS. Another anti-caking agent used in some salts contains cyanuric acid. Avoid this as well. Also be sure the salt contains no iodine, because while this will have no negative effect on the fish, it may damage beneficial bacteria. Table salt is available in both iodized and non-iodized forms: use the latter. On the other hand, the drying agent sodium aluminosilicate that is added to some salts is safe.

Uses: Salt is used to eliminate ciliated protozoan parasites, curb the absorption of nitrite, and reduce the osmotic pressure exerted by fresh-water on any hole in the skin or gill.

Dosage and Dosing: Dosing salt is simple. To produce a 0.3% solution, use 1 tablespoon per gallon. This is the concentration used to control most protozoan parasites. To produce a 0.6% solution, use 2 tablespoons per gallon. This is the concentration for salt-resistant *Trichodina*. To produce a 0.9% solution (commonly called for in German texts), use 3 tablespoons per gallon.

Before you dose an aquarium with salt, remove any live plants of value. Also perform a significant water change (50%) before starting, because you will want to avoid water changes if possible after salting in order to maintain a stable concentration. It is best to gradually introduce the fish to the salt, so the total dose will be divided into three one-third doses, added to the aquarium over a twenty-four-hour period. Choose a suitable starting time. Dissolve one-third of the total salt dose in a small bucket of water, and after it is completely dissolved, pour it into the aquarium.

Wait twelve hours while the fish acclimate, then apply the second salt dose. Once again, it will be one-third of the total dose and once again you should dissolve it in advance in a small bucket of water.

Add the final dose in exactly the same way twelve hours later. The whole amount has been added over

twenty-four hours, which reduces the shock on the fish or filter. However, if the fish are dying off quickly, it is advisable to add the total salt dose all at once. This may have a negative impact on filter bacteria but may be life-saving in the case of *Chilodonella*, *Costia*, or even ich in smaller fishes.

Precautions: Is it possible to apply too much salt? Of course, but it is difficult, since Goldfish will survive salt concentrations up to 0.9% and higher. This is, however, a stressful salt concentration and should only be used when absolutely necessary. Small, weak fish do best at a 0.3% concentration, with observation. "Not worse" is a good result. If the fish are surviving after a day or two at a concentration of 0.3%, then you can, if necessary, raise it to a 0.6% concentration without losses.

TRAMISOLE

Description: Tramisole is levamisole phosphate. It is available from a veterinarian.

Uses: Tramisole is a safe and effective deworming medication.

Dosage and Dosing: Dose at 0.5 PPM, added directly to the water.

Precautions: None. Tramisole will not harm the fish or the biological filter.

Topical Treatments

Topical treatments are of considerable importance to Goldfish keepers. Indeed, in perhaps no other species of fish will we see fish recover solely through the use of topical medications. Use discretion in repeated application of topical treatments to wounds. Once the wound has stopped bleeding, seems less red, and the edges seem to be "organizing" into a thick white rim, do not reapply any topical treatment, or you will disrupt the necessary migration of epidermal cells across the wound, which is the only way that large sores will heal. Daily scrubs of wounds prevent healing.

MALACHITE GREEN

Description: Malachite green is a dark green liquid or paste that stains deeply.

Uses: Malachite green is occasionally used as a paste or liquid topical treatment in the management of minor fungal infections. Make certain that you are treating a fungus, since it is ineffective against bacterial ulcerations.

Dosage and Dosing. Swab fungal lesions with malachite green daily or every other day until the fungus disappears.

Precautions: Care should be taken to avoid exposure to

CALICO AND RED-CAP ORANDAS.

malachite green as it is a carcinogen and causes birth defects. Wear protective eyewear while applying this medication to prevent the fish from flipping some into your eyes.

MERCUROCHROME

Description: Mercurochrome is a red liquid disinfectant that is readily available from the local pharmacy.

Uses: Mercurochrome is a good topical treatment for fish wounds because it does not stain very intensely and it stays on for a while after application.

Dosage and Dosing: If this is the topical treatment you choose, simply remove the fish from the water, blow on its wound to remove extraneous water, and then put a few drops of mercurochrome on the wound. Do not blot or scrub the wound. Scrubbing of the wound is indicated only during the initial recovery phase to remove dead tissue and debris from the wound and if performed after this first treatment actually inhibits healing. Mercurochrome should be applied to a wound on a daily or every-other-day basis until the center of the wound is pink instead of red.

Precautions: None.

PANOLOG

Description: Panolog is a combination of an antibiotic, an antifungal agent, and a cortisone compound that reduces inflammation. Panolog is not always available any longer, but your veterinarian will be able to supply you with a generic or similar product.

Uses: Panolog is used to treat wounds on fish with good results. Panolog will not work alone on most ulcers; to be successful, the fish must also have perfect water quality and minimal crowding. Use Panolog on any skin lesion, superficial or deep, that is infected or slow to heal.

Dosage and Dosing: Simply capture the fish and apply the Panolog to the wound, without rubbing, on a daily basis. Panolog is fairly hydrophobic and remains on the wound for up to two hours after application.

Precautions: None.

POTASSIUM PERMANGANATE

Description: Potassium permanganate is a caustic alkali that is purple when dissolved in water. It is usually found in a powder or granular form.

Uses: Potassium permanganate is a superb topical disinfectant for wounds. If a wound is deep, meat red, and bleeding, then you should favorably consider scrubbing once with potassium permanganate. This is especially true if the wound appears slimy or has strands of dead tissue trailing from it.

Dosage and Dosing: Place a small amount of the dry powder in the bottom of a paper cup. Then add a few drops of water to the powder and stir with a wooden stirrer. When the potassium permanganate is mixed and pasty, it can be applied to the wounds of the fish. This treatment effectively clears parasites that might be living in and deepening the wounds of the fish. Potassium permanganate has the ability to kill 99% of surface bacteria. It is also a potent oxidizer, which may have some benefit in the removal of dead tissue and debris from the wound. Potassium permanganate is an excellent topical treatment for the initial scrubbing of wounds, but should not be used on wounds that have been scrubbed once and are beginning to heal.

Precautions: Potassium permanganate is caustic to the eyes and protective eyewear is recommended. Avoid getting this under the gill cover when used as a topical. It could be fatal.

TINCTURE OF IODINE

Description: Tincture of iodine is available in several strengths. A 2% solution is commonly available in the drug store, but your pharmacist may be able to supply you with a 7% solution, which is excellent for cleaning wounds.

Uses: Iodine is an excellent topical disinfectant for wounds.

Dosage and Dosing: Swab the wound with the iodine, taking care to avoid using it near the gill, as it may seep under the gill cover and damage gill tissue. It does not seem to damage the eyes of the fish, though it is harmful to human eyes (see below). Apply tincture of iodine only once in most cases.

Precautions: Tincture of iodine stains intensely but does not hurt the skin. It can cause serious eye damage in humans, however, and you should wear protective eyewear when applying it.

Injected Treatments

Injection of Goldfish affords you complete control over every aspect of medication. With injection, there is no question when the fish got the medicine, or how much was actually delivered to its system. Injection was new to ornamental fish hobbyists in the mid-nineties, though now it is commonplace. The following section of the Formulary provides information on several antibacterial drugs.

It is pointless to inject over and over again without reward. If a drug is not working, the diagnosis should be reevaluated or a culture and sensitivity test performed.[7] I have given dosages for injecting fish as small as 2 inches, but if you do not feel comfortable injecting such small fish, do not attempt it. Remember, each time you inject a fish you are subjecting it to the stress of capture and handling.

7. A culture and sensitivity test refers to the process by which a microbiologist collects samples of tissues from an infected fish and attempts to culture the bacteria found in those tissues in a petri dish. "Sensitivity" refers to the second process, in which the scientist treats the bacterial culture with various antibiotics to determine which ones the bacteria are sensitive to. This is done by putting small samples of different antimicrobials on the petri dish and looking for areas of inhibited growth.

AMIKACIN

Description: Amikacin is an aminoglycoside antibiotic. Resistance to this class of drugs is rare. It is sold through veterinary suppliers, and a generic is available and has equal results. It comes in liquid form, and the customarily available strength is 50 milligrams per milliliter. Amikacin is safe for intraperitoneal injection and is also safe for you to handle.

Uses: Use Amikacin for any kind of infection of body, mouth, fin, or other bacterial outbreak that responds to the drug. I do not use Amikacin to treat very small fish. I consider it the drug of choice in freshly imported fish that are under direct and heavy attack by bacterial infections.

Dosage and Dosing: For a 2-inch Goldfish, reduce the 50 milligrams per milliliter strength of Amikacin with sterile water by half. Using this 50% solution, inject the fish intraperitoneally with 0.05 milliliters. Inject a Goldfish with a body length of 3 inches with a 0.1-milliliter dose of the 50% solution. Inject a 6-inch fish intraperitoneally with 0.1 milliliters of the undiluted Amikacin. Inject a 12- to 14-inch fish intraperitoneally with 0.3 milliliters.

You may inject once every other day for a total of three injections.

Amikacin is also effective when injected in alternation with Azactam, each antibiotic injected on alternating days for a total of six injections, three of each, over a six-day period.

Precautions: This drug accumulates quickly in the body of the fish and has been associated with considerable toxicity when dosed daily for more than three to four injections. Signs of overdose include sudden death, and neurological disorders such as bent back, abnormal swimming, twitching, convulsions, and rigidity.

AZACTAM

Description: Azactam was brought to my attention by Dr. Galen Hansen, a Koi hobbyist with a medical background. I tried it in Koi and Goldfish and became impressed at its safety and effectiveness. Azactam (also known as Aztreonam) is a "monobactam" antimicrobial produced by Squibb Labs and is used in human medicine against resistant bacterial infections. Like chloramphenicol, Azactam kills bacteria, and does not simply impair or stun them. Azactam is not very expensive. It is an injectable liquid antibiotic, available from a veterinarian in 1-gram bottles that can be reconstituted at 100 milligrams per 1 milliliter, but several sizes and strengths are available.

Uses: Use Azactam for any infection that shows sensitivity to it. Azactam is a good choice for very valuable Goldfish with body sores and symptoms of systemic

infection. It is the drug of choice for bacterial pop eye and dropsy. Azactam can be used in small fish.

Dosage and Dosing: Inject small fish with a dose of 5 to 10 milligrams. Dose the 100 milligrams per milliliter concentration as follows.

Inject a 2-inch Goldfish intraperitoneally with 0.05 milliliters. Inject a 3-inch Goldfish in the same manner with 0.2 milliliters. Inject a 6-inch Goldfish with 0.3 to 0.4 milliliters. Inject a 12- to 14-inch fish with 0.6 milliliters.

Inject once daily for two or three injections and then inject every other day for another three to four injections.

Azactam is also effective when injected in alternation with Amikacin, each antibiotic injected on alternating days for a total of six injections, three of each, over a six-day period.

If you are combating bacterial gill disease, inject once daily for at least three days. A single injection of Azactam is a good choice as a prophylactic treatment for new fish, too.

Precautions: Azactam can be frozen after reconstitution for long-term storage. If not refrigerated, discard any unused amount after three to four days.

BAYTRIL

Description: Baytril is a quinolone antibiotic and is in the same family as oxolinic acid, nalidixic acid, and ciprofloxacin. It is marketed by Bayer and is sold as a clear, thin 2.27% solution through veterinary channels. It has a wide-spectrum effectiveness against many gram-positive and gram-negative organisms that infect Goldfish. It is safe to dose and handle. Best of all, it lasts forever on the shelf.

Uses: Use Baytril for gram-negative and gram-positive bacteria and the control of any other infection that responds to it. It is an excellent choice when importing fish and in the treatment of body sores and fin rot.

One of the most effective uses of Baytril is in the post-shipment stress of larger fish. While large fish generally survive shipment better than smaller fish, the smaller fish that do make it usually adapt more rapidly to their new environment. On the other hand, many large fish arrive in the country safely but simply retire to the bottom of the quarantine tank, moving only when prodded. Their fins may begin to develop red streaks. Such a fish is probably developing a bacterial septicemia. Many factors can contribute to this, including a concurrent parasitism and poor water quality in the shipping container. Check your water quality first to make sure it is perfect, and then consider Baytril as an effective therapy for this condition.

Dosage and Dosing: Inject a 2-inch Goldfish intraperitoneally with 0.05 milliliters. Inject a Goldfish with a body length of 3 inches with a 0.1-milliliter dose. Inject a 6-inch fish intraperitoneally with 0.2 to 0.3 milliliters. Inject a 12- to 14-inch fish intraperitoneally with 0.5 milliliters.

You may inject a single dose daily for two or three days, and then inject a single dose every other day for a total of three to four days.

Precautions: None.

CHLORAMPHENICOL

Description: Chloramphenicol is one of the original injectable antibiotics used for ornamental fish, and it became widely used because it was very safe in

Goldfish. In the past it has been used as a water treatment, and was available in tablet form. I do not recommend its use in this form, since there is a risk in handling this drug (see below). Veterinarians can supply chloramphenicol in a 1-gram vial that can be reconstituted with sterile water for injection.

The antibiotic spectrum of chloramphenicol is broad, and particularly effective against gram-negative bacteria. Chloramphenicol is advantageous because it is bactericidal ("bacteria killing") instead of bacteriostatic ("bacteria stopping")—that is, an antibiotic that immobilizes bacteria for the immune system to clean up, or just stops the bacteria's function.

Chloramphenicol is absorbed from the intraperitoneal area and modified in the body into another compound (a thiamphenicol) that has potent antibiotic capabilities. The drug can penetrate many tissues and areas of the body and fights internal infections as well as external ones.

Uses: Use chloramphenicol in any case of bacterial infection in Goldfish. See the section on bacterial pathogens for the signs that alert you to the presence of a bacterial infection. I have used chloramphenicol since 1992 with excellent results. It is true that this drug is losing ground with the bacteria that infect Koi, but as a medicine for Goldfish the results remain good.

Chloramphenicol is the drug of choice for smaller Goldfish because it is relatively safe. It can also be used to treat routine infections and traumas. It has no negative side effect with extended use.

Dosage and Dosing: Prepare a stock solution of chloramphenicol by mixing a 1-gram vial with 10 milliliters of sterile water. Inject approximately one-tenth milliliter per body length (excluding tail) for fish 3 inches and larger. Inject a 2-inch Goldfish intraperitoneally with only 0.1 milliliters. Inject once daily for two or three days, and then inject every other day for three to four additional injections.

Precautions: Injections of chloramphenicol into people can cause a human blood disorder called Gray's Syndrome. Be careful not to accidentally inject yourself, though obviously this would be very hard to do. In some cases, breaking tablets of chloramphenicol and breathing the dust can have a negative effect on an unborn fetus.

To preserve its potency, chloramphenicol should be reconstituted with sterile water and frozen when not in use. If chloramphenicol is not refrigerated, it should be discarded within a few days of reconstitution.

Do not attempt to use this medication for dropsy, which is usually incurable.

DEXAMETHASONE

Description: Dexamethasone is a potent corticosteroid used in human and animal medicine in the treatment of shock. In fish, it has been used in some cases of "jumpers" and other causes of acute, life-threatening trauma. Dexamethasone is available in liquid form from a veterinarian, customarily in a 2 milligram per 1 milliliter strength, but there are variations.

Uses: Dexamethasone is not useful in treating fish succumbing to chronic or end-stage disorders. For example, a fish that has been suffering with bacterial infection for a week and is finally dying will not be salvaged by an injection of dexamethasone. Dexamethasone will not offset the effects of a caustic or toxic stress.

Dexamethasone has been used successfully in the management of fish that are near death after jumping from their aquarium, in fish that have been recovered from pH crashes, and fish that have been severely cold stressed. Do not use dexamethasone for any fish that can swim and right itself.

Dosage and Dosing: Inject a 2-inch Goldfish intraperitoneally with 0.05 milliliters. Inject a 3-inch Goldfish in the same manner with 0.1 milliliters. Inject a 6-inch Goldfish intraperitoneally with 0.2 to 0.3 milliliters. Inject a 12- to 14-inch fish with 0.5 milliliters.

In all cases that merit the use of dexamethasone, the most rapid absorption of the drug is essential. To achieve this, the dosage should be expanded in sterile saline or lactated Ringer's solution, warmed, and then injected. This is a job for a veterinary professional.

Precautions: After the initial dose of dexamethasone, the fishes' immune system will be completely annihilated. Indeed, dexamethasone is used to suppress the immune function in many animal and human autoimmune disorders. Fish that have been treated with dexamethasone should be protected from secondary bacterial infection with daily injections of Baytril.

GENTAMYCIN

Description: Gentamycin is an aminoglycoside antibiotic in the same class as Amikacin. Never use it in treating Goldfish.

VITAMIN C

Description: Vitamin C (ascorbic acid) is available in an injectable form, usually in a strength of 100 milligrams per 1 milliliter, from a veterinarian. It should not be overlooked in the treatment of Goldfish diseases.

Uses: Ascorbic acid injection is an excellent adjunct to the treatment of any bacterial infection in Goldfish.

In testing done by Dr. Lovell at Auburn University, it was discovered that supplementation of ascorbic acid to fish stimulated the immune system. Many fish-food manufacturers are adding larger amounts of vitamin C, and especially its stabilized forms, to foods.

Dosage and Dosing: A single injection is sufficient. Inject a 2-inch Goldfish intraperitoneally with 0.05 milliliters. Inject a Goldfish with a body length of 3 inches intraperitoneally with a 0.1-milliliter dose. Inject a 6-inch fish intraperitoneally with 0.2 to 0.3 milliliters. Inject a 12- to 14-inch fish intraperitoneally with 0.5 milliliters.

Precautions: Ascorbic acid precipitates, so it does not mix with very many antibiotics, and I recommend that you inject it separately.

Oral Treatments

Oral medication is a safe and effective method to get medications into Goldfish. One advantage of oral medication is that it does not contaminate the environment as a bath treatment may, negatively affecting fish, filter bacteria, and algae growth. Another advantage is that when you medicate orally the fish gets a full, measurable dose. An obvious disadvantage of orally administered medications is that most sick fish won't eat, though this can be overcome by force feeding through a stomach tube, a technique called entubation that can provide much-needed nutrition along with medication. Another disadvantage is that digestive absorption of some of the most effective medications is poor, which means they must be injected.

BLACK HAMA NISHIKI.

LIONHEADS.

MEDICATED FOOD

Oral antibiotics in food are only recommended if the manufacturer mills them into the food. Some hobbyists attempt to add antibiotics to pelleted food by first mixing the antibiotics with some kind of edible oil, and then top dressing the food with this oil and antibiotic mixture. Unfortunately, most of the oil separates from the food, carrying the antibiotics with it.

There is a good medicated food called Romet-B which has sulfadimethoxine and ormetroprim sulfa milled into it during manufacture. The sulfa antibiotics are often effective against some of the more common bacteria affecting Goldfish, but unfortunately the strains of *Aeromonas salmonicida* that are often encountered in bacterial ulcer disease in Goldfish have acquired considerable resistance to sulfa antibiotics. Another medicated food, MediGold, combines the two antibiotics in Romet-B with oxolinic acid and kannamycin and is well accepted by Goldfish.

ENTUBATION

Entubation offers a superior means of supplying food and medicines directly to the digestive tract. To perform entubation, you will need a red rubber feeding tube (which your veterinarian can supply), a tuberculin syringe, and a nutritional supplement called NutriCal. This is a high-calorie protein and vitamin supplement available from your veterinarian that may also stimulate appetite and keep fish from starving. This supplement is helpful for fish that have flipped over and are losing weight as a result of their inability to eat normally. A 0.2-milliliter serving is appropriate for a 3- to 5-inch (body measurement discounting tail) Goldfish.

It is impractical to try to entubate a Goldfish of less than 3 inches because a feeding tube small and thin enough to fit in the esophagus would simultaneously not be rigid enough to enter and pass down the esophagus. If you must try with a smaller fish, I'd suggest a "Tom Cat" catheter, which is considerably more rigid, available from a veterinarian, attached to a 1-cc tuberculin syringe. Extra care must be taken not to rupture the digestive tract of smaller fish, and I would strongly recommend attempting this method on large Goldfish first.

Here's a step-by-step description of the entubation technique:

You may sedate the fish, but it is not necessary.

Select a red rubber feeding tube that is one-half the diameter of the pupil of the Goldfish's eye. The pupil of a Goldfish happens to approximate the size of its gullet.

Preload a 1-cc tuberculin syringe with NutriCal, NutriCal mixed with antibiotics, or whatever medicine you are trying to dose. Push some of the syringe contents down the tube until you can see some at the tip. Note how much remains in the syringe because this is how you measure what the fish will get. The amount in the tube itself will not be part of the dose.

The "stomach" of the Goldfish is really nothing more than a wide spot in the distal esophagus. Goldfish have no true stomach with muscular sphincters like ours. This "stomach" is just behind the pectoral fins. Lay the tube on the side of the fish and mark the tube where the mouth will be when it is "in" the stomach. This will help you avoid inserting the tube too far into the fish.

Slide the red rubber feeding tube straight into the back of the throat. Avoid any deviation or the tube will soon emerge from under the gill (this is harmless but useless).

When you encounter the back of the throat, there will be some resistance, but you will feel the gullet yield and the tube will slide on in. Slide the tube to the point you've marked so you know the tip of the tube is in the stomach.

Depress the plunger to release the food. Withdraw the tube slowly. Replace the fish in the water.

PANDA TELESCOPE.

Chapter 6

Symptoms, Causes, and Solutions

BLACK RANCHUS.

This chapter is organized by symptoms—by what you see when you observe your sick fish. This "quick reference" does not tell you all you need to know about the situation you are confronting. Please refer back to the disease and the treatment, where the detailed information you'll need for successful health management is to be found.

I hope the reader will imagine that each solution below begins with "Check your water-quality parameters." This is the secret to keeping healthy Goldfish and curing sick ones.

Here is a finding list of the symptoms included in this section. When possible, I have placed the word for the afflicted body part first ("Fins Red" instead of "Red Fins") to help you find the symptoms more quickly.

Abdomen Mushy
Abdomen Swollen, No Raised Scales
Baby Fish Dying in Large Numbers
Back Kinked

Belly Red
Color Changes: Color Loss, Blackening
Comportment Changes
Eye Loss or Damage
Eyes Bulging
Eyes White or Cloudy
Fins Clamped
Fins Red
Fins Split
Flank Sucking/Picking
Flashing/Scratching
Flipover/Floating
Gasping at Surface
Gill Cover Holes
Gills Pale
Gills Swollen Open
Head Down, Tail at Surface
Head Up, Hanging Just Under Surface
    Lethargically
Jumping

Large Sores on Body
Mouth Rot
Red Spots
Scales Standing Out All over Body
Scales Standing Out on Part of Body
Sitting on Bottom
Skin Milky
Spitting
Stool Changes
Swimming with Mouth Wide Open,
    Unable to Close
Ulcers
Wasting Away
Waxy, White Teardrops on Skin
White Fuzz/Tufts
White Spots on Skin
Worms Under Scales

A FISH WITH A SWOLLEN ABDOMEN.

Symptom: ABDOMEN MUSHY
Causes: The causes of this very serious condition are numerous, including bacterial infections in the abdomen, starvation caused by liver damage, internal damage, or organ displacement. Cancers will also cause emaciation and collapse of fat stores and liver mass. When opening most mushy abdomens in a necropsy, one finds emaciation of the fat reserves and liver and the abdominal cavity filled with thin or mucousy amber fluid, depending upon the cause of the mushiness.
Solutions: If the abdomen is mushy but the fish otherwise appears healthy, increase the number and amounts of feedings with nutritious foods such as krill, green peas, and bloodworms. If the fish appears sick, inject for a bacterial infection. At present there are no means of treating cancer or internal organ failure.

Symptom: ABDOMEN SWOLLEN, NO RAISED SCALES
Causes: A swollen fish such as this suffers from fatty liver or egg impaction, or possibly cystic kidneys.
Solutions: Surgery is the best solution.

Symptom: BABY FISH DYING IN LARGE NUMBERS
Causes: This is usually caused by ich or flukes infesting the gills in huge numbers. Goldfish fry do not withstand any ammonia accumulation or other water-quality disorders.
Solutions: Add salt to the water to make a 0.3% concentration. Crush a whole fry under a cover slip and check for flukes with a microscope on the lowest setting. Simultaneously, check and improve water quality if necessary. If flukes are found, you're facing a difficult situation, because fry don't handle most medicines used for flukes very well, though there is some anecdotal evi-

dence to suggest that Droncit is effective without harming the fry.

Symptom: BACK KINKED
Causes: Kinked backs (scoliosis) are a common sight in Goldfish tanks. There are numerous causes for this condition, the most common of which is genetic. In a million Goldfish fry, there will be those that develop abnormally and are kinked, almost doubling back upon themselves.

A normal fish that is developing well and suddenly begins to show a deviation in back shape may be demonstrating signs of a nutritional deficiency. Scoliosis can be caused by deficiencies in Vitamin C, Vitamin E, Vitamin A, and the amino acid tryptophan. In other cases, chemical medications may have caused such forceful muscular contractions adjacent to the spine that the spine fractures. Overdosages of organophosphates (such as neguvon, dipterex, trichloracide, trichlorfon, malathion, fenthion, and masoten) will cause this syndrome. The organophosphates act as a cholinesterase inhibitor, and acetylcholine builds up at the nervous synapse until the muscles approach complete tetany (permanent contraction). At their most intense contraction, the spine breaks.

Electrocution may also cause bent backs. See the discussion on this topic in the section "Other Threats to Goldfish Health."
Solutions: This is probably an incurable condition.

Symptom: BELLY RED
Causes: Red belly is a symptom of an advanced bacterial infection in which the bacteria have invaded the internal organs. This is very characteristic of *Aeromonas* infections.
Solutions: Injections are required to save such fish, and even then, it's too late for the really advanced cases. Injections are recommended for all fish in the

A FISH WITH A KINKED BACK. RIGHT: AN ORANDA SHOWING SIGNIFICANT MELA-NOPHORE MIGRATION.

collection, even healthy specimens, which have been exposed. Refer to the section on bacterial pathogens.

Symptom: COLOR CHANGES: COLOR LOSS, BLACKENING
Causes: If the color change is from orange or black to white, it may be pigment loss due to lack of sunlight. Red Cap Orandas frequently lose the red in the cap, and it is exceedingly rare for Black-and-Red Orandas to remain two-toned. Most turn orange over the years. Orange Comets also develop large white areas on heads and sides.

Blackening of the fins or body is commonly reported by hobbyists when fish have been treated with some medication or there have been recent water-quality problems. It is also seen in fish that have recently been shipped long distances. The color may just appear on the fin tips or extend all over the body. The fish has suffered some surface irritation, and the blackening is actually a sign of healing of the fish's epidermis. This phenomenon is called "melanophore migration." Black pigment cells, or melanophores, are erroneously responding to the presence of leukine, a chemical produced by the body that attracts and stimulates fibroblasts, the primary cells that replace and repair damaged tissues.
Solutions: In cases of loss of pigment or blackening related to healing, check water quality, activity level, appetite, and whether fins are clear and erect. If these are all acceptable, you have nothing to worry about.

If the "discolored" areas are depressed or raised, however, you may be facing bacterial infections, parasitism, a skin tumor, a viral wart such as carp pox or lymphocytes, and further diagnosis is recommended.

Symptom: COMPORTMENT CHANGES
Causes: A Goldfish that is listing to one side is usually suffering from water with high nitrates. Remember that a slight list may be within the range of the fish's normal behavior. This is especially true of very large Ranchu, which may list while at rest, and as long as their energy levels and appetite are good, there is little to worry about.

Changes in comportment can also be caused by intestinal parasites, which could be causing weight loss or damaging the intestines.
Solutions: Test all water parameters immediately and correct any problems. If you determine that your water is perfect, perform a fecal examination to check for intestinal parasites.

This may also be a precursor of "flipover." See the entry "Flipover/Floating."

Symptom: EYE LOSS OR DAMAGE
Causes: The loss of one or both eyes may be caused by catching on tank décor, the attack of a tank mate, or a bacterial or fungal infection.
Solutions: The loss is usually followed by two days of reduced activity, and then life seems to go on as usual. There may be considerable bleeding from the eye socket at the time of loss, but this subsides quickly and requires no surgical attention. Eyeless Goldfish maneuver around their tank with aplomb and find food with ease.

Symptom: EYES BULGING
Causes: Bulging eyes are related to dropsy, or water accumulation in the body. Another cause for bulging eyes is trauma to the eye, which causes swelling in the

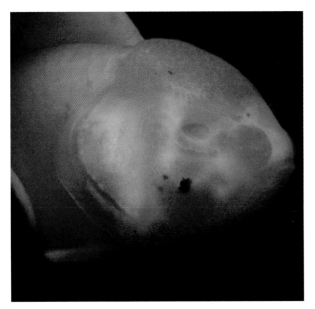

EYE LOSS.

CLOUDY EYES.

blood vessels behind the eye and will go down in a week or so.

Solutions: The condition may be transient and can be benefited by salting the water to a concentration of 0.3%. Bulging eyes PLUS dropsy is terminal.

Symptom: EYES WHITE OR CLOUDY

Causes: White eye is almost always one of two things: a flexobacterial infection secondary to trauma to the eye, or a caustic inflammation from exposure to ammonia or formalin. In addition, a recently shipped fish may have suffered some eye trauma, in which case the lesion will probably be only a corneal edema.

Cloudy eye is a common condition in all Goldfish varieties, but it is most prevalent among the varieties with protruding eyes such as Telescopes. When Goldfish are netted and sized in Asia, they are often slid across sizing and counting tables, and this easily causes abrasions on the protruding eyeballs of Telescopes. Then the fish are flown on a twenty-four-hour journey across the ocean to the wholesaler. The ammonia in the bags burns the fishes' abraded eyes, causing them to whiten and become slimy in the next few days.

On the other hand, hobbyists who own a previously clear-eyed Black Telescope that suddenly develops white eyes in an established tank should check their water quality, which has probably deteriorated in some way. In many instances, white eyes show up in Telescopes after you've already been treating the other fish with a compound containing formalin.

Solutions: Injections, perfect water conditions, and temperatures in the mid-seventies are usually curative for flexobacterial white eye. White eye that is the result of caustic trauma from an overdose of formalin or an ammonia burn responds well to Stress Coat, a 0.3% salt solution, and possibly an injection of Azactam, chloramphenicol, or Baytril. For those without the ability or inclination to give injections, consider furazone green. White eye that is actually a lesion caused by a shipping accident will only be resolved with time, though antibiotic injection won't hurt. See the Formulary for details on all these medications.

Symptom: FINS CLAMPED

Causes: Clamped fins are caused by parasitism or poor water quality, especially pH crash.

Solutions: Check water quality. Check for parasites under the microscope. If a microscope is not available, treat with a 0.3% salt solution first, and then for flukes.

Symptom: FINS RED

Causes: Fins with dilated red vessels or a reddish tinge to them can be a sign of several things: stress, poor water quality, parasites, or systemic bacterial infection.

Solutions: Test your water quality. If that's fine, perform a 50% water change and add salt to your tank to a 0.3% concentration.

Symptom: FINS SPLIT

Causes: Split fins can indicate flukes.

Solutions: Check and, if necessary, treat for flukes. To repair a split pectoral fin on a large Goldfish, you can anesthetize the fish and suture the fin back together with a fine 3-0, 6-0, or finer suture, by weaving the suture through the rays of the fin and eventually closing the gap. The suture breaks down in a week underwater and the fin is as good as new. The fish must be anesthetized or the thrashing of the tail will tear up your work.

Symptom: FLANK SUCKING/PICKING
Causes: Flank sucking or picking can start with a tiny lesion on the fish that becomes attractive to other fish because of the hemorrhage. These lesions may come from abrasions received during normal activity, breeding behavior, and so forth. If you are underfeeding the fish you may find them becoming unduly interested in weaker fish or chewing at each other. Care must be taken in the interpretation of lesions, however. Do not assume that a sore on a fish is caused by other fish picking on it. Indeed, the ulcer may be the primary symptom of a parasitism and secondary bacterial attack, and the fish picking at the sore may be an innocent bystander.
Solutions: Check and correct water quality. Check for parasites.

Symptom: FLASHING/SCRATCHING
Causes: A fish that hovers for a moment, almost motionless over an aquarium surface or tank ornament, and then briskly rolls onto its side and scratches itself on the surface or ornament is described as "flashing." The fish seems to be running sideways into objects in an effort to dislodge some skin irritant. The fish may display this behavior as rarely as once daily or as frequently as every five minutes. Any flashing seen more than once per day can be considered cause for water-quality evaluation and a check for parasitism.

Fish will "flash" and scratch when they have flukes, *Trichodina*, or an anchor-worm infestation. Almost any parasitism can cause fish to flash or scratch on things. Rapid changes in water quality can cause flashing. A large addition of fresh water can cause flashing as the fishes' skin adapts to a slightly higher or lower pH. Residual chlorine or metals in new water can cause flashing. Goldfish brought to shows often flash very actively, irritated by the new water in the show tank. Still, keep in mind that a parasite could also be the cause, so caution and quarantine are recommended.

Finally, black plastic water lines that contain large amounts of UV stabilizers and elasticizers can cause irritation sufficient to cause excessive flashing.
Solutions: Check for parasites, use a dechlorinator when changing water to bind irritating ingredients in your water and alleviate irritation, and never allow your fish water to come into contact with a novel plastic.

Symptom: FLIPOVER / FLOATING
Causes: "Flipover" and "floater" are two terms commonly used to describe a condition in which the

Goldfish may begin to list to one side or swim and float upside down for a short period of time. Eventually you begin to notice that the inversion becomes more and more common and when the fish is at rest, the tail begins to rise or the fish rolls onto its nose while resting. Finally, the fish spends most of its time rolling onto its nose and floating upside down.

There are at least three theories about why flipover occurs, and each may be accountable for some cases, alone or in combination. In some cases, flipover seems to be due to a loss of lower-body mass due to intestinal parasitism or harm to the liver, such as is caused by tuberculosis. As the fish's appetite and absorptive capabilities wane, it loses its ventral ballast, and soon it begins to flip over and float to the top.

In other cases, impaction of the gut is the culprit, and feeding green peas is sometimes effective. Flipover can sometimes be prevented by feeding small, more frequent feedings with variations in protein and fiber content instead of a processed staple diet.

But in many other cases, no cause can be determined. One of the most interesting recent theories, as yet unverified, suggests that high levels of nitrate affect air-sac control. According to this theory, the accumulation of nitrates in the water can adversely affect the normal buoyancy of the air sac and cause the sac to hyperinflate and flip the fish over. The reason for this lies in the physiology of fishes' ballast system. Goldfish possess an air sac. The air sac, located in the abdomen, buoys the fish up in the water. It has two lobes. One of the lobes is nearer the tail (the caudal sac) and the other is in front of it (the anterior sac). The air sac fills with air as tiny capillaries that supply the air sacs deposit tiny amounts of air through the walls in the posterior chamber. As the fish desires to rise or fall in the water, there is a natural and automatic adjustment in the amount of air in the air sac. When the sac needs to lose air to allow less buoyancy, small amounts of air can be expelled into the air sac and then into the esophagus. The air can be "burped" out, or in some cases may pass through the digestive tract.

High nitrate levels are thought to cause dilation of the capillaries (vasodilation) in the walls of the air sac. They become inflamed and this swelling can impede transfer of air from the caudal sac to the anterior one. It can also impede the exit of air from the air sacs into the esophagus. This causes an excess of buoyancy that may result in the floater or flipover syndrome.

This theory has been advanced because so many cases of flipover are discovered in water contaminated with extremely high nitrate levels, and many "borderline" flipover cases are rapidly returned to normal when moved to nitrate-free water. Still, it remains only a theory at this point, since no scientific testing of this hypothesis has been carried out to date.

Solutions: Flipover has been successfully reversed by removal of the affected fish from nitrate-rich water, heavy feedings with varied foodstuffs, and a surgical process called quartz-implant coeleotomy, in which we simply implant some quartz stones in the ventral abdomen. This procedure is discussed, with illustrations, in the "Surgical Procedures" section.

Symptom: GASPING AT SURFACE

Causes: The water may have inadequate dissolved oxygen. Decay of uneaten food, plant material, and so forth can consume massive amounts of oxygen. Formalin, contained in many generic medications, consumes oxygen. Finally, warm water and crowding result in low levels of dissolved oxygen. If oxygen levels are fine, pH crash, parasitism, chlorine toxicity, damage caused by excessive use of medications, and other caustic traumas to the gills may be decreasing oxygen transfer.

Solutions: Check all water parameters and correct as necessary. Increase agitation of the water. You can use a strong pump with a Venturi valve that increases oxygen levels. If the water is over eighty degrees, cool it. If the water quality is good and the temperature cool, treat with a 0.3% salt solution.

Symptom: GILL COVER HOLES

Causes: Consider tuberculosis or *Aeromonas* bacterial infections. Holes in the gill covers are among the most common signs of tuberculosis I have seen in fish, probably because it is the only external symptom. Other tuberculosis lesions are internal, found in the liver and other organs. Tuberculosis is only occasionally transmissible to people, usually to the elderly and those with compromised immune systems. Even in these cases, the tuberculosis must gain entry through wounds on the hands or other skin surfaces in contact with the water.

Solutions: Tuberculosis in fish is not treatable. *Aeromonas* may respond to injections of antibiotics, but the hole will not close. Check for parasites and treat as necessary. For best results, insure optimal water quality, temperature, and aeration.

Symptom: GILLS PALE

Causes: Flukes can damage the gills to the point where the fish is basically bleeding to death through microhemorrhages in the gills. Fish with the IHN virus will also develop pale gills as they die.

Solutions: Check microscopically for flukes, and treat accordingly. There is currently no treatment for IHN.

Symptom: GILLS SWOLLEN OPEN

Causes: This is almost always a fluke infestation. Some rare exceptions are bacterial gill disease, and the two conditions often occur together.

Solutions: Check for flukes under the microscope and treat accordingly. Also check the gills of fish for signs of bacterial gill disease and, if present, treat as described in that section.

Symptom: HEAD DOWN, TAIL AT SURFACE

Causes: This is a symptom of a bacterial infection or it could be an early warning sign of flipover disease.

Solutions: Check your water and make sure you check your nitrates. If the readings are normal, you should treat with injections as for a bacterial infection. You may lose the head-down fish within a week to ten days if a bacterial infection is the cause. Other exposed fish will die later if you do not eliminate any parasites (which probably precipitated the infection) and bacterial invasion of the fish.

Symptom: HEAD UP, HANGING JUST UNDER SURFACE LETHARGICALLY

Causes: If the fish are hovering lethargically with heads at the surface, not gasping but just hanging there, check your pH at once. This can be a symptom of pH crash. Very often the pH is falling and the fish will hang under the water surface, then start getting a milky skin. Check all other water parameters as well and correct as necessary. You should also follow up with an examination of gill tissue with the naked eye and also microscopically.

Symptom: JUMPING

Causes: Jumping behavior suggests the fish have a problem with parasites or their water. You'll see fish jumping when the pH is dropping, or when some other irritant, such as ammonia, is accumulating in the water.

Solutions: Perform water tests first. If the water is perfect, check for parasites, particularly flukes, and treat as indicated by the diagnosis.

Symptoms: LARGE SORES ON BODY

Causes: These are ulcers and are caused by bacteria such as *Aeromonas* and *Pseudomonas*, which often get into the skin via parasitic attack, assisted by poor water conditions.

Solutions: Restore water quality to near-perfect conditions. Check for parasites with a microscope. Treat the parasites first, then inject the fish with antibiotics to cure the infection. The sores may be swabbed with potassium permanganate, hydrogen peroxide, Panolog, mercurochrome, or another topical treatment. The UV sterilizer has been the biggest advance in the treatment of ulcers since the advent of injections. By making the water as sterile as possible we can hasten recoveries from ulcer disease by up to a week.

Symptom: MOUTH ROT
Causes: The initial cause of mouth rot is often a parasitic attack, but it can also arise from overcrowding and nose rubbing on the tank sides or decor. Treat aggressively and be sure to select a treatment that will eliminate flukes.
Solutions: First, make certain your water quality is perfect, with plenty of aeration, minimal organic material, no ammonia, and a stable pH. Injections are strongly recommended for the affected fish. You don't have to remove the fish from the main tank, but you should consider a potassium permanganate treatment for the entire tank.

You may swab the mouth wound once, but don't scrub too hard or repeat. Avoid letting any topical medication run down the gullet to the gills.

Symptom: RED SPOTS
Causes: Red spots or sores represent the earliest stages of bacterial infection (ulcer disease) in the skin of Goldfish. Sometimes abrasions sustained in the breeding frenzy can become infected. This is particularly true if the spawn has fouled the water or if the fish are crowded. In addition, some red spots are very commonly caused by infectious parasites that attack the skin, such as *Argulus* or *Lernea*, opening it to infection. Flukes are another excellent possibility.
Solutions: Check for bacterial infection and parasites and treat accordingly.

Symptom: SCALES STANDING OUT ALL OVER BODY
Causes: This is dropsy, which is terminal.
Solutions: None, at present.

Symptom: SCALES STANDING OUT ON PART OF BODY
Causes: Breeding activity or parasites have broken the skin and bacteria are starting to infect the areas. *Costia* infections may also cause raised areas of scales but a microscopic biopsy is required to confirm this.
Solutions: Check water quality. If it is normal, add salt to the water to make a 0.3% concentration. I also recommend a single injection of Amikacin.

Symptom: SITTING ON BOTTOM
Causes: Goldfish that rest on the bottom of the tank can be divided into two categories, each requiring different treatment. The first category includes fish that have to struggle to swim into the mid-water or to the surface. They have a swim bladder problem, sometimes due to

bacterial infection and sometimes due to defects in the swim bladder. (Necropsies show that some of these fish have water in the air sac instead of air.)

The second category is fish that swim fine when disturbed. These fish usually carry a massive fluke or *Costia* burden and are being weakened by the parasites. They rest on the bottom, which further assists the parasites in proliferating on the skin and gills, and the fish eventually dies.

Electrocution can cause this symptom as well.
Solutions: Check for bacterial infection and parasites and treat as necessary. Also check for electrical current in your system.

Symptom: Skin Milky
Causes: Milky skin is the result of excess mucus production. Parasitism is one cause. In long-established collections to which new fish have not been introduced, it can be caused by plunges in pH. When the pH plunges, fish hover at the surface and get milky skins. Their eyes can even turn whitish.
Solutions: Please refer to the sections on pH and carbonate hardness. If you have a stable pH but some new arrivals to your collection, consider parasites and ammonia burn caused by increased biological load. In either case, a 0.3% salt solution will help considerably. In fact, salt is the answer in many cases because it controls so many parasites. If milky skin continues despite salt treatment and a thorough check of water quality, a salt-resistant *Trichodina*, *Costia*, or a fluke infestation may be the culprit. Use a microscope to diagnose and treat accordingly.

Symptom: SPITTING
Causes: The fish will eagerly take food, then immediately spit it out without eating it. Some fish will take and spit out food at each feeding, never actually eating a thing! This may be a sign of an advancing fluke infestation, of something lodged in the gills, or an ulcer in the mouth.
Solutions: Perform an oral exam of the mouth including the roof of the mouth and look for an ulcer. Examine the gills, looking for swelling, paleness, and streaks of white around the edge of the gill or through the gill tissue. Look for a foreign body, such as a piece of hair or string intertwined in the gill arches, or even a stone in the mouth. Then perform a gill scrape and examine microscopically for flukes and treat accordingly.

Symptom: STOOL CHANGES
Goldfish stool is normally brown and crumbly. Deviations from this quality of stool are not always a sign of disease, but it is good to be aware of the diagnosis and correction of potential problems indicated by stool changes.

SYMPTOMS, CAUSES, AND SOLUTIONS

Stools, which change according to the color of the food that is being fed, may indicate a digestive problem in which the food is not broken down or absorbed. The most common cause for this is intestinal parasitism. You can collect a stool from the Goldfish by placing it in a white tub with its own tank water. As soon as it has a bowel movement pipette the stool onto a glass slide and compress it with a coverslip. Examine the stool under the microscope. If you see eggs, worm the fish with Tramisol or Droncit, both of which are extremely safe and effective regardless of the species of intestinal worm.

Stools that are hollow, white, and stringy are called "casts" and are seen when a fish has not been eating well for a while or has an intestinal infection. Such casts may also be seen in perfectly healthy Goldfish that are kept in a tank with a sand substrate.

If fish kept in a tank with a gravel substrate have white casts, check the stools for worms. Watch closely, and if the fish exhibit any signs of illness, consider using an injectable or oral antibiotic to prevent a worsening condition.

Green stools are common and normal in Goldfish that receive high quantities of vegetation and algae in their diet. Stools that are light green or very loose may suggest a bacterial intestinal infection in the Goldfish. Usually, the stool does not hang together or form a strand. It seems to disintegrate as it is extruded. Stool condition is not the best way to diagnose a systemic infection, because stools are usually scant in infected fish, which have a reduced appetite.

Symptom: Swimming with Mouth Wide Open, Unable to Close

Causes: Three out of four times such fish have a foreign body lodged in the mouth. The remaining cases usually have an ulcer or sore on the roof of the mouth.

Solutions: Examine the mouth, and if you find a foreign object, gently push it forward and out of the mouth through the gill cover. The fish will tolerate this better under anesthesia. In the case of an ulcer, carefully swab with hydrogen peroxide, making sure no excess peroxide gets on the gills, and inject the fish intraperitoneally with Baytril or one of the other antibiotics listed in the Formulary.

Symptom: Ulcers

Causes: True ulcers are open sores on the body caused by bacterial infection. Flukes usually contribute to this condition.

Solutions: Make sure your water quality is perfect. Check your pH and ammonia as well as your nitrite and nitrate readings. Then, removing any plants, salt the tank to a 0.3% concentration. Check for flukes, which almost certainly contributed to the problem, with a microscope and treat if necessary. Injections and topical treatments are also recommended.

Symptom: Wasting Away

Causes: Many fish that seem to waste away are burdened by flukes. In the absence of any other stress, such as poor water quality, Goldfish can carry large numbers of flukes, but they slowly lose body condition as they bleed to death through their gills. This is especially common among smaller fishes of the one-year size. Larger fish that exhibit wasting may have an internal pathology. Wasting can be caused by tuberculosis of the liver, other liver pathology, or poorly formulated diets.

Solutions: Diagnose for flukes and check diet.

Symptoms: Waxy, White Teardrops on Skin

Causes: Viral dermatosis is commonly caused by a herpes virus of Goldfish and Koi, also known as carp pox.

Solutions: These lesions will only respond to heat. See the section on papillomatous lesions.

Symptoms: White Fuzz/Tufts

Causes: White fuzzy areas or tufts can be tough to diagnose without a microscope, since fungus, *Epistylis*, and bacterial *Columnaris* (sometimes called cotton-wool disease) all produce this appearance. Under a microscope, fungus looks like strands of human hair, while the usually abundant *Epistylis* organisms feature a long, slender stalk and a body that looks like a wineglass or goblet. *Columnaris* bacteria are harder to identify without special stains or a very high-powered microscope.

Solutions: Fungus is best treated with potassium permanganate. *Epistylis* responds well to a 0.3% salt solution, and *Columnaris* should be treated with injections and water treatments such as potassium permanganate and furazone green.

Symptom: White Spots on Skin

Causes: White spots are caused by ich. The spots caused by ich are tiny, pinhead-size spots; if the spots are larger and resemble droplets of wax, check the symptom Waxy, White Teardrops on Skin.

Solutions: Diagnose and treat ich.

Symptom: Worms under Scales

Causes: These are anchor worms (*Lernea*).

Solutions: Treat with Dimilin, which will eliminate anchor worm in only a few days.

Surgery for Goldfish is a developing, constantly changing field. Though for most veterinarians it is new, Dr. Greg Lewbart at North Carolina State University has been performing it for several years. I am among the first private practitioners to effectively perform routine elective surgeries on fish.

Egg impaction and "flipover" or "floater" syndrome are two conditions that respond well to surgery. I have also performed surgery to remove tumors, repair split fins, and pare away excess headgrowth.

This section is not intended as a surgery textbook. I have described selected surgical procedures to offer guidelines and, I hope, encouragement to professional veterinarians who are considering performing fish surgery. I do not recommend that the hobbyist attempt any of these procedures.

Anesthesia

Fish respire through their gills, and the success of surgery depends upon being able to supply oxygenated water that also carries anesthetic to the gills. We do this by mixing the anesthetic into a vessel of oxygenated water and flushing it across the gills with a tube attached to an adjustable pump. Larger fish may require a larger pump; for smaller fish, we use a paper cup and dribble the water continuously on the upper gill arch as the fish lies on its side.

For very small fish, we do not use a water reuse system. For very large fish we use a special table that catches the water and returns it to a vat for reuse.

The technical-support staff for the surgery monitors the anesthesia very closely, reporting immediately if the gill movements become too rare. The water-circulating pump is transferred from the maintenance anesthesia water to the clear water and back again as needed to maintain the necessary level of anesthesia.

Surgery for Egg Impaction

Description: The surgical approach to the abdomen of a Goldfish is through the belly wall off the midline (there is a large vessel on the ventral midline) and above (to the outside) the ventral and pectoral fins.

Equipment: Anesthetic, anesthetic delivery pump, tubing, three buckets of tank water, maintenance solution, induction solution of anesthetic, scalpel, holder, surgical abdominal pack, Liga Clips, Liga Clips appliers,

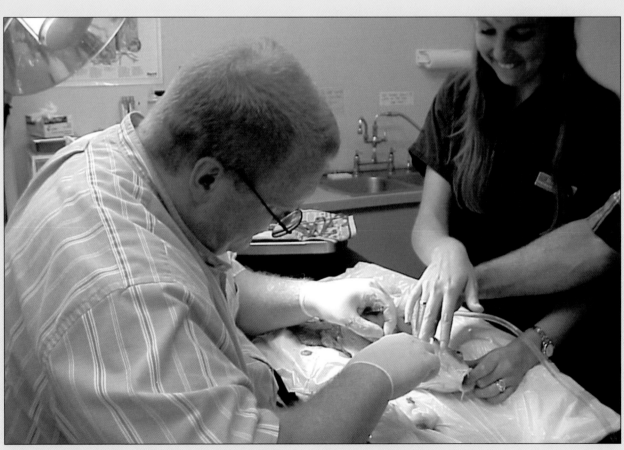

gauze, 3-0 absorbable suture for fine abdominal work, 0 nonabsorbable suture (Braunamid) for the abdominal wall coming out, bright surgical light with flexible neck, plastic bag to wrap the fish in during extended-period surgeries, and two extra pairs of hands.

Procedures: Once inside the abdomen, it is imperative to use extreme care to prevent damage to the intestines, which are pale pink and very fragile.

The success of this surgery depends on recognition of several anatomical landmarks, and detailed instruction is beyond the scope of this book. Many surgical failures among amateurs can be attributed to a failure to consult on and learn these surgical landmarks. The most conspicuous one is the large ovarian artery that passes between the front and back lobe of the air sac and that supplies the egg sac. When one resects the egg-impacted ovary from the fish, a failure to find and ligate this vessel guarantees failure. The problem is that the heart beats so rarely that there is no dramatic spurt of blood to attract the surgeon's eye.

Surgery for Air-sac Pneomonocytis

Description: Air Sac Pneumocytis is an important factor in the management of "floater syndrome," in which a fish becomes inverted and floats helplessly on the surface. Many factors contribute to this condition.

Some "floaters" can be cured by a procedure called air-sac pneumocentesis. In this process, the air sac is defined within the body of the fish and is drained of air without risk to any important vascular structure or digestive entity.

Equipment: A sterile 22-gauge needle on a 3-milliliter syringe.

Procedure: The sterile 22-gauge needle on a 3-milliliter syringe is used to extract the air, but hitting the air sac without damaging another structure is of paramount importance. The needle is introduced perpendicular (90 degrees) to the side of the fish to a depth of approximately half the fish's body width. If you cannot pull back on the syringe's plunger, you are NOT in the air sac. It is almost impossible to miss the air sac when you use the landmarks described below.

Define your vertical axis by observation of the first ray of the dorsal fin and coming straight down the side of the fish from this ray. Define your horizontal axis by coming across from the eye to a point slightly below the lateral line, where it crosses your vertical axis.

Insert the needle at this intersection and withdraw as much air as you can. In large fish, 3 to 6 milliliters of air can be expected.

The fish will have lost all its buoyancy when returned to the tank and will sit on the bottom of the tank lethargically. There should be very little bleeding from the needle stick.

If the fish is still inverted, give it time. The air sac will usually refill within twenty-four hours. If the fish refills completely, it will be floating upside down again the following morning. Hopefully, the fish will not refill completely and will be swimming normally the following day.

If the case resists this treatment and returns to an overly buoyant and inverted condition, you will need to repeat the air-sac pneumocentesis and then perform and quartz-implant coeleotomy.

Quartz-Implant Coeleotomy

Description: Quartz-implant coeleotomy is the technique of choice in righting a flipover or floater fish. Small pieces of uncolored quartz are implanted in the fish to provide it ballast. In earlier trials, stainless-steel implants were rejected, but uncolored quartz aquarium gravel proved to be irritating enough that the body covered the stones with fibrin and safely retained them.

Equipment: Oil of cloves, a clean plastic bin, a clean jar with lid, 3-0 absorbable suture material, scalpel blade and holder, 2 gallons of water, 4 to 5 pieces of uncolored quartz aquarium gravel of a slender, oval shape.

Procedure: Note: If you do not fully understand the gravity or technique of the following, then this information is not for you.

Get a clean plastic bin with aquarium water and place exactly 2 gallons of water in it.

To prepare the anesthetic, place 10 drops of oil of cloves into the clean jar with a small quantity of water. Cap the jar and shake it until it looks like thin milk, thoroughly mixing the oil of cloves with the water.

Place the fish in the bin. Place the jar in the bin and under the water, open the cap and allow the mixed oil of cloves to mix with the water in the bin. In a few minutes the fish will become lethargic. Do not wait until the fish is motionless to begin.

Pick up the fish and make a small incision through the belly wall. The incision need only be wide enough to slide in the ballast implants.

Do not damage structures underneath your incision. You can more safely widen and deepen the incision with a pair of hemostats.

There will be some bleeding. Do not get rattled. It's all right if the fish moves. Fish do not have a spinothalamic tract and feel no deep pain.

Using hemostats, pick up two or three slender, clean pieces of uncolored quartz aquarium gravel and insert them into the incision, sliding them downward

ABOVE: ORANDA WITH HEADGROWTH COVERING THE EYES.
BELOW: ORANDA WITH EXCESS HEADGROWTH SURGICALLY REMOVED.

dling. At that point let the fish fall to the bottom, where it should sit upright.

Eventually, the fish's air sac will fill sufficiently to lift it from the bottom of the tank and allow it to rejoin its mates, upright and eating. Until that point, you may have to feed it a sinking food such as bloodworms or krill.

Precautions: Never incise across the midline. A giant blood vessel is located there. Do not force the stones into the abdomen in any way, as you may sever the colon. And finally, erring on the side of using less anesthetic and seeing a little squirming is better than killing the fish with excessive anesthesia.

Surgery for Removal of Excessive Headgrowth

Description: The cap or headgrowth of some fancy varieties of Goldfish can grow so large that it covers the eyes of the fish. In most instances, this does not affect the fish. Blind fish can apprehend food as effectively as their sighted tank mates, though they are often less active. Still, some hobbyists may wish to have excess head growth removed, and this can be done surgically.

Equipment: Oil of cloves, a #10 scalpel or a pair of iris tenotomy scissors.

Procedure: Induce anesthesia with oil of cloves. Once the fish is still, lift it from the water. Introduce the blade adjacent to the eye and cut at an angle to the eye, removing the tissue around the eye. Extreme care must be employed to avoid lacerating the eye globe; this may be difficult, because you cannot see where the tip of your blade is. With practice, you can complete the trimming within four to five minutes.

You can also use a pair of iris tenotomy scissors to pare away the excess growth over the eye.

The headgrowth is never attached to the eye globe at any point. Indeed, it is possible to cut away too much of the headgrowth, and you may find the eyes protruding without support.

If the fish begins to struggle during the procedure, place it into the aerated oil of cloves solution again. If the fish is not struggling but has been out of the water for more than ninety seconds, place it into well-aerated normal tank water for a "breather," then resume where you left off. In all instances, you should maintain the fish under fairly deep anesthesia, with gill movements at less than one flex per several seconds. (During many of my surgeries, gill movements occur at an interval of less than one per minute.)

No sutures are needed. The fish will bleed very nominally after the procedure.

with minimal force to the midline, under the organs. You are trying to provide ballast to keep the fish from floating, and you will find it takes only a few pieces of gravel to right the fish. I've never had to use more than 4 pieces. Again, don't just shove them in, slide them along the belly wall down to the ventral (lower) midline.

Set the fish back in the anesthetic and see if it's belly-down. If not, add another stone.

Once you've added enough ballast to keep the fish upright, or at least listing upright, sew the incision closed using a fine, 3-0 or 4-0 suture. Use a simple basting stitch and tie it gently, not tightly, closed. Leave the stitches in for one week and remove them.

An injection of an antibiotic is recommended at this point. Since you've opened the peritoneum, an intramuscular injection is mandated.

Place the fish back in its main aquarium. There is some wisdom in walking the fish, very gently, in moderate current, holding it upright until it resents your han-

Appendix

GOLD-AND-BLACK ORANDA.

DOSAGE MEASUREMENTS AND CALCULATIONS

Water Treatments

Use the following formula to determine water volume precisely. Make sure to use the interior, not exterior, dimensions of the vessel.

For a rectangular box of water, multiply length x width x depth (recorded in inches) and then divide the product by 231. This gives a result in U.S. gallons.

$$[(L") \times (W") \times (D")] \div 231 = \text{U.S. gallons}$$

For a cylindrical, vat or bowl, multiply pi π, approximately 3.14, x the (radius)^2 in inches x depth in inches and divide that product by 231 to arrive at U.S. gallons.

$$[(\pi) \times (r^2) \times (D")] \div 231 = \text{U.S. gallons}$$

Doses

Doses are calculated by converting common measurements. Here are some important and commonly used conversions:

General Equivalents

1 PPM (parts per million) is the same concentration as 1 milligram per liter (mg/L).

1 milliliter (1 ml) of most fluids weighs 1 gram.

1 milliliter (1 ml) is considered equivalent in volume to 1 cubic centimeter (1 cc)

30% purity represents 300 milligrams per milliliter or 300 milligrams per gram

Weight Equivalents

1,000 milligrams = 1 gram

1,000 grams = 1 kilogram

2.2 U.S. pounds = 1 kilogram

1 milliliter (1 ml) of most fluids weighs 1 gram

Volume Equivalents

3.79 liters = 1 U.S. gallon

4.55 liters = 1 British gallon

1.06 liters = 1 U.S. quart

1 liter = 1.13 British quarts

1 liter = 2.1 pints

1 liter = 33.8 fluid ounces

1 milliliter (1 ml) is considered equivalent in volume to 1 cubic centimeter (1 cc)

1 teaspoon = 5 milliliters

1 tablespoon = 3 teaspoons

1 tablespoon = 15 milliliters

1/4 cup = 60 ml = 12 teaspoons

1 cup = 240 ml = 16 tablespoons

1 drop = 0.1 ml or 25 drops = 2.5 ml

CONVERSION OF "PERCENT SOLUTIONS" TO MG/ML

A 20% solution contains 200 milligrams of medication per milliliter of solution.

A 20% pure compound contains 200 milligrams per gram of compound.

A 50% solution contains 500 milligrams in one gram.

Dosages are often expressed in PPM, for example, "Dose with COMPOUND at 4 PPM." The label on your medication COMPOUND tells you that the solution is of 30% purity. Here is one example of using the above conversions to calculate this dose correctly.

First, remember from the above that 1 PPM = 1 mg/L

Therefore: 4 PPM = 4 mg/L

Convert your gallons to liters: 1 gallon = 3.79 liters

I have 30 gallons in my tank = 30 gallons x 3.79 liters/gallon = 113.7 liters

I need 4 milligrams per liter, so: 4mg/L = x mg/113.7L and solve for x

I need 454.8 milligrams of COMPOUND.

My stock solution is 30% pure. Using the above charts, I get:

30% solution = 30 milligrams per milliliter.

So I set up another equation: 30mg/ml = 454.8mg /x ml and solve for x

Therefore I will require 15.16 ml of the 30% COMPOUND to treat my 30-gallon tank.

These calculations are not really complex, but there is plenty of room for error, so be careful to check your arithmetic several times.

PART TWO

Keeping and Collecting Fancy Goldfish

Chapter 7

Keeping Fancy Goldfish: Commonly Asked Questions

Richard E. Hess

CALICO ORANDAS.

Over the past twelve hundred years, the Chinese, and later the Japanese, have developed the small Asian river carp species *Carrassius auratus* into the Goldfish, with its tremendous variety of beautiful shapes and colors. Goldfish make excellent pets, and they have many advantages in addition to their beauty that busy people today will appreciate. They aren't noisy or destructive, as

neglected dogs can be; they don't shed or need a place for their litter box in a cramped city apartment. Just give them good clean water and a stable environment, and they will greet you every time you walk into the room, swimming eagerly to the front of the aquarium. A Goldfish tank can be an attractive addition to your home, and watching your fish swim gracefully through the water is relaxing and a good way to relieve stress. It can be an educational tool for children, teaching them not only about caring for living things, but about genetics (for those who breed fish), chemistry (especially with regard to water quality), and mechanics (working out your filtration and other support systems). You'll enjoy the satisfaction of seeing them grow and thrive under your care. When kept well, Goldfish can live a long time. You may even venture into breeding them. There are dozens of varieties and color patterns to choose from, and as you observe your pets you'll discover that not only each variety but also each individual fish has its own distinct personality. In short, Goldfish collecting is a wonderful hobby that has many different things to offer to many different people.

Over the years I've talked with Goldfish keepers ranging from the beginner who saw a pet-shop Goldfish she just had to take home, to the experienced collector who has had his Goldfish pets for ten to fifteen years. I've answered many questions for the beginners and even for the experienced collectors. I have also asked questions from the best and most experienced hobbyists and breeders, including experts in Japan and China. In this section, I would like to share these questions and answers with you, organizing them around some of the topics that come up most frequently.

The Goldfish Environment

The first step to keeping Goldfish is setting up a suitable environment for them to live in. This includes the container, usually an aquarium, and everything that goes in it, from water to equipment to decoration. Establishing a good, stable, and safe environment is the key to success in keeping Goldfish.

THE AQUARIUM

Because of limited space and climate factors, among other reasons, most Western collectors today keep their Goldfish in indoor aquariums. The Goldfish aquarium can be an enjoyable "entertainment center" in your home, and it also allows you to control your Goldfish's environment carefully. Aquariums are widely available in all shapes and sizes today, but some are more suited for Goldfish than others.

What's the best size tank for Goldfish?
The size of your aquarium depends upon the number of Goldfish you plan to keep. A good rule of thumb is one Goldfish per 10 gallons of water. While 10 gallons per fish is a good general rule, obviously a really large fish will be better off with more water and a very small

fish won't need as much. Some people follow the rule of 3 gallons of water for each inch of fish, not including the tail. The more space you can give your pets the better. We all want to have a large collection of fish, but in kindness (and fairness) to your pets, don't crowd them.

You should also consider the shape of the aquarium when choosing a tank for Goldfish. Choose an aquarium with maximum surface area. A shallow, long, wide aquarium is more desirable than a deep, short, narrow one, because it will have more surface area. Goldfish seem to prefer to swim back and forth rather than up and down, and a shallow tank is also much easier for you to keep clean and to work in. If the tank is deeper than the length of your arm, you'll have a hard time cleaning the gravel and the glass, or catching the fish when necessary.

It is also much easier to control water quality in a large aquarium. When something goes wrong in a small volume of water, the entire system will be affected very quickly. When there is more water, not only do you have a chance to see problems starting but the larger amount of water also acts as a buffer that actually prevents some problems from arising at all.

Is it true that the size of my tank will limit the size of my Goldfish?
It doesn't seem so. In an experiment conducted with Channel Catfish, researchers placed five or six small Catfish in a 15-gallon tank under perfect conditions. The Catfish grew the entire length of the tank with no room to turn around—their tails were touching one end and their noses the other. The average hobbyist probably cannot duplicate the perfect conditions in which the laboratory Catfish were raised, but with excellent water and high-quality food, most Goldfish will grow quite large in an aquarium. Tank size does not seem to significantly limit fish size, except for the very important fact that it is extremely difficult to keep a crowded tank and its water clean—and those factors will have an effect on your fishes' growth, and maybe even their survival.

A more important factor may be genetics and the conditions the Goldfish were raised in during their first year. Some individual fish just grow larger than others. Also, fish grow tremendously in their first year, and those fish that are fed and kept well in that period will have a big head start on those that aren't. The smaller fish may in fact never keep up.

Also remember that different varieties of Goldfish have different adult sizes. Comets and Wakins, for example, can easily grow to be a foot in length. Orandas, Lionheads, and Ranchus can also grow into relatively large fish. Celestials and Bubble Eyes, on the other hand, don't grow as large.

To repeat: Give your fish the most space you can afford. They will reward you with not only size but also increased health and beauty.

Where should I locate my aquarium?
A good location for your aquarium is a quiet place with indirect rather than direct sunlight that is convenient to electrical outlets and as close as possible to plumbing fixtures, which will save you a lot of work when doing water changes. Direct sunlight is not necessarily bad for your aquarium. It will promote the growth of a coat of green algae on the sides and bottom of the tank, and that can contribute to good water quality. But too much sunlight will overheat your water, so if you are going to place the aquarium near a window, it should be one that doesn't get too hot and is equipped with some means to control the amount of light and heat, such as blinds or curtains.

Set your tank on a stable, strong, flat surface. I use a layer of 1/2-inch blue Styrofoam underneath my aquariums, for two reasons. The first and most important reason is the Styrofoam forms a very good cushion and protects the aquariums from any unevenness of the stand. The second reason is that the Styrofoam gives the bottom of the aquarium a very nice blue color.

You need to be sure that not only the aquarium stand but also the area of your home where you place your aquarium can bear the weight. A 125-gallon tank filled with water weighs about one thousand four hundred pounds. Some homes are not built to support this weight.

My grandfather is a smoker and every time he leaves my home I spray with an air freshener. Will this hurt my fish?
Be very careful what you spray around your aquarium. Air fresheners, window cleaners, and spray furniture polish can all cause problems—as can tobacco smoke! It's not just that the vapors may land on the surface of the water; your air pump is drawing air from your room and pumping it into your water through air stones or your filtration system.

If you have any pesticide spraying done in your home, make sure that the compounds used are safe for fish, or skip the room in which you keep your aquarium (and make sure any central air conditioning or heating systems are off when spraying is done).

Can I use sponges from my supermarket to clean my aquarium?
Be very careful what kind of sponges you buy. Some contain an anti-bacterial agent that will kill your Goldfish. Read the labels carefully.

Be careful about everything that goes into your tank, including your hands. Make sure you are not wearing any lotion or perfume when you place your hands in the aquarium. Don't use any plastics or other materials that are not safe for fish. If you fill your aquarium with a hose, make sure it's a hose that can be used for drinking water. If you use your watering can, make sure there are no remnants of plant food in it. If there are children in the house, try to teach them not to throw toys or anything else into the tank.

I put my hands in my fish tank to clean the front glass and got a shock! What's happening and will it hurt my fish?
It can hurt and even kill both you and your fish. Some ungrounded aquarium equipment, such as pumps, heaters, and even lights, can cause stray current or serious electrical shock. The safest thing to do is to make sure all outlets near your aquarium, or which you use for your aquarium equipment, are fully grounded outlets. (You can also buy extension cords with this feature.) Any short will trip the circuit and turn off the current, preventing electrocution. If you have many tanks, each with many electrical appliances, it isn't a bad idea to check with your electrician to see if you are in danger of overloading your household circuits.

Some appliances start to short out slowly, and you may feel only a slight tingle when you place your hand in the water. This is a warning to shut everything off and examine the pumps, heaters, and lights carefully for any problems. If your aquarium light is exposed to the surface water of your tank, splashes of surface water can hit the electrical connections and cause current leaks and shorts. Place a lid or a Plexiglas protector between lights and water.

Stray current, even in small amounts, can irritate and even deform your fish.

WATER
What is the most important factor in keeping Goldfish healthy? That's easy: water quality. I once talked to a very successful Goldfish collector who has fish that are eight and ten years old. His oldest fish lived to be fourteen! I asked him his secret for keeping Goldfish alive for such a long period of time, expecting to hear a secret recipe for his homemade food, but his answer surprised me: "Rick," he said, "I'm not sure how much I know about Goldfish, but I know a lot about water quality. I feed the same food every day, always making sure I never overfeed to foul the water. I maintain superb quality water and the Goldfish take care of themselves."

These are simple words, but they are wise ones. Remember, water quality is the secret to success with your fish.

MATTE RED-AND-WHITE
VEILTAIL WITH A FEW
MATALLIC SCALES.

The serious Goldfish hobbyist should test his or her water, or have it tested. You need to know what kind of water you are offering your fish. Two important elements of water quality are pH and hardness. The pH of water is a measure of hydrogen ions in the water. On a scale of 0 to 14 a pH of 0 is the most acidic and a pH of 14 is the most alkaline. A pH of 7 is considered neutral. Our Goldfish like a pH from 7.2 to 7.4. A higher pH of 7.8 to 8.5 will not harm your fish but will make any ammonia in your aquarium more toxic to them. A low pH can harm the fish and the good bacteria in your aquarium.

Hardness is the concentration of mineral ions in the water, calcium and magnesium being the most prevalent. Water-test kits for hardness are available at your local fish store. Water that has a general hardness (GH) of from 0 PPM to 75 PPM is regarded as soft water. Moderately hard water ranges from 75 PPM to 150 PPM. If your water measures from 150 to 300 PPM, it is regarded as hard water. Water over 300 PPM is very hard water, and not suitable for Goldfish.

A very important part of water hardness is what is called the carbonate hardness (abbreviated as KH), which is the amount of carbonates in the water. There are test kits available that test carbonate hardness separate from general hardness. Carbonates act as a buffer, holding the pH of the water at a stable level. The less carbonates there are, the more chance you have of having a sudden drop in pH. Goldfish collectors with water of low carbonate hardness should test pH daily. Some medications are also more toxic in soft water. Please refer to the first part of the book for more information on this subject.

These are the main water-quality parameters that come with your water source. If you use well water, you should have it tested for contamination by pesticides, fertilizers, and heavy metals.

If you use city or town tap water, you can be certain that your city water department has added chemicals to your drinking water to make it safe for human consumption. Unfortunately, our Goldfish can't survive in this treated water. The two additions you must worry about the most are chlorine and chloramines. Most chlorine can be removed by heavy aeration for twenty-four hours. Chloramines, which are chlorine with ammonia (bleach) added, are much harder to remove. Fortunately, there are many good water conditioners on the market that will remove both chlorine and chloramines. Call your city water department to find out what is added to your drinking water, and then select the dechlorinator that removes those chemicals.

My pH is 8.2 and I am having a very hard time keeping it at the recommended 7.2 to 7.4. What should I do?
Goldfish are highly adaptable creatures, and they can thrive in water of considerable pH range, but they don't like sudden changes in their environment. You are probably stressing your Goldfish more by trying to regulate your pH level than by just leaving it alone. An 8.2 pH level will not harm your Goldfish, but remember to watch your ammonia levels at all times, since ammonia is more toxic to fish at a high pH.

The pH of my tap water is very low. I'm using a pH adjustor, but I'm still having problems.
A low pH is definitely a problem you must be aware of, and there are several ways to address it. The most reliable

RED ORANDAS.

is periodic testing of the pH and the carbonate hardness of your aquarium water and the regular use of high-quality commercial pH buffers. The quick-fix pH adjustors sold at pet stores are not the answer.

When I receive new Goldfish the pH in the bag is always much lower than the pH in my aquarium. Will a sudden rise in pH hurt my fish?

Some hobbyists place some water from the aquarium into the bag to help the fish adapt more easily to its new environment, but the sooner you remove the Goldfish from the bag after the temperature matches your aquarium water the better. Please remember—and this is very important—you can always place a fish from a low pH into a higher pH with no problems; but never place a fish from a high pH into a low pH. This will cause them great harm and probably kill them. If you are going from a high pH to a low pH, bring the low pH up with a buffer.

FILTRATION

Our Goldfish are kept in a closed environment, and they do not have the advantage of a large ecosystem to naturally maintain good water conditions. They depend on us for that. No matter how hard we try, we'll never come close to the efficiency of nature in providing clean water, but we do our best with filtration. There are basically three different kinds of filtration available to us: mechanical, biological, and chemical.

Mechanical filtration is necessary to remove floating particles in the water. Biological filtration is carried out by bacteria that reduce toxic ammonia and nitrites into less toxic nitrates. Chemical filtration is the use of absorbent materials such as charcoal and zeolite to remove ammonia and other toxins from the water.

Many filters on the market these days combine all three functions. Today there are four basic types of filters in common use: canister filters, wet-dry biological filters, undergravel filters, and hang-on filters. Sand and bead filters are also growing in popularity. Bead filters are presently only practical for very large systems of hundreds or thousands of gallons. Sand filters provide only biological filtration, but they are very efficient and come in sizes and at prices that make them practical as supplementary filtration for home aquariums.

One way to think of your filters is as small sewage-treatment plants, and in fact there is much technology in common between aquarium filters and sewage treatment systems. Goldfish hobbyists tend to have strong opinions about what the best filtration system is, but the short answer is: none. All filters are a compromise and none are perfect. Goldfish excrete much larger amounts of body wastes than tropical fish or saltwater fish, and the best way to keep their water clean is to make frequent, regular water changes. Your filters are important, but they are really only a stopgap measure between the all-important water changes.

Hobbyists who purposely overstock their tanks must have extensive filtration systems, but they take a risk in doing so: filters (and electric power) can fail, jeopardizing the entire collection. It's wiser to be "old-fashioned": stock lightly, change water regularly, and look at your filters as your helpers in maintaining water quality, but not the main factor, which is water changes.

Should I use charcoal in my filter?

Many people use carbon and charcoal in their filters on a regular basis, but it becomes useless very quickly and if not changed frequently becomes contaminated, doing more harm than good. For the home hobbyist, large and frequent water changes are much better for your Goldfish than depending on charcoal to filter your water. It would be of much more benefit to your Goldfish to replace the charcoal with some kind of medium with a surface on which to grow nitrifying bacteria.

ULTRAVIOLET STERILIZATION

Ultraviolet sterilizers can be a very valuable tool for creating a better environment for your Goldfish. We all keep our Goldfish in confined quarters under unnatural conditions that are perfect for cultivating bacteria. Of course the bacterium keep multiplying, and a single bacteria can produce 250 million bacteria in just a 24-hour period! Importers and collectors across the country have proven the effectiveness of ultraviolet sterilizers, using them to dramatically cut back on fish disease and death.

Is it true that if I use an ultraviolet sterilizer on my aquarium, I'll never be able to place my Goldfish back into regular aquarium water again?
Not at all. An ultraviolet sterilizer has no effect on your Goldfishes' immune system, which remains intact. The function of an ultraviolet sterilizer is to greatly reduce the number of bacteria in your aquarium and to make your aquarium as bacteria free as possible. Ultraviolet sterilizers kill some of the bacteria floating in the water, thus reducing the bacterial load of your closed system and creating cleaner, better water conditions. An ultraviolet sterilizer does not create a one-hundred-percent sterile environment. The bacteria on the side of your aquarium and in your filter will not be killed by ultraviolet sterilization.

How do I know what size ultraviolet sterilizer I need?
The most common mistake people make in determining the type of ultraviolet sterilizer (U.V.) to buy is to look at the wattage instead of the microwatts. Microwatts are what kill the bacteria, so look for the appropriate number of microwatts: 28,000 is a good standard.

The next important factor is what is called exposure time, the length of time that a certain amount of water is exposed to ultraviolet rays, usually measured in seconds. The exposure time is determined by the capacity of your pump and the amount of water your U.V. unit holds. In order for your U.V. unit to be effective—to kill most of the bacteria we are concerned about—the aquarium water must be exposed to an ultraviolet light of 28,000 microwatts for at least five seconds. To calculate exposure time, you must determine how much water your U.V. holds and the pump flow in gallons per second.

Let's try with an example of a U.V. that holds 3.3 gallons and a pump that circulates 180 gallons of water per hour. First let's find out how much the pump circulates per second. We start by dividing the 180 gallons per hour by 60 minutes and find that it pumps 3 gallons per minute. Then we divide those 3 gallons by 60 again, to get the amount of water pumped per second: in this case, 0.05 gallons. Finally, we divide the amount of water the U.V. holds (0.33 gallons) by 0.05. The answer is 6.6, which means that the water in the U.V. unit is exposed to ultraviolet rays for 6.6 seconds. This is sufficient exposure to kill all the bacteria and parasites that Goldfish collectors need to be concerned about. For a U.V. to be effective in killing most bacteria and parasites, a minimum exposure time of 4 seconds is required.

Not all U.V. units are created equal. Some brands of bulbs have lower microwatts, a shorter life, and are difficult to find replacements for. Different brands of units hold different amounts of water. It is very important to check on these things when purchasing a U.V. unit. If you do, you will have an effective tool for keeping your water clean and your fish disease free.

AERATION AND WATER CURRENT

Aeration in an aquarium is one of the most important components of a healthy aquarium.

It is also the one that is most often neglected. Some Goldfish collectors think that if they have plenty of filtration they do not need extra aeration. That belief may be wrong, depending upon the means of filtration you use. If the water exiting your filter vigorously agitates the surface of the water in your aquarium, it will produce some aeration by water-air contact. But if the water exiting your filter is below the waterline of your aquarium and causes little surface-water movement, the aeration benefit of that filter is nil.

Oxygen enters the water at the surface, where the tank water and the air in the room meet. Agitation of the surface creates exchange between these two media, and oxygen is mixed into the water. Any way you keep the surface of the tank water vigorously moving will produce aeration.

One good way to aerate is to hook up your filter so that the water returned to the tank vigorously agitates the surface. Canister filters are often set up to return water through a spray bar, which can be aimed across the surface of the tank to create maximum surface agitation and gas exchange. You could also set a small powerhead on the bottom of the tank and aim it to the surface.

Underwater air stones or diffusers are another excellent way of getting the water surface moving and picking up oxygen from the air. They are a good means of supplementing any surface agitation your filter return may provide. When using air stones or diffusers, finer bubbles generally produce more air-to-water contact at the surface, so they are superior.

Moving water to oxygenate it means producing water current inside the tank, and this is another important factor to consider in Goldfish keeping. Though the Carp that Goldfish originated from are a river fish, the highly developed strains of fancy Goldfish we keep have many features such as long fins, large heads, and short, deep bodies that make them poor swimmers. Some water current is beneficial, but strong water current can be an easily overlooked problem. Goldfish that have to be constantly fighting water current will become stressed, and stressed Goldfish are susceptible to illness.

How do you know if there is too much water current for your fish? Watch them. If the fish are all staying in one corner or to one side of your aquarium and the current pushes them about when they stop swimming, the current is too strong. Your Goldfish should swim actively throughout the entire aquarium.

There are many ways to reduce the current of your filters. The output of a powerhead can be directed against the back of the aquarium, for example. You can reduce the current output of a hang-on filter by draping a piece of filter floss over the overflow into the tank. Air stones are an excellent means of producing water-air exchange without creating strong currents. Experiment, checking your fishes' swimming patterns to judge your success. Some fish enjoy playing in a current that is not too strong and will swim under the outflow, or allow themselves to be carried up through the water by the bubbles from an air stone. Make sure they are not short of oxygen, but otherwise, don't worry too much about this behavior. It may be left over from their ancestors' days as strong river swimmers.

Some hobbyists find that they can direct the output of powerheads and other filters across the very top level of tank water, creating good oxygen exchange but leaving the lower levels relatively current free. Make sure in this case that the intake of your filters is close enough to the bottom to insure full circulation throughout the tank.

How much oxygen do I need in my aquarium?
The more the better. I recommend using several air stones or diffusers to maximize the amount of oxygen available to your fish. Also remember that warm water carries less oxygen than cold water, and if your tank temperatures rise because of the season or because you are treating your fish for disease, make sure you have sufficient aeration to compensate.

TEMPERATURE AND HEATERS

The ideal water temperature for Goldfish is seventy-two to seventy-four degrees. The metabolism of a Goldfish starts to slow down in water colder than sixty-five degrees. On the other hand, water that is too warm contains much less oxygen and greatly enhances the multiplication of bacteria, so maintaining correct water temperature is very important.

When doing water changes it is extremely important that the temperature of the water you are adding is very close to the temperature of the water in your tank.

Goldfish can adapt to a wide variety of temperatures if the changes are gradual. A change of five degrees per hour is regarded as the maximum safe temperature change.

If you can maintain the temperature of the water in your aquarium between seventy-two and seventy-four degrees, you have no need for a heater. A slight drop of a few degrees overnight should not affect the health of your Goldfish, and may even be beneficial. A temperature above seventy-two degrees is necessary for the "good" bacteria that keep your biological filtration system operating well.

If you do use a heater to maintain an even temperature in your aquarium, make sure it is unplugged before doing major water changes. When the water line goes below the heating unit, the glass housing will shatter!

What is the normal body temperature of a Goldfish?
Fish cannot regulate the temperature of their blood like mammals. Their body temperature is the same as or very close to the temperature of the water they are in.

In the summer, sometimes the temperature in my tank reaches ninety-five degrees. Will this hurt my fish?
Goldfish can stand a temperature of ninety-five degrees or higher if they are not crowded, but remember, the warmer the water, the less dissolved oxygen there is in it. If Goldfish are to survive in water this warm, they must not be overcrowded and you must have plenty of air-water surface exchange in the aquarium. An excellent way to help hold the temperature down in your tank in an emergency is to fill two 1-gallon jugs with water and freeze them. Take one out of the freezer and float it in your aquarium. When it thaws place it back into the freezer, and float the other, frozen one in your aquarium. Make sure you keep an eye on the temperature, because you don't want to overcool the water.

LIGHTING

As I mentioned earlier, the Goldfish aquarium can be placed near a window if you can control temperatures with blinds or curtains. This allows them to have some natural light, which is definitely beneficial to their health, activity level, and color. If your Goldfish cannot get natural light, they will benefit from full-spectrum lighting that approximates natural sunlight. Many such fluorescent bulbs are now available, stimulated by the saltwater-fish hobby.

Do Goldfish sleep?

Yes, they do, though their eyes don't close. You may see them "sitting" in the water at night, moving just enough to stay in place. This is your Goldfish asleep. Keep your fish on a cycle of twelve to sixteen hours a day of light, and try to allow them to rest peacefully in darkness for the remaining hours.

GRAVEL, PLANTS, AND TANK DECORATIONS

A bare-bottom aquarium is the easiest to maintain and the safest for your fish, though many feel that a layer of gravel adds to the beauty of an aquarium. If you are determined to use gravel, first be prepared for more frequent cleanings and a lot of extra work at cleaning time; if you still are determined to use it, I suggest large (at least one-half inch in diameter) natural, smooth gravel, and just enough to cover the bottom of the tank.

The worst thing you can do is to place two inches of fine gravel in your aquarium. Fine gravel can become lodged in the Goldfish's throat and choke them to death. In addition, a deep layer of gravel will clog with fish waste and deteriorating food, releasing toxins into your aquarium water. Deep gravel is also very hard, if not impossible, to keep clean.

What kinds of rocks and stones are safe to use in decorating my Goldfish aquarium?

It is very important that decorative rocks and stones are smooth so that your Goldfish don't injure themselves. Don't use stones such as sandstone, which will disintegrate in the action of the water. Rocks and stones that leach elements into the water, such as limestone and marble, can prove fatal to your fish. Smooth pieces of granite and slate are the best choices for aquarium decoration.

I do not recommend using driftwood in your tank. You never know where it came from, how it was treated, or what it will leach into your water. Also avoid ceramic and plastic ornaments. Even those sold at

RED-AND-WHITE RYUKINS.

pet stores to be placed in aquariums may have toxic paints, bonding agents, or other chemicals that will harm your fish.

Do you recommend live plants in aquariums?

Some Goldfish collectors like live plants, but they can cause several problems. The Goldfish will tear them apart and or eat them. They get stuck in the filters and make a real mess. They can introduce parasites and harmful bacteria into your tank if you are not very careful in disinfecting them. If you really like the look of plants, add some of the beautiful, lifelike, artificial plants that are now available.

For those addicted to natural greenery, there is nothing better for your fish and their water than cultivating a nice smooth coat of green algae on the sides and bottom of the tank!

Selecting and Buying Goldfish

SOURCES FOR GOLDFISH

In the United States there are two sources from which you can purchase Goldfish: your local fish store and mail order importers specializing in Goldfish.

Some ninety-nine percent of the Goldfish sold in the United States are imported from Asia; less than one percent are raised in the United States. Wholesalers import millions of Goldfish every year. Because of the tremendous volume of Goldfish the wholesalers receive every week, they must sell them fast to make room for their next shipment. Most Goldfish are shipped from the wholesaler to your local fish store in less than forty-eight hours after they arrive in this country—itself a journey of at least twelve, and more likely twenty-four, hours. When they arrive at your local fish store the fish are very stressed from their long trip and most of them have heavy loads of parasites. A good local fish store will rest, treat, and quarantine these Goldfish before they offer them for sale. A local fish store that doesn't know how to care for these fish, or doesn't care, will offer these Goldfish for sale the very same day they arrive.

Local Goldfish stores who do this play a large part in ruining the enthusiasm of new Goldfish collectors. A new collector buys a Goldfish that has never been treated or quarantined, takes it home, and within a week it is dead. They try again, and maybe even a third time, until they blame themselves and leave the hobby in frustration. This happens to thousands of would-be Goldfish collectors each year.

If you are buying a fish from a local fish store, you're going to have to take responsibility for quarantining your new fish and treating it for disease. Try to purchase the fish the day it arrives. Select the healthiest looking fish, one that is swimming with its dorsal fin up and is active. Take the fish home and place it alone in a tank of at least 10 gallons. Make sure the water has been treated to eliminate chlorine and chloramines, has plenty of aeration, and a good—preferably already biologically active—filter. Add 1 teaspoon of salt per gallon of water each day for three days, to achieve a 0.3% salt solution. Test your water every day for ammonia and nitrites. If they are high, do a water change and replace the salt in the equal proportion to the water you removed. (In other words, for each gallon of new water you add, also add 1 tablespoon of salt.)

By keeping the salt at a concentration of 1 tablespoon per gallon for twenty-one days, you are killing most of the small parasites that your new Goldfish may carry. A salinity meter makes it easy to measure the exact salt concentration (you will need a salinity meter for measuring fresh water; those designed for saltwater tanks will generally not read these low levels). Remember, a salt concentration below 0.3% will not kill the parasites, and a salt level too high above 0.3% can stress your Goldfish. That is why a salinity meter is so important.

Observe your new Goldfish carefully during the quarantine period and watch for signs of disease as outlined in part 1 of this book. If you follow this system of quarantine and treatment, combined with excellent water quality and nutritious food, you will have a happy, healthy Goldfish in a month.

Importers that specialize in Goldfish and sell them through the mail are the second source for Goldfish. Some only offer price lists, others produce videotapes of new fish, and some also offer photographs of their fish on the Internet. Most of these importers import directly from China, and some of the bigger ones also import from Japan. As is true with all businesses, there are bad ones, good ones, and superior ones. Some quarantine their Goldfish only two weeks; others do so for thirty days. Some are more experienced at treating Goldfish diseases. Today the major importers have websites, and you should check them out to see what their customers have to say.

No matter where you purchase your Goldfish from, YOU must quarantine them. Never place a new fish in the same tank with the fish you already have.

How do I choose a healthy fish?
Before you buy a fish from the local fish store, first ask yourself the following questions:
• What is the condition of the aquariums at the store? Are they clean? Do they have clear water? Do they have plenty of aeration?
• How do the Goldfish in the aquariums behave? Are they active and swimming with their dorsal fins up? Are they resting on the bottom? Are they gasping for air at the top of the tank?
• How do the Goldfish in the aquariums appear? Do they have torn or bloody fins? Are there body sores or white spots on the fish? Is their color bright and clear? Are there dead fish in the tank?
• Does the salesperson seem to really know about fish?

Also find out whether the store treats incoming shipments, and if it does, what it treats for and what medications it uses. Try to get an honest answer, because it will affect how you treat any fish you buy there.

The source I purchase Goldfish from quarantines them. Do I have to quarantine them too?
Yes. You must quarantine them for at least thirty days. During this period, you should check them for parasites and watch for any bacteria problems. No matter where you

buy your Goldfish, never place new fish in with the fish you already have. That is a disaster just waiting to happen.

VARIETIES OF GOLDFISH

Goldfish come in many shapes and sizes, and there are more than a hundred different colors and color patterns throughout the world, some of which have never been seen outside their native lands in Asia. The most frequently found colors are red, white, orange, calico, black, blue, lavender, and chocolate, and various combinations of these. Goldfish have two different types of scales: metallic scales and transparent scales. Most Goldfish have metallic scales all over their body. A Goldfish with a mix of metallic scales and transparent scales is often called "nacreous," because it gives the impression of mother-of-pearl. A Goldfish with transparent scales all over the body is called "matte." Many Goldfish loosely described as matte actually have a few metallic scales sprinkled over the body.

The Pearlscale Goldfish have a special scale structure in which each scale is rounded, like a pearl embedded in the fish's body.

I will briefly describe in the following pages some of the most popular varieties of Goldfish in the West in alphabetical order. There are many, many more varieties, but these are the ones you are most likely to encounter.

GOLDFISH CHARACTERISTICS

Goldfish are bred with so many body types, features, and colors that anyone would be hard pressed to catalogue them all, but here is a short alphabetical list of some of the most frequently found terms for Goldfish characteristics. Many of these are also the names for Goldfish varieties.

BROADTAIL: a long, horizontally set, undivided caudal fin
BUBBLE EYE: an upward pointing eye with a large sac of fluid hanging below it
BUTTERFLY TAIL: a double caudal fin that is set on a horizontal or near horizontal axis
CALICO: a color pattern that includes red or orange, black, and blue or white, usually of nacreous (mixed metallic and matte) scalation
CELESTIAL EYE: an eye oriented upward
DEMEKIN: the Japanese name for Telescope Eyes
DRAGON BACK: a back without a dorsal fin
DRAGON EYE: the Chinese term for Telescope Eyes
DOUBLE TAIL: A caudal fin with two lobes
EGG SHAPE: the Chinese term for a fish with a round or oval body and no dorsal fin
FANTAIL: a long quadruple caudal fin
FLAT HEAD: a head with no head growth
FRINGETAIL: a long caudal fin
FROG FACE: a fish with eyes resembling a Bubble Eye but with very reduced sacs
FROG HEAD: same as Frog Face
GOOSE HEAD: headgrowth concentrated on the top and front of the head
HIGH HEAD: the general Chinese term for headgrowth
JADE SEAL: a pattern with an oval marking on the top of the head, like a Chinese seal

LIONHEAD: headgrowth all over the head and cheeks with a hood on the top
MATTE PATTERN: a fish with only transparent scales (no metallic scales)
METALLIC SCALE: a shiny, reflective scale
NACREOUS PATTERN: a scalation pattern that combines metallic and matte scales
NARIAL BOUQUET: a fleshy appendage at the nostril, often in pairs
PEARL SCALE: a domed scale
POMPOM: a fleshy appendage at the nostril, often in pairs
POPEYE: synonym for Telescope Eyes
QUADRUPLE TAIL: a caudal fin with four lobes
RED CRANE: a white fish with a red cap
REVERSED GILLS: gills that bend outward at the edge
RIBBON TAIL: a long quadruple tail with deeply indented lobes
SINGLE TAIL: a single-lobed, vertically oriented caudal fin
SKY-GAZING EYES: same as Celestial
SWALLOW TAIL: A long, single, forked caudal fin
TANCHO: Japanese for Red Crane
TELESCOPE: protruding eyes
TIGER HEAD: uniform growth all over the head
TOAD HEAD: Same as Frog Head
TRANSPARENT SCALE: a non-metallic scale that allows body color to show through
TRIPLE TAIL: a caudal fin with three lobes
VARIEGATED: Calico
VEILTAIL: a long, draping tail
VELVET BALLS: large, exaggerated Pompoms, usually in pairs

BUBBLE EYE This unique Goldfish lacks a dorsal fin and has large pouches of skin filled with fluid attached under its eyes. The bubbles jiggle like Jell-O as the fish swims. Bubble Eyes come in many color patterns—red, red and white, black, and calico are some of the most popular. Bubble Eyes are poor swimmers and their bubbles can be easily sucked into the filter intake, so they need a special environment to flourish, and cannot compete with more active fish. Bubble Eyes are one of the smaller varieties of Goldfish.

CELESTIAL The eyes of this variety are turned upward so that they seem to gaze up at the sky. They lack a dorsal fin and are, like Bubble Eyes, unable to compete with more vigorous varieties for food. They come in all colors, and they are a relatively small variety.

COMET This is the most common Goldfish variety in the United States, and it is said to have in fact originated here. The Comet has a long, slim body with a long, single tail. Popular colors are red and red and white (often called *sarasa*, a Japanese word). They can grow up to 12 inches in length and are a very nice pond fish.

JIKIN This is a rare Japanese variety hardly ever available outside Japan. It has a long, cigar-shaped body that is white, with red lips, fins, and gill covers. Jikin are not born with this coloration. They are "made" by removing red scales when still young. Jikin grow to be about 9 inches in length.

LIONHEAD These are the gentle giants of the Goldfish world, and they look like little whales as they swim through the water. Their headgrowth and nice fat cheeks give them a puppy-dog face, and indeed they were bred by the Chinese to look like the mythical lion-dog of China (as was the Pekingese). Lionheads have no dorsal fins, tremendous headgrowth, and relatively straight backs. They can grow to a large size and are a great fish to collect. They come in a variety of colors. As you can tell, they are one of my favorites.

PHOENIX This is a Chinese variety with an egg-shaped body, no dorsal fin, no headgrowth, and a long tail. It comes in all colors and scale types.

ORANDA Noted for its headgrowth and long fins, the Oranda is one of the most popular Goldfish varieties in the West. This deep-bodied, large Goldfish (up to 12 inches) usually has a long quadruple tail and occurs in many colors, such as orange, red, red and white, red and black, black, blue, and calico. Recently the Chinese have developed Telescope Orandas, which combine the protruding eyes of the Telescope variety with the Oranda's headgrowth.

PEARLSCALE The most characteristic feature of this Goldfish is its thick, domed scales, which look like pearls. The body of the Pearlscale is as round as a golf ball and can grow as large as an orange! It can be found without headgrowth, with Oranda-like headgrowth, or with two large bubble domes (the latter variety is called a High-head Pearlscale or Hama Nishiki). Pearlscales may have long or short finnage and come in every color variety. They can reach a size of about 8 inches.

RANCHU The Ranchu is similar to the Chinese Lionhead, but its back is more arched and its tail is much shorter and tucked in at a sharp angle. The Ranchu is perhaps the most highly prized variety in Japan, and standards there are very strict. Ranchus may be orange, red, or red and white. Recently calico nacreous Ranchus (Edo Nishiki) and red-and-white nacreous Ranchus (Sakura Nishiki) have also been developed. So-called "black Ranchus" are produced in China and Southeast Asia.

RYUKIN This is a hardy and beautiful variety of Goldfish. It is very deep bodied and has a hump on the back behind the head. There are long-finned and short-finned varieties, and it comes in many different colors, though red and white is the most popular. It has a quadruple or triple tail, and is a fine aquarium fish, growing to a size of up to 8 inches.

TAMASABA The Tamasaba, also called the Sabao, is an uncommon Japanese variety with a body shaped like a Ryukin and a very long, flowing, single tail. The most common colors are solid red and deep red and white. Very attractive and strong, they make a very good pond fish as well as aquarium fish.

SHUBUNKIN The Shubunkin is of Japanese origin with calico coloring (red, white, blue, and black) and nacreous scales (a mix of metallic and transparent scales). It is a single-tailed fish reaching a length of 12 inches. In the West, there are three distinct types of Shubunkins. The American Shubunkin has a long, pointed, forked tail and long fins. The Bristol Shubunkin has a moderately forked tail with rounded lobes shaped like the letter B. The London Shubunkin has a short, round tail and fins. Shubunkins are another very hardy variety that make excellent pond fish.

TELESCOPE Also called Popeye and Demekin, these fish have protruding eyes, deep bodies, and long, flowing fins. They come in many colors, such as red, red and white, calico, black and white, chocolate, blue, lavender, chocolate and blue, and black. Black Demekin are also called Moors. A deep solid black color is hard to find, though it is more stable on the Moor than any other Goldfish variety. Telescope Goldfish can grow quite large, but they don't see well and should not be kept with more active varieties of fish. Because of their delicate projecting eyes, make sure their aquarium has no sharp, pointed objects in it.

TOSAKIN This Japanese variety is almost never seen in the United States. It has a body shape like a Ryukin, but its tail fin opens so flat and wide horizontally that the front ends flip under, sometimes twice. It swims clumsily and requires special care, but is a real beauty when seen from above. Tosakins come in red, red and white, white, and black (actually iron colored) and grow to a medium size.

VEILTAIL As its name implies, this beautiful Goldfish with a modified Ryukin-shaped body is known for its extra-long, flowing tail, which is square, with no forking or indentation between the lobes, and a high dorsal fin. The Veiltail is believed to have originated in Japan, but has been bred in the United States, as the Philadelphia

Veiltail, for decades. Though it almost became extinct at one time here, the Philadelphia Veiltail is being revived by hard-working hobbyists. The Chinese also breed Veiltails in several varieties and many colors, and there are also European strains. They can grow to be very large, up to 12 inches.

WAKIN This Japanese Goldfish variety is very similar in shape to the River Carp ancestor, and it is also common in China and the rest of Asia. They are a very strong and hardy fish, growing to a foot in length. The most popular Wakin colors are red and red and white. There are also calico Wakin, but they are not common. Because they are so hardy and have such intense red coloring, they make great pond fish.

Setting Up and Maintaining Your Goldfish

Now that you have your new aquarium and all the accessories to run it, you are ready for the water and the Goldfish. Fill your aquarium two or three days before you add your fish and use plenty of aeration, which will help remove unwanted gases from your water. If you use treated tap water, you must remove the chlorine and chloramines your local water department adds to your drinking water, as we discussed earlier, with a good dechlorinator.

CYCLING A NEW AQUARIUM
Your Goldfish will be excreting bodily wastes, primarily ammonia, through their gills and their waste products. Any amount of ammonia is harmful to your fish, and high levels of ammonia will kill them. Fortunately, there is a natural waste-reducing cycle that we can make use of in our aquariums to eliminate the ammonia. A particular variety of bacteria consume the ammonia the fish produce, converting the ammonia into nitrite. Unfortunately, nitrite is also toxic to your fish, though less so than ammonia, but a second kind of bacteria consumes nitrite and converts it into nitrate, a relatively harmless compound that you can then reduce by regular

BLUE ORANDA.

water changes. Dr. Johnson discusses the nitrogen cycle in greater detail in part 1 of this book.

When you set up a new tank, you need to get this cycle up and running. It usually takes from four to six weeks for enough good bacteria to become established for the cycle to be complete. During this time, your fish are still producing ammonia, and so they are susceptible to ammonia poisoning. You have to test your aquarium water daily during this time for ammonia, and perform frequent water changes to keep it from reaching harmful levels.

Normally, after a few weeks your ammonia level will test negative, but you will have high nitrite-test readings. This means that your first good bacteria, the ones that change ammonia into nitrites, have been established. Now you must watch your nitrite levels very closely, since high levels of nitrite will also kill your Goldfish. Again, the best way to keep the nitrite level down is by doing frequent water changes. In a week or two the second good bacteria, which changes your nitrites into nitrates, will become established and your tank will be cycled.

What is new-tank syndrome?

This refers to the problems we run into before a tank is fully cycled: the ammonia levels shoot way up, followed by the nitrite levels. Both of these are harmful to fish. The tank water may also become cloudy and take weeks (or months!) to clear. This is a crucial time in getting a tank up and running, and it is important not to expose too many or too valuable fish to the hardships of new-tank syndrome.

You can sometimes reduce the time it takes to cycle a tank by "feeding" it with good bacteria from another healthy tank, but this is not always successful, and you do run the risk of introducing diseases or parasites that lay hidden and inactive in the "healthy" tank. Some hobbyists try a few teaspoons of garden soil; this runs the same risks. There are also several commercial bacterial starters, but so far they have shown mixed results.

The best solution to new-tank syndrome may just be that old-fashioned virtue of patience and water changes.

I'm setting up my new 55-gallon aquarium. How many fish should I start with?

Keep just a few fish for the first six weeks. Too many fish will increase the ammonia level to lethal levels before your first good bacteria become established. Of course it depends upon the size of your tank, but I suggest starting with just two or three of a hardy variety.

What are the most important tests I must perform the first two or three weeks after setting up a new tank?

Test for ammonia and your pH on a daily basis. When the ammonia level drops, start testing for nitrites. Every Goldfish collector should have a minimum of four test kits: ammonia, nitrite, nitrate, and pH. For further information, see the section on water quality in part 1 of this book.

I set up my new aquarium about ten days ago, and my ammonia readings are very high. What should I do?

High ammonia readings mean that your first good bacteria have not been established. You must do frequent water changes to bring the ammonia level down to prevent harming your fish. If you try to cycle a tank with too many fish in it, you will quickly find yourself in a double bind. The fish produce so much ammonia that they quickly make their environment (their aquarium water) toxic to themselves. As a result, you have to change water to eliminate ammonia. At the same time, you need ammonia in the tank in order to initiate the cycle.

This can be avoided by starting with just a few fish. They will produce enough ammonia to get the cycle started but not so much that they are in danger of poisoning themselves.

Also be careful not to wash your filtration materials in chlorinated tap water, which will kill any bacteria that have started to grow. Wash filter materials that you want bacteria to colonize only in dechlorinated water.

In my experience, the two points noted above—overcrowding and killing good bacteria while washing filter materials—account for nine out of ten problems or delays in cycling aquariums.

ADDING FISH

This is the fun part of the hobby—at last you have your fish and are ready to place them in the tank. If the tank is a new, empty tank, you can introduce them directly. Never add new fish to an established collection, though, without quarantining them for a month.

How do I introduce new Goldfish into my tank?
First make sure that the temperature of the water in the bag is the same as the temperature of your aquarium water by floating the bag containing the fish in your aquarium for about ten minutes. Then open the bag and with your hand, not a net, remove the fish from the bag and place it into your aquarium. Never, never put any of the water in the bag into your aquarium. The water is contaminated with the fish's waste, and it may also contain bacteria. This small precaution can save you big problems.

Are all Goldfish varieties compatible?
They are in a general sense—they won't battle like male bettas, for example—but because of the highly adapted body forms of some varieties, they are often best segregated. A good example is Bubble Eyes, which cannot really see or navigate very freely because of their huge eye sacs. They should be kept with other Bubble Eyes or similarly "visually challenged" fish. Many collectors advise keeping Telescope Goldfish in their own tank, because they can't see well, either. A general rule is that the long-bodied, large-growing, powerfully swimming varieties such as Comets and Shubunkins should not be kept with the "mellower" round-bodied varieties such as Lionheads and Ranchus. Judge how to mix your collection based on your fishes' mobility and ability to compete for food.

RED-CAP ORANDA.

Much could be written about feeding your Goldfish, and it is a controversial subject. Fortunately, we are long past the days when dried ant eggs were sold as the staple Goldfish food! Today there are many fine manufactured foods in pellet, gel, and frozen forms. I recommend a varied diet of top-quality manufactured foods. Some hobbyists go to great pains to make their own foods, but it is hard to really know the nutritional content of such foods, and even harder to preserve it over time.

What is the proper method to feed Goldfish?
The method that works best for me is to feed adult Goldfish all they can eat, a pinch at a time, for two to three minutes. Make sure none of the food goes uneaten. The healthiest Goldfish are always a little bit hungry—not starving, but a little hungry. When you walk into the room, your fish should come to the front of the aquarium and greet you with open mouths.

Do you have a favorite recipe for homemade food?
The ingredients in some gel-food recipes are unbelievable—everything from liverwurst to spaghetti. I believe that if you are feeding adult Goldfish a high-quality manufactured Goldfish food, you do not need a supplement food. In recent years, much research has been undertaken to find out what keeps Goldfish healthy, and there are excellent prepared foods on the market.

To be on the safe side, keep at least two or three kinds in stock and vary them.

Cooked rice and skinless green peas are commonly given as treats to Goldfish, and in Asia traditionally Goldfish have been fed extensively with live foods, but this is changing now as the quality of manufactured foods has increased and the quality of live foods is threatened by environmental pollution and development.

How can I keep my manufactured Goldfish food fresh?
I do not recommend freezing Goldfish food. The fatty acids in the food may become rancid, giving the food a bad odor after it is thawed. It is important, however, to know if your source of Goldfish food freezes their food. If they do, you must keep it frozen and only feed the food directly from your freezer to your Goldfish.

The best way to maintain the quality of your food is to store it in a vapor-locked container in a cool, dry, dark place. High-quality, freshly milled foods such as Sho-Gold, made here in the United States, will last a year under these conditions. Many Goldfish foods are imported to the United States and you don't really know how old they are.

Should I feed my fish live foods?
In my opinion, feeding live foods is an invitation to trouble. There is too much of a chance that you will introduce bacteria or other disease-carrying organisms. Many hobbyists swear by live food, but most importers and

CALICO BROADTAIL PEARLSCALE.

others who handle large numbers of fish don't—partly because it is more expensive and time consuming, but also because they have consistently had disease problems when they fed live foods, even frozen or freeze-dried ones. This is a controversial subject, so "let the keeper beware."

Should I soak pellet foods before feeding?
Some believe that feeding pellet foods can cause Goldfish to float. There is no harm in soaking a hard, dense pellet in water for a few minutes before feeding it, and it may make the pellets easier for the fish to eat. More crumbly pellet foods (such as Sho Gold) will disintegrate if soaked, however, and don't need to be soaked.

I advise against feeding any pellet food that causes fish to float in the first place. In addition, if your fish are floating, consult the discussion of this problem in part 1 of this book.

I'm going on vacation for a week. Should I buy an automatic fish feeder, or just have my neighbor feed my Goldfish?
Don't buy an automatic fish feeder; if something goes wrong it could very easily overfeed your fish.

It's not usually a good idea to ask someone who doesn't also keep Goldfish to feed your fish. Inevitably, they give the fish too much, and you come home to find your Goldfish sick and swimming in dark, foul-smelling water. (One Goldfish collector toldl me that her father fed one and one-half pounds of Goldfish food to six Goldfish in just ten days.)

About twenty-four hours before you go on vacation, do a 50% water change. If you are going on vacation longer than five days, place the amount of food that you would feed your fish at one time in a zip-lock sandwich bag. Mark the day of the week and the date on it that you want the caretaker to feed it to your fish. Do not place more feed in the bag than you would normally feed at one time if you were home. Feeding the fish once every five days while you are gone on vacation for a week or two will be enough. Hide the rest of the food, or your caretaker might feel sorry for the fish and give them more.

Now that feeding is taken care of, make sure your caretaker knows how to monitor such appliances as the air pump and the filter, and ask him or her to make sure that your power doesn't go out unreported for any length of time.

REGULAR MAINTENANCE
By this time you are up and running and all systems are go. Now you're in the nuts and bolts of Goldfish keeping, which is really the most important part: keeping everything running smoothly by regular, careful maintenance.

Can I offer a word to the wise on a related subject? Maintenance is very important, but if you have too many tanks to maintain, you aren't going to enjoy your hobby. Goldfish collectors tend to accumulate fish faster than Imelda Marcos did shoes, but she had a full-time staff to keep her closet organized. Keep your Goldfish keeping enjoyable—and successful—by knowing your limits and keeping your hobby within them. Never try to keep more fish than you can give the maintenance time they require and deserve.

How frequently should I change water, and how much should I change each time?
Changing about 25% once a week is a good guideline. Make sure the new water is well aerated, free from chlorine and chloramines, and the same temperature as the water in your aquarium. Experienced Goldfish keepers in Asia advocate "seasoning" your fresh water by letting it sit for a few days, preferably in the sun, before using it to make the water change, but this is not practical for apartment dwellers and those with limited storage space, or in the winter in cold climates. You can, however, let your water sit in a large plastic garbage can with aeration for a day if you have the space to do so.

If you have a small aquarium, you can use a bucket and a siphon for water changes, but if your tank is larger than 55 gallons and you're more than a few steps away from a sink, invest in a pump or powerhead and a length of plastic tubing. To empty your tank, place the pump in your tank and the end of the tubing in a sink, bathtub, or toilet. (Make sure to secure it or you'll have water all over the floor!) Start the pump and remove as much water as you want, then shut it off and remove it from the aquarium. (If your drain is lower than the tank, as is usually the case, the water will continue to siphon out of your tank by the force of gravity, so make sure to remove the pump from the tank.)

Then place the pump in your replacement water and pump it into the aquarium. To be safe, it's better to use one plastic tube for removing the old water and another for pumping in the fresh. You should regularly clean out the plastic tubing by placing it and the pump in a bucket with water and a few capfuls of bleach and running the pump until the tubing is clean. Then make sure to run it again in a bucket of clean water, to get rid of any traces of bleach before using it again. NEVER use the same tubing for more than one tank. You're just asking for an outbreak of disease.

You will perform larger water changes when you are having water-quality problems or treating for diseases.

Dr. Johnson discusses such situations at length in his section.

I use buckets to do my water changes, but it's so much trouble. Is there an easier way?
You can also use the siphon system on the market called the Python. It is plastic tubing that connects to your water faucet and uses the flow from your tap as a source of suctioning power that you can use to empty and fill your aquarium. It's a great product and works well if it can be attached to your faucet fixture. Remember, you should not use the same hose for removing and adding water. If you are going to use a Python or similar system, buy two—one for siphoning out and one for refilling.

The Python system will not work for adding water to your aquarium if your tap water is treated with chlorine, chloramines, or anything else, because you should remove those chemicals before adding water directly to your tank.

How often should I clean my filters?
This depends on so many variables—the size of your tank, the number of fish, how much you feed, the kind of filter—that there is no one good answer, but as a general guideline, I recommend the following, as a minimum:

HANGING FILTERS: Rinse or replace cartridges when the water from the overflow slows down. If the filter has a biological filter component, rinse it in aquarium water whenever it seems to be getting clogged with debris.

CANISTER FILTERS: Rinse media with aquarium water every six weeks.

SPONGE FILTERS: Squeeze out and rinse the sponge in aquarium water once a month, but not too much; you do not want to lose all your good bacteria.

WET-DRY BIOLOGICAL FILTERS: Same as canister filters.

SAND FILTERS: No maintenance necessary, but rinse out the sponge prefilter of the pump feeding the sand filter as often as you would a sponge filter.

Always err on the safe side in filter maintenance—in fact, in all maintenance tasks!

How often should I perform water tests?
In a cycling or newly set-up aquarium, I suggest daily water tests. After the tank is established, you can drop down to weekly, just prior to your weekly water change. If you have soft water, you may need to test your pH

more frequently. At any sign of disease, immediately test your water.

How often should I clean the sides of my aquarium?
I suggest cleaning the front of the aquarium when you do your weekly water change, but allow algae to grow on the other sides and the bottom of the tank. You will probably never have to clean them off, since the Goldfish will keep them nicely "mowed."

How often should I clean my aquarium gravel?
If you have gravel, clean it weekly, before or during your weekly water change. Gravel is a real trap for dirt and disease organisms, and even frequent cleaning will never really get it clean.

Observing Your Fish

The reason that most of us keep Goldfish is we enjoy watching them. To be a really good Goldfish keeper, you should try to develop merely watching into observation. Get to know how your fish behave. This will help you spot any strange new behaviors that may be signs of illness or stress. Watch how they swim and how they hold their fins. Monitor their level of activity, and observe how they interact with other fish in the tank. At feeding time, check to make sure they are interested in their food, eating, and getting their fair share. Pay attention to where they are in the tank. A fish always at the surface might be telling you it's not getting enough oxygen, and you may have water problems or it may have parasites in its gills. A fish always sitting on the bottom of the tank may be sick, too. If your fish are always only on one side of the tank, check to make sure you don't have overly strong water current that is keeping them away from the other side.

Different varieties of Goldfish behave somewhat differently, too. Be aware of this and pay attention to it. As you observe your fish, you'll come up with lots of questions. Here are a few I have frequently fielded over the years.

How can I tell the sex of my Goldfish?
Sexing Goldfish less than one year of age is very difficult. As the fish approach maturity, it's much easier to determine the males from the females, because the male will develop very small white bumps or tubercles on the gill covers and on the leading edge or first ray of the pectoral fins. Some varieties, like the Oranda and Lionhead, have so much headgrowth that it will hide the gill covers and make the tubercles very difficult to see, but they can still be seen on the pectoral fins. Many

new hobbyists mistake these small white spots for the parasite known as ich. Breeding tubercles are restricted to the gill cover and first ray of the pectoral fin. If you see white spots anywhere else on the fish's body, then it might have ich.

The only completely positive way of sexing a female fish is to actually observe her lay eggs. Other methods, not quite as reliable, include viewing the fish from the top. A female may appear more rounded on one side as she fills with developing eggs. Very smooth pectoral fins with no bumps can determine a fish to be a female, but it could also be a late-developing male. Another method used by skilled Goldfish collectors in Asia is viewing the anal opening. The male opening is small and oval, while the female opening is larger and circular in shape and projects slightly from the body. Mastering this method takes many years of practice and is not reliable for the novice.

I have three fish that keep chasing one fish all the time. Is this normal?
What you probably have are three aggressive males pursuing an outnumbered female, which is not a good situation. The males may actually chase your female to death, causing her to die from exhaustion and stress. I recommend you place the female into a separate aquarium.

I put a new fish in my tank and the next morning there were white spots all over everything in the tank. What are they?
Your new fish was a female and has spawned, which sometimes happens when a gravid female is placed in a new environment. These white spots are eggs, which the fish will eat.

My Lionhead has white spots on its head. Is it sick?
If the white spots are located on the hood of your Goldfish and nowhere else on its body, your Goldfish is probably healthy and just producing new headgrowth. Dr. Johnson discusses this at length in part 1 of this book.

One of my Goldfish is very aggressive toward my other fish. I would like to separate him from the other fish until I can find him a new home, but I don't want to set up another aquarium. Any suggestions?
One of the best methods of temporarily separating a Goldfish from the rest of your fish is to float a small plastic basket in your aquarium. Make sure it has no sharp edges. Place the Goldfish you want to isolate inside. I do not recommend this method for treating sick fish, because you should remove a sick fish from your aquarium and get it away from your healthy Goldfish.

My Goldfish has torn a fin. Will it heal?
Fins will grow back as long as the spines or ribs of the fins are not destroyed. The clear tissue between the ribs almost always regenerates.

My Goldfish lost some of its scales when it was shipped. Will they grow back?
Yes, the scales will grow back, but may not be as perfect as the original scales.

I noticed my Goldfish have a line running along both sides of their body. Is this normal?
The line is called the lateral line. It runs from the start of the tail into the head. The lateral line is a sense organ that fish use to determine direction and water currents.

My Goldfish is 3 inches long. How old is it?
It is very hard to tell the age of a Goldfish from its size. I've seen 3-inch Goldfish produce eggs. Some Goldfish become stunted from lack of proper nutrition and poor water quality and never reach the maximum size of their particular variety.

When I handled my Goldfish to introduce it to the tank, it felt slimy. Is it sick?
The slime coat is a protective suit of armor your Goldfish produces on its body to protect it from the bacteria in your aquarium. That is why you do not want sharp decorations in your aquarium that would cut into the slime coat. Any opening in the slime coat is an invitation to problems. Excess slime can also be a sign of a health problem. See part 1 for a detailed discussion of this.

I've watched my Goldfish eating, and it seems to "chew," but I've never seen any teeth in its mouth. Does it have any?
Goldfish don't have teeth embedded in their jaw as some other fish do, but they have what are called pharyngeal teeth situated far back in the mouth. These teeth are shed and replaced throughout the life of the Goldfish.

Breeding Your Goldfish

Several of the questions in the section above are related to Goldfish breeding, a subject that most hobbyists eventually grow interested in and try their hand at. Though I have bred Goldfish on many occasions, I turned to Dr. Streamson Chua, an experienced breeder of several fancy varieties, to present a brief outline of the steps in breeding Goldfish and raising fry.

Hand Spawning Goldfish: The Reasons and the Mechanics
by Dr. Streamson Chua

There are several good reasons for hand spawning Goldfish. By hand spawning, you can avoid having the fish spawn in a show tank or another tank that is not set up for raising fry. Hand spawning allows you to know the parents of the fry. It is also a good idea when the male or males do not chase well and have demonstrated low fertility in previous spawns.

The Prelude to Spawning

The male and female fish should be housed in the same tank, since the males' sexual development is influenced by the presence of the females. The fish need to be prepared for spawning by feeding them heavily over several weeks: three to four meals every day, providing them with as much as they will eat over fifteen to thirty minutes. Females will develop a rounded, gravid look due to enlargement of the developing eggs. Males will develop white tubercles on the gill covers and the leading edges of the pectoral fins. The tubercles are rough to the touch, like sandpaper.

Though Goldfish will spawn of their own accord, you can help them along by keeping the water around seventy degrees and making frequent small water changes (about 15% two to three times a week). This is actually necessary for the health of the fish due to the heavy feeding regime. When the females look really full and heavy, you can try to induce them to lay eggs. I have found that egg laying occurs about two to three days after a low pressure system brings a thunderstorm and heavy rainfall. I take advantage of the change in barometric pressure by performing large water changes (50%) every day for three days. Since I work during the week, I look up the weather forecast for the week and start water changes on Wednesday night or Thursday morning so that the fish will spawn around Saturday or Sunday. If this doesn't work, wait a week until the weather forecast looks good. Keep trying until they spawn. Since well-fed females will spawn every seven to fourteen days, it isn't a disaster if you miss the first spawn. The second spawn can be timed so that you will have a chance to catch the fish in the act.

The Mechanics

On the second day after starting the water changes, make sure to wake up a little before or just at sunrise, because Goldfish spawn early in the morning, just around sunrise. You might see just a few eggs if the female just started, or thousands of eggs if the spawning is nearly over.

I use a plastic shoebox made of polycarbonate for the hand spawning since polycarbonate sinks in water due to its buoyant density. A shoebox of polypropylene (the box will have a PP symbol inside the recycling symbol) is acceptable but the box will need to be weighed down since polypropylene has a tendency to float.

Get the male into the box along with enough tank water to fill the box with about three inches of water. Hold the male with both hands, left hand over the head and right hand near the ventral fins, making sure that you can see the vent clearly. (If you're left-handed, reverse the position of the hands.) Using your right hand, gently squeeze the male about two-thirds down the length of the body so that you see the milt coming out. The milt is a white fluid that looks like milk. Swirl the milt with your hand or the fish's tail. A very fertile male will provide so much milt that the water will become cloudy. (A male that is not kept with females does not produce any milt, in my experience.)

At this point, bring the female into the box by transferring her in your hands or inside a small quart container. I would recommend that you wait until the female has released most of her eggs before you start hand spawning, because a fully gravid female is extremely fragile. I have lost several females by hand spawning them too early in the spawning process. The fish died several weeks after spawning from peritonitis, probably as a result of ruptured ovaries. Hold the female in the same position as you did with the male. Squeeze the female's abdomen very gently—even more gently than you did the male—until you see a small stream of eggs coming out. Most of the time, the female will squirm in your hand and the eggs will come streaming out without any pressure at all.

Immediately swirl the eggs around with the female's tail. The reason is that the eggs swell and become sticky upon exposure to water. If the eggs are not separated, they stick to each other and do not develop properly. Collect about 300 to 500 eggs per shoebox. Another male can be used to fertilize the eggs of the same spawning female if you wish to test the qualities of two males. Leave the parents alone for about five to ten minutes to recover, then gently transfer them back to their home tank. Rinse the eggs with fresh tank water three to four times to remove the excess milt and residue from the parents.

INCUBATING THE EGGS

Place the shoebox with the eggs in a 30-gallon or larger tank that contains established sponge filters, along with an air stone to provide circulation inside the shoebox. Under no circumstances should the eggs be incubated in the small quantity of water that the shoebox will hold. If you do this, the fry will develop into bottom swimmers or worse. The water should be kept at a constant seventy degrees for optimal development. Development of the fertilized eggs can be followed under a low-power microscope. The first cell division occurs within thirty minutes of fertilization. Bad eggs or unfertilized eggs will become opaque in about eight hours and develop fungus.

Fungus can be a problem if the fertilization rate is low, but it can be minimized by using an ultraviolet sterilizer for the first forty-eight hours of incubation. I use a circulation rate of about 200 gallons per hour for a 30-gallon tank with an 8-watt lamp. The ideal system would be to run the water with an airline at low flow rates such that the fry are not subjected to high flow rates. If more than 300 eggs hatch, the egg contents released will make the water cloudy and smelly, necessitating a water change. I perform two 50% water changes on the same day with a siphon that has a sponge over the intake end to prevent losing any fry. Leave the fry alone for about two days until they are free swimming and ready for their first meal.

RAISING GOLDFISH FRY

The First Two Weeks: Feed Brine Shrimp Nauplii and Algae

Let's say that you now have a thousand fry from a recent spawning of your prized show-quality Goldfish. The fry are currently split into two 30-gallon tanks. The fry should be swimming horizontally a few days after hatching. They will start grazing on microorganisms as soon as their mouths have developed. If you look very carefully with a magnifying glass, the fry do not have mouths when they have just hatched. There is no point to feeding them before they are ready to eat!

By about the second day after hatching, the fry will be ready to eat. The general consensus among all fish breeders is that freshly hatched brine shrimp nauplii are the best food for young fish fry, and this has been my experience as well. Fry that are fed brine shrimp nauplii grow faster and develop more massive bodies. This enhanced growth is probably due to the palatability of brine shrimp and their movement, which stimulates the fry to hunt and eat. The only drawback to brine shrimp is their cost and lack of availability.

The solution to this problem is to raise your own brine shrimp. Anyone who is serious about raising Goldfish fry should invest in a one-pound can of quality brine shrimp eggs and use them for a season's worth of growing fry. Since brine shrimp nauplii will last for several hours in fresh water, a large number of nauplii can be fed at one time, allowing the fry to "graze" over the course of several hours. There is also less fouling of the water with live food; the nutrients of prepared food, whether commercial or homemade, start leaching into the water as soon as the food hits the water.

Brine shrimp eggs can be hatched by many different methods. Most eggs come with instructions by the packager, and these are usually quite accurate. My preference is to use a tall cone-shaped beer glass that is very well aerated with an air line. The water should be made up with 1 tablespoon of non-iodized salt to 1 quart of water. Do not use salt preparations that have a declumping agent since the agent will make the water cloudy. The eggs will hatch in twenty-four hours if the temperature is kept at about eighty degrees. At lower temperatures, the eggs will take longer to hatch. Freshly hatched brine shrimp have the highest nutrition value, and my preference is to hatch a batch of eggs each day, so that the fry are fed fresh brine shrimp daily. The brine shrimp can be harvested by allowing the culture to settle for a few minutes. The hatched eggshells will float, unhatched eggs will sink to the bottom, and the nauplii will gradually settle as a layer on top of the unhatched eggs. The brine shrimp can be pipetted out and strained through a fine net or a funnel made from disposable paper towel. Rinse the nauplii in fresh water before feeding. In general, a teaspoon of brine shrimp eggs will be sufficient for about 500 fry at three to four weeks of age.

The fry should be fed as frequently as possible, ideally with fresh brine shrimp every four hours. Most Goldfish fanciers, however, cannot follow such an arduous schedule. As an alternative, it is possible to feed the fry twice a day very heavily since the allure of the brine shrimp keeps the fry hunting as long as the brine shrimp are alive and swimming. Excess brine shrimp will die and should be siphoned off to prevent fouling of the water.

Growing algae in the tank will provide an alternative food source to promote continuous growth of the fry. While the algae may have lower nutrition value than brine shrimp, it has several advantages. First, it grows by itself in the tank. Second, a coat of algae helps to convert fish wastes (nitrates) into fish food. Third, as vegetable matter it complements the nutrition of the brine shrimp. Finally, it is always available to the growing fry, providing a continuous source of calories between brine-shrimp feedings. Algae growth can be promoted by placing strong light sources over the tanks.

The water should be changed as often as necessary. Ideally, two 25% water changes should be performed each week. A larger volume may be necessary if the number of fry exceeds a thousand. In such cases, the fry should be split into two or more tanks to minimize the likelihood of developing poor water conditions and to maximize the growth potential of each fry. Sponge filters should be the only filtration as the fry are unable to withstand the intake of power filters.

The Second Two Weeks: Add Microworms to the Diet

The fry should be gaining mass quickly and should be developing their finnage at this time. The color pattern may also be discerned: metallics, calicos, and mattes can be distinguished with careful inspection. The metallics start developing a metallic sheen over their bellies while the calicos and mattes will appear to have a translucent glaze over certain regions of their snouts and other areas.

Continue with at least twice-daily offerings of brine shrimp nauplii in quantities such that even the slowest of the group develops a bulging belly after ten minutes of feeding. By this time the constant grazing of a large number of fry will probably have reduced the algae in the tank to a minimal layer that is insufficient to provide for the growing mass of Goldfish fry in the tanks. This is the time to add microworms to the feeding regimen.

Microworms will last for many hours in water—several hours longer than brine shrimp. Although the fry like the microworms less than the brine shrimp, they will still graze on the worms. The worms will be a supplemental food that provides calories to all fry after the more aggressive feeders have devoured all the brine shrimp nauplii. It will help to prevent runts, since all fry will have a better chance at getting food. Feeding big chunks of homemade foods will promote the gorging by a small number of robust feeders while the smaller, more delicate fry will be unable to compete with their larger siblings. While the fast-growing fry may become the larger fish, it usually happens that the prettier ones are the ones that are in the middle of the growth curve. These desirable fish will have a chance to develop their

potential if their food is provided in small packages that are dispersed around the tank and accessible to each fish.

Microworm cultures can be obtained from fellow aquarists who have cultures or ordered from mail-order supply houses. The worms are readily grown in moist cornmeal or oatmeal that is placed as a layer on the bottom of a plastic shoebox. The worms feed on the yeast and bacteria that grow on the meal and can be easily seen crawling on the sides of the shoebox.

The Second Month: Start Culling

At the end of the first month, the fry will start to look like Goldfish. This is the time to start culling, since it is literally impossible to raise all of the fry from a large spawning to adult size. One adult Goldfish needs at least 10 gallons of clean water. Since a large spawn can hatch out over a thousand fry, raising each and every fry to become an adult fish means that the Goldfish fancier will need at least 10,000 gallons to raise all of his fish. This amount of water is equivalent to a decent sized in-ground swimming pool! If that doesn't give you pause, think about doing the weekly water changes for that many fish!

Generally, you will want to raise only 1% to 5% of the fry. If you have 1,000 fry, then, you will raise from 10 to 50 highly selected fish. Along the way, you must carefully examine the fry to identify those with the best potential to become high-quality adults. Generally, small faults in a small fish become big faults in a big fish; at the same time, a fish may grow out of some of its faults. Knowledge about the potential of a given fish can only come about from experience in observing the development of a lot of fish over a length of time. It is best to exercise prudence when culling until you have acquired that experience.

Most commonly, culling is done by looking at each fish and rejecting those that are obviously defective. I suggest a strategy of positive selection, however, because I believe it is easier to accurately recognize a small number of nice-looking fish than to evaluate a lot of poor ones.

I suggest the following method. First select the from 25 to 50 of the best fry from each of the two tanks and place them in their own 30-gallon tanks for a week. Over that week, observe the selected fry as well as the fry left in their original tanks. This will give you a chance to look over all the fish before discarding any of the fry. Fish can be moved between tanks depending on their perceived potential. At the end of the observation period, keep all of the fry in the selected group and cull the rest.

Since now only a fraction of the fry remain, you will be relieved of a tremendous burden of water changes and feeding. In addition, the remaining fry are select specimens that hold the greatest promise for developing into beautiful adult Goldfish.

For certain varieties, it may be necessary to subdivide the fry even further. Long-finned fry tend to grow more slowly than short-finned fry. For the long-finned fish to grow adequately, it is necessary to provide them with their own tanks. In addition, feeding live foods exclusively is probably the only way to get these fish to develop deep bodies. The growth of finnage appears to take precedence over the growth of the body. Under suboptimal feeding conditions, the fish end up with long fins and small bodies. Therefore, it is of paramount importance to feed long-finned Goldfish varieties very well during the early growth period.

The Next Four Months: Feed Heavily, Change the Water Very Often, and Make the Final Cull

Raising Goldfish to adult size is simply a matter of feeding the right number of calories. Assuming that an adult Goldfish weighs about 500 grams (about 1.1 pounds) and that the efficiency of feed conversion is 10% (10% of the ingested calories is converted into body mass; this feeding efficiency is simply an approximation), then it requires about 5,000 grams of food (about 11 pounds) to produce a fish of that size. This calculation also tells us the amount of waste the fish produces: in this case, some 10 pounds of excrement that has to be removed from its environment. These calculations emphasize the fact that growing Goldfish eat a lot of food and produce a lot of waste. For the average Goldfish keeper who keeps fish that are not actively growing, limited feedings minimize the waste that is produced by the fish. For the fancier who is raising a bunch of Goldfish fry to become breeding-size adults, food and water changes are the overarching concerns. Goldfish fry grow as quickly as their feeding regimen allows. More food equals faster growth. Furthermore, for those varieties that develop deep bodies (Ryukins and Veiltails) or headgrowth (Ranchus and Lionheads), heavy feeding is mandatory. For long-finned varieties (Ryukins and Veiltails), insufficient feeding leads to the overgrowth of finnage at the expense of body growth and the end result is a stunted fish that is useless for breeding purposes.

As the fish grow, power filters can be added to aid in water circulation and filtration. However, care should be exercised to minimize the effects of high currents on the fish. In general, fish over three months should be able to tolerate power filters. Always observe the fish when you start to use a power filter to make sure they are strong enough to swim against the current without tiring. If the fish don't seem ready for the current, try again in a few weeks.

The heavy feedings will necessitate frequent water changes to maintain water quality. The easiest measure of deteriorating water quality is pH. Fish produce and excrete metabolic acids that are buffered to a certain extent by the mineral salts in the water. However, once this buffering capacity is exceeded, the pH will drop inexorably. The only way to keep the Goldfish growing is to change the water. On the conservative side, water changes of 50% of the total volume of the tank twice a week will minimize the accumulation of metabolic wastes. Additionally, you will probably need to shift the fish to larger tanks as they grow unless you decrease their numbers through continual culling. My experience has been that it is best to let the fish develop to a healthy size before making a final decision about its fate, so I transfer the fish to bigger tanks as they grow. Ideally, place the growing fish outside in large ponds so that they have the benefit of sunlight and access to additional live foods. The fish will grow even more rapidly and develop richer colors.

At the end of the summer, the fish should have attained a good mass and size. Any faults in coloration, body shape, and finnage can be readily evaluated in fish at the age of four to six months. A final evaluation should be made at this time to select the eight to twelve most promising individuals from a given spawn. The procedure described above will select the top 1% of the Goldfish that are produced from a spawn. It is still possible, however, that these fish may not be as good as the parents. Several factors contribute to the development of a high-quality Goldfish, including genetics, a nurturing environment, and luck. All three elements have to be working in unison to develop beautiful fish, and sometimes it can take several tries before they work together. The Goldfish breeder soon learns that the expression "one in a million" is no exaggeration when describing the show-winning fish he or she is aiming for.

I've heard that microworms are an excellent food for fry. How can I cultivate them?

Next to brine shrimp, microworms are one of the best live foods available for raising fry and they are very inexpensive. Years ago when I first started raising show guppies, I never even considered using microworms. Back then, the methods of raising and harvesting microworms were very primitive. You took a culture of microworms, placed it in a cottage cheese container, and waited until the microworms crawled up the sides of the container. Then you used either your finger or a butter knife to scrape the microworms off the sides of the container and dipped your finger or the butter knife into the tank of fry. This method had two major flaws. First, you never had enough microworms to feed all your fry, and second, every time you dipped your finger or knife back into the container of microworms, you contaminated the entire culture. Even today, when fish breeders think about feeding microworms this old method comes to their minds, and that is why very few use them. I discovered and perfected a new method of raising and harvesting microworms, however, that I call the "Inverted Railroad," and here is what I do.

Depending on how many fry I am going to be raising, I buy four to eight plastic shoeboxes with lids, a box of tongue depressors, a turkey baster, rolled oats, yeast, and the microworm culture. (Note: You must submerge the new rails and the new tongue depressors in very clean aquarium water for at least one hour before using them.) I drill three 1/4-inch holes in each side of the lids of the shoe boxes. Then I cut two 3/4-inch by 1 1/4-inch pieces of wood (the rails) the same length of the shoeboxes. I place the "rails" 3/4-inch side up in the shoebox about 3/4 inches from the sides of the box. Now I add the food for the microworms. I buy the biggest box of Quaker rolled oats I can find and a 1-pound package of yeast (the same kind you use for baking). I add enough dried rolled oats to the shoebox to cover a little less than half the depth of the rails, and add 1 heaping tablespoon of yeast. (Note: the rolled oats will rise after adding the water and yeast, and you do not want the mixture touching the bottom of the tongue depressors that are going to be placed on top of the rails.) I add just enough warm water (hot water will kill the yeast) to give the mixture a texture thick enough to be able to pour, like a thick cake batter.

Then I add my microworm culture. All you need is about 1/4 cup. Gently mix the culture into the food. Now place the tongue depressors (the "railroad ties") across the top of the "rails," close enough so that they are touching one another for the length of the entire box.

Put the lid on the box and place it in a warm (seventy-four degrees to seventy-eight degrees) location. Open it in about two to three days. The tongue depressors should be crawling with microworms.

To harvest the microworms, take a measuring cup and fill it almost full of clean, healthy aquarium water. Pick up each tongue depressor and swish it in this water until the microworms are removed. Repeat this process until all the tongue depressors are clean. Place the tongue depressors back on the "rails" and close the lid. Now you should have a measuring cup brimming with microworms. The more shoe boxes you use, the more microworms you can harvest. You could have so many microworms that the water in the measuring cup will now look like skim milk.

To feed the microworms to your fry, use the turkey baster. Do not touch the water in your tanks with the baster. This avoids cross contamination. The best feature about feeding microworms is that if your fry do not eat all of them, the microworms will gather at the bottom of your aquarium like grass and remain alive. You can feed microworms in the morning, go to work, and your fry can graze on them all day.

In about two weeks, the microworm culture becomes old and begins to smell. When the odor gets very strong and the food mix turns watery, it's time to mix up another batch. (A word of advice: dispose of the mixture out of the house, or your spouse may do the same to you!) Just save about a quarter of a cup of the old mix for each box you plan to restart, and add it as you did before to start your microworm supply all over again. As long as you keep saving a small amount of old culture to mix with the new rolled oats and yeast, you'll never have to buy a new culture of microworms. In addition, you can set up as many shoeboxes as you need to supply live food for your fry. Microworms make an excellent food for newborn and growing fry, and this system is a very easy, efficient way to raise and harvest microworms.

In Closing

I've organized this chapter around questions and answers. Let me offer one more question that I hope sums everything I have to share with the reader.

In your opinion, what are the most important factors in keeping healthy Goldfish?
1. Water quality.
2. Do not over feed.
3. Do not over crowd.
4. Quarantine ALL new fish at least 3 to 4 weeks.
5. Do not over medicate.

POMPOM TELESCOPE.

The more you know about your Goldfish the better your chances will be of caring for it successfully. The Goldfish fancy will always owe a debt of gratitude to the hobbyists all over the world with questing minds who have been experimenting with and investigating feeding, housing, and breeding techniques for centuries; today, with advances in fish medicine and increased communication among Goldfish fanciers around the world, we are more likely than ever to enjoy long-term success in keeping Goldfish as pets.

Goldfish make delightful little pets and can live many years. They make very few demands on their owner, and they provide years of enjoyment. They can definitely endear themselves to and become part of the family.

Whether your interest in Goldfish is as a single companion pet, as a breeder, or as an exhibitor, you must use your interest in the hobby to ensure the future of these fascinating little pets. Using a combination of love, common sense, and the information in this book, you should be able to keep your Goldfish healthy and happy for many years. Enjoy!

Chapter 8

Appreciating

and

Evaluating

Chinese

Goldfish

Jackie Chan

and Louis Chan

Appreciating Beautiful Goldfish

The beauty of the Goldfish, with its exceptional form, coloring, movement, and charm, has won it the devotion of connoisseurs as an object of aesthetic appreciation. Because of this, new essays on Goldfish appreciation and new monographs about Goldfish culture are being written constantly in Chinese and other languages, but opinions about standards for evaluating the beauty of Goldfish vary widely. Nonetheless, if we look back over the history of Goldfish connoisseurship, we will see that connoisseurs' judgments about aesthetic standards for Goldfish are intimately connected to the ceaseless evolution of its external form.

The great Song-dynasty poet Su Shi (1036–1101) wrote:

> I didn't see you at your golden carp pond,
> So I went right away and sought you out at
>   Dingshan Village.

At the time that he composed those lines, Su Shi was especially enamored of golden carp, a natural sport of the wild ancestor of the Goldfish that was first introduced to cultivation at this time. Su Shi admired the carp for their beautiful gold coloring, and this was the first feature of Goldfish to be appreciated aesthetically. Over the centuries that have passed since then, Goldfish coloration has steadily evolved, and new and beautiful colors and color combinations are constantly appearing on the scene. There have also been dramatic changes in the physical forms of Goldfish. The earliest was the appearance of double and triple tail fins, from the original single tail fin of the ancestor carp; later, such distinct and wonderful forms as the High Head, Bubble Eye, Pompom, and many others were developed.

The rich beauty of form that Goldfish varieties display has delighted connoisseurs. For example, in the late Qing-dynasty work, *Random Notes from the Bamboo Leaf Pavilion* (1893), Yao Yuanzhi records that Bao Wufeng had special methods for raising Goldfish as well as four criteria for classifying and appraising Goldfish: (1) a thickset, well-proportioned body, (2) a large, straight tail, (3) evenly set, symmetrical eyes, and (4) a regularly shaped, rounded body. These early standards of appreciation and classification were based on the physical characteristics of Goldfish developed at that time. In later years, a plethora of new varieties were created, characterized by a wide range of distinctive features and individual styles of movement and personality, and two additional concepts or principles were added to the aesthetic standards for judging Goldfish: beauty of movement and charm.

In 1930, the Goldfish connoisseur Zhou Shoujuan wrote a poem in which he used Goldfish as a metaphor for expressing his feelings of homesickness. Using the sophisticated rhetorical devices characteristic of classical Chinese literature, Zhou's encomium to Goldfish provides a clear description of the beauty of their form and charm. "Charm" (*shenyun* in Chinese) has long been a much sought-after quality and important concept in Chinese painting theory and criticism. Ling Xu, a painter from Suzhou, painted a long scroll that depicted one hundred Goldfish in great detail, including attractive and symmetrically shaped Dragon Eye Goldfish, innocent and playful Red-Cap Goldfish, the brilliantly colored vermilion Phoenix, and the luminous Pearl Scale. Ling's depiction is utterly lifelike and portrays these fish in every possible attitude, still and in motion, in a carefree and natural spirit. He has captured the beauty of the Goldfish's charm and movement in a masterful fashion.

We can see from the above that critical standards of Goldfish aesthetics have developed over the course of history. As the external form of Goldfish has evolved, so, too, has the aesthetic appreciation of Goldfish become ever richer, and the standards of Goldfish beauty are becoming higher and more comprehensive by the day. Since there are no limits to the possible evolution of Goldfish, our ways of evaluating and describing the beauty of Goldfish are also limitless. At the same time we need to bear in mind that all standards of Goldfish beauty are firmly bound to a particular historical period. In addition, any given Goldfish aficionado's judgments will be influenced by his personal taste and by his level of connoisseurship. Tastes differ, levels of expertise differ, and each individual will have a different appraisal of the same aesthetic object. We have been engaged in the business of breeding and selling Goldfish for many years, and over those years we have striven to hone and deepen our awareness of Goldfish aesthetics, employing both careful observation and thoughtful analysis. This has led us to propose that contemporary standards for judging the beauty of Goldfish should rest on the three principles of quality, size, and rarity. In other words, the beauty of contemporary Goldfish depends on the harmonious combination of fine quality, large size, and precious rarity, and that beauty will be flawed if it does not demonstrate all three of these principles in a harmonious balance.

The Beauty of Quality

The beauty of quality is perhaps in need of definition. We use it to indicate a harmonious unity of form, color, movement, and charm. Beauty of form requires balance, first and foremost. This balance is reflected in the fish's ease of movement, steadiness, and firmness. When the fish is still, it should retain its balance and exhibit poise and graceful carriage. Generally speaking, such a fish has a thick caudal peduncle and symmetrical, well-set tail finnage. It opens its tail fins naturally, and they neither droop down nor rise up. Such a fish will always

A WELL-BALANCED HAMA NISHIKI.

APPRECIATING AND EVALUATING CHINESE GOLDFISH

be able to maintain its balance and stability, and will remain on an even, horizontal keel whether swimming or at rest. If the caudal peduncle is too slender, the tail fins will droop. Not only will the fish need to exert a lot of energy to move its tail fins, but when it does the tail will rise while the front portion of the body tilts downward in compensation. The result is that the swimming fish appears to be diving, and in Chinese we say it looks like a scallion sticking out of the ground. A fish with a tail that floats, on the other hand, will swim as if darting upwards, its nose pointing up. All of these factors can

affect the beauty of the fish when it is swimming, and are no doubt the basis for Yao Yuanzhi's principle of "a large, straight tail."

Many Goldfish varieties have exceptional, distinctive forms, such as the Bubble Eye, High Head, Butterfly Tail, and others. Because of the plump bodies for which they are prized, they have a great ability to maintain their physical equilibrium. This makes them capable of gracefully bearing increased weight at head and tail, allowing for distinctive head and tail growth to become more pronounced. This is what Yao Yuanzhi meant by "a thickset, well-proportioned body." Chinese people today still describe Goldfish with the saying, "whether long or short, only plump beauties can make the grade." Nonetheless, if the characteristic that defines a variety is too exaggerated, the structural arrangement of the body as a whole will lose its harmony. The center of gravity will be thrown off, either because the weight carried by its head is too great, or because the tail fin is too large or too long. This in turn can have a detrimental effect on the beauty of the fish when it is in motion. When, for example, the head of a Bubble Eye is weighed down by bubbles that are disproportionately large, the fish cannot move freely and spends its time resting at the bottom of the aquarium, which naturally detracts from its visual appeal.

One can see from the above that there is an intimate connection between the harmonious arrangement of the structures of every part of the fish's body and its ability to maintain its physical equilibrium. Whatever

A Red Wenyu with good conformation. Photo by Tung Hoi Aquarium Company.

An excellent Dragon Eye (Telescope). Photo by Tung Hoi Aquarium Company.

the strain of Goldfish, the physical features that characterize its variety must be fully and strikingly developed. At the same time, the other parts of the body must have developed correspondingly in such a way as to allow the fish to maintain its balance. We must not overemphasize the development of one feature to the detriment of the total harmony of the fish and its physical grace.

One of the essential qualities of a beautifully formed fish is symmetry. A good fish appears natural and complete. All of its features—mouth, eyes, nose, gill covers, trunk, and fins—contribute to the impression of an organic whole. There is an easy test for this quality. If either adding to or taking away from any part would disturb the balance of the whole, then its features are in true harmony and proper proportion. Let us look, for example, at the Chinese Wenyu Goldfish, a category of fish with dorsal fins, open tails, normal eyes, and scales.[1] The overall shape of the Wenyu is a pair of triangles: the head is pointed like that of a mouse, and the body is short and deep, forming the first triangle. The caudal peduncle is narrow, spreading out into the broad tail, forming the second triangle. This body type is entirely consistent with the aesthetic principle of symmetry, and it gives the Wenyu its distinctive beauty. It is for precisely this reason that aficionados will reject a Wenyu with a blunt, round head or a low back. On the other hand, practically every part of the body of an excellent Dragon Eye, as shown above, including the bases of the fins, is

cylindrical. The body is formed of an arrangement of large and small cylinders according to certain principles: the lengths are symmetrical, the proportions harmonious, and the general impression is similar to the polished refinement of controlled, melodious singing or masterful Chinese calligraphy. If a Dragon Eye has a large head but a sunken mouth, or if its protuberant eyes are unequal in size, or if the shapes of the features vary, or if the head is large and the eyes are small, it cannot be considered a beautiful example of its type. By the same token, the bubbles of a Bubble Eye Goldfish, the Pompoms of a Pompom Goldfish, and lobes of the tail fin of a Butterfly Goldfish must be symmetrical in size and set. The headgrowth of an Oranda must not lean to one side; it must be symmetrical both back-to-front and side-to-side. This is the basis for Yao Yuanzhi's principles of "evenly set, symmetrical eyes" and "a regular, rounded body."

In judging individual fish, it is important to remember that Goldfish are always growing and changing. A Bubble Eye Goldfish, for example, may have very well-formed bubbles while the fish is young, but some time after the fish reaches the age of two or three years, the bubbles may become uneven in size. On the other hand, a fish that does not appear to be very good at birth can, after the age of two or three, grow to be symmetrical.

As one learns to appreciate Goldfish, it is relatively easy to learn to appreciate and value the regularity and symmetry of all a fish's features—the mouth, nose, eyes, fins, gill covers, bubbles, wens, pompoms, and so forth. What people often overlook, however, is the importance

1. We do not use this category in English. The Veiltail and the Ryukin are perhaps the most typical examples of Wenyus, with their pointed heads, deep bodies, and long, full tails.

of the overall harmony and balance of all of these features in the structure and arrangement of the entire fish. This is failing to see the forest for the trees, and it is a sign of a low level of expertise or being overly focused on the distinctive characteristics of a particular variety.

In addition to balance and symmetry, a fish of high quality should have a muscular and regular body. This is primarily seen in three features. The first is a thick and well-set caudal peduncle. This is a necessary feature for achieving a Goldfish with an outstanding body type. A Goldfish with a thick caudal peduncle is healthy and full of vitality. Furthermore, the direction in which the tail fin grows affects the balance of the fish's body, and it plays an important role in determining the attitude of the body when the fish is swimming. A well-formed and properly set tail fin provides stability and balance to the fish.

Second, each and every fin should be well formed and fully developed. Fins should spread naturally without obvious folds. Fish that have dorsal fins (such as Wenyus) must have dorsal fins that spread easily and stand up straight. Those that lack dorsal fins (such as Eggfish) must not have vestigial fins or spurs. The ideal Butterfly Tail Goldfish has a short body, long fins, and a tail fin as thin as a cicada's wings. When it spreads its fins, it is the epitome of beautiful finnage. Some of the possible causes of defects, damage, or folds in the fins, with the exception of hereditary factors, can be attributed to rough picking at the fish farm, carelessness in packing and handling, or to disease.

Third, the fish should have well-formed, even, and regularly arranged scales. Scalation is especially important, of course, in the Pearl Scale. A first-rate Pearl Scale should have scales spreading evenly and densely from behind its gill covers to the base of its tail, and from back to belly. On the other hand, if scales have sloughed off, or are of uneven sizes, or if the rows are not straight, the fish will not be pleasing to the eye.

The special characteristics that typify a variety should be strong and pronounced. The existence of a wide variety of fish characterized by different special features ensures that there are Goldfish to satisfy the aesthetic preferences of connoisseurs of all tastes. The Oranda, a large-bodied variety, has a high dorsal fin, a big, tall "hat" on its head, and a long, broad tail fin. Its movements are smooth, and it has an elegant, poised beauty. Small-bodied varieties, such as the Bubble Eye and Pompom, display a gentle, graceful beauty. The Butterfly Tail, the Ryukin, and other similar varieties, with their distinctive tail fins and their dancing and fluttering movements in the water, exhibit a refined and lovely beauty. The Ranchu and Lionhead varieties are the "strongmen" of the Goldfish kingdom, and theirs is a powerful and forceful beauty. The body of the Pearl Scale is perfectly round, and pearl-like, well-defined scales cover it entirely. Each "pearl" seems more dazzling than the next, and their beauty is that of something entirely new and fresh.

There are too many varieties of Goldfish to mention them all, but each stands apart from all other varieties by possessing characteristics that are particular to it. Thus, the stronger and more pronounced those special characteristics are the better. This is particularly true for those strains of Goldfish that are the result of crossbreeding between two different varieties. It is especially necessary for these hybrids to display varietal characteristics as strongly and prominently as possible. Otherwise, they will not be distinctive and will appear to be "neither horse nor donkey." For example, the Calico Celestial Goldfish is a new strain that is a hybrid of the Calico Dragon Eye Goldfish and the Celestial Goldfish. Though this new strain displays the coloration of the Calico Dragon Eye Goldfish, it remains a Celestial, and the focal point is the characteristic eye placement of the Celestial. Though a combination of two strains, it has a strong identity of its own.

Beauty of color is another important standard for evaluating the quality of a Goldfish. Chinese Goldfish are renowned worldwide for their rich variety of brilliant colors. China's first Goldfish connoisseur, Zhang Qiande, in his *Cinnabar Register of Fish*, catalogued a wide range of Goldfish varieties, in all their colorations, splendor, and magnificence. As he wrote:

> Some Goldfish have white bodies, red wens on their heads in the shape of the character *wang* 王 and red heads and tail fins. There are Goldfish whose bodies display a crystalline translucence,[2] and whose heads and tail fins are white. There are Goldfish with crystalline translucent bodies, half red and half white; other Goldfish that have red backs and white bellies; and others still that are pure white all over. Some Goldfish are pure white with the exception of a red line running down their backs. There are calico Goldfish whose entire bodies are spotted with colors like the stars in the sky. And there are Goldfish whose bodies are as richly suffused with color as a beautiful sunset. Some have golden-yellow backs, others have silver-white backs. Some have golden-yellow round markings, and some have silver-white round markings. Some are completely covered with multicolored patches. There are so many different kinds that it is hard to list them all.

2. This is a poetic way of referring to nacreous scalation.

RED-AND-WHITE POMPOM ORANDA. PHOTO BY TUNG HOI AQUARIUM COMPANY.

There is an old saying in China, "A myriad variations cannot alter the essence"— which is to say that no matter how many different colors and complex patterns Goldfish display, they can all be assigned to one of two categories: solid colored or multicolored. The solid colors are: red (red-orange), black, bronze (or chocolate), orange (or gold), blue (blue-gray), white, and iron color. Of these, white and iron-colored fish have mostly been allowed to die out, due to the lack of visual appeal of these dull colors. The multicolor combinations are: red and white, red and black, black and white, bronze and blue, tricolor, and calico.

For a fish to have beautiful coloration, its color must be rich, strong, and bright, its markings must be clear, and the shapes of its markings must be arranged harmoniously and with interest and variety. If a fish fulfills these conditions, it will accord with our aesthetic standards. Practically speaking, it is not difficult to find solid-color fish that are bright and dazzling. When there are two colors, one color might be set delightfully like jew-

els in the other, or the colors might be evenly matched in tone, or they might contrast brightly with each other. A calico fish should have all colors represented—blue, white, red, and black, but red in particular should be present. The red-and-white Oranda, above, has stunning coloration, the deep red and white of the body setting each other off perfectly.

But what, in the end, is the most beautiful coloration? This question may be unanswerable. Goldfish connoisseurship is an emotional activity, involving the connoisseur's aesthetic experience, background, and even culture. These vary widely, and hence the individual aesthetic responses to the various colorations of fish vary as well. Some people admire ornate beauty, while others prefer simple beauty. Some people are fond of one coloration, while others prefer another. As the old Chinese saying goes, "Some like radishes, and some like cabbages."

There is one complication in appreciating and evaluating Goldfish coloration, and that is that some Goldfish colorations are not stable, including black, black and white, bronze and white, blue and white,

A BLACK DRAGON EYE GRADUALLY TURNING FROM BLACK TO RED. PHOTO BY TUNG HOI AQUARIUM COMPANY.

bronze and red, red and black, and tricolor. During the course of the fish's growth, or as a result of changes in water quality or temperature, the original colors may change, even to the extent that the fish may lose the qualities that attracted the connoisseur to it in the first place and it will no longer please him. Take for example the red-and-black Dragon Eye shown here on the left. When the fish was a juvenile, its body was solid black. But as the fish aged and experienced changes in water temperature, the black on its body began to fade, starting at the belly. Ultimately, the fish has become a red-and-black Dragon Eye, and it may go on to become completely red. In light of this phenomenon, when a Goldfish connoisseur buys a fish, he should inquire about the fish's bloodlines and the farm where it was bred. If he knows what coloration changes to expect, he can purchase a Goldfish that is more likely to remain the coloration he desires.

In addition to the Goldfish's ability to delight the heart and please the eye with the beauty of its form and color, the Goldfish possesses even more important kinds of beauty: those of movement and charm. There are those who compare the beauty of the Goldfish's movements to that of an accomplished dancer. They consider this to be the epitome of the Goldfish's beauty, because Goldfish are living, moving creatures that we observe swimming about in the aquariums that we have painstakingly designed and built for them. Goldfish give their owners—their audiences—endless joy as they perform a living comedy, displaying in their infinite poses and movements humor, absurdity, drama, and grace. We can look upon the Goldfish's movements as a splendid stage performance: the physical form of the Goldfish, which depicts its style of movement, is equivalent to the dancer's talent; its flowing fins are its costume, and its bright colors are its makeup. Surely everyone has seen Goldfish that were as silly as clowns, or as lively as mischievous children, or as calm and dignified as cultivated gentlemen, or as poised and confident as well-bred young ladies. Every inch of their bodies, even in the tiniest movement, is the embodiment of beauty in motion.

To give a specific example, most Orandas are large-bodied fish, such as the red Oranda on the facing page. This fish has a very large head, which is nearly perfect in form and gives it an appearance of outstanding bravery. The fish's dorsal fin is tall, the tail fin is big and broad, and the wens are abundant and elastic.[3] When swimming, the fish appears cool and calm, full of confidence, and naturally endowed with a style echoing that of a splendidly attired medieval knight. The Butterfly

3. This is a term used in both China and Japan to describe a wen that has a soft, plentiful appearance, as opposed to a "hard" or "rigid" wen, which is small and tight.

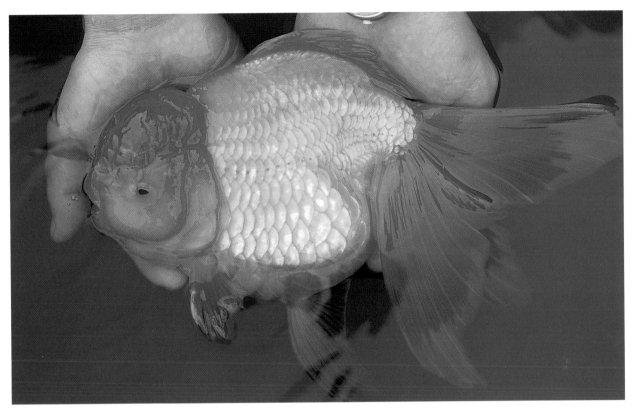

ABOVE: A LARGE RED ORANDA. PHOTO BY TUNG HOI
AQUARIUM COMPANY.

BELOW: RED-CAP ORANDA. PHOTO BY TUNG HOI
AQUARIUM COMPANY.

Tail is a small-bodied variety. It often flutters its lovely tail fins like a girl in the flower of her youth taking a leisurely stroll—all innocence, vitality, and not a hint of worry or sadness. Words simply cannot do it justice. The short-bodied Lionhead, with its stubby body and large head, seems to limp along. Seeing its comic gentleness and earnestness, one cannot help but laugh. And then there is the small, exquisite Pompom Goldfish. A pair of fleshy "flowers" bloom like colored balls on either side of its mouth, waving from side to side as the fish swims through the water. Like a pretty page boy coming to greet an important guest with fresh flowers, the Pompom creates an atmosphere of boundless happiness, good fortune, and abundant joy. The Red Cap Oranda, loftily elegant, aloof but bighearted, inspires one to pleasant thoughts and reveries.

Such limitless attitudes and beauty of movement make Goldfish infinitely appealing. It is this appeal, combined with the natural grace and poise of the fish, that forms the quality of charm, another important aspect of its beauty. Chinese people have always emphasized the beauty of the movement and charm of Goldfish. All of China's famous arts and crafts have taken the Goldfish as their subject, including the brocades of Hangzhou, the stone and boxwood carvings of Qingtian in Zhejiang Province, the lacquerware of Fujian, the litchi-wood carvings of Guangdong, the glasswares of Dalian, the embroideries of Hunan and Suzhou, the decorative paper cuts of Taohuawu, and the porcelain of Jingdezhen in Jiangxi Province. All of these have vividly recreated the beauty of the Goldfish's charm, representing its lively form and capturing its wit and humor in scenes of frolicking Goldfish.

DECORATIVE PAPER CUT WITH A GOLDFISH MOTIF. PHOTO BY TUNG HOI AQUARIUM COMPANY.

The Beauty of Size

Zhang Qiande's *Cinnabar Pictorial Catalogue* elucidates the way in which early Chinese Goldfish connoisseurs regarded large size as a measure of beauty: "The beauty of a Goldfish depends not only on its coloration, tail fins, markings, and body being distinctly different from ordinary Goldfish. Whether the fish has long or short tail fins, it should be plump and solid looking, and it should be large of body in order to fulfill the standards of beauty." Seen from a contemporary perspective, this statement is overly simplistic. We believe that "the beauty of size" rests not only in the size of the fish but also in the size of the particular feature or features that characterize the particular variety. It is the combination of these two distinct measures of size that constitutes the beauty of size. The Goldfish as a species is a relatively small animal, and most individual Goldfish are also small; consequently connoisseurs have prized fish that are relatively large. Size makes a fish stand out from its fellows and also reflects its vigor and robustness—qualities that engender a powerful aesthetic response.

But when it comes to evaluating the beauty of a Goldfish's size, one must have a grasp of three principles. First, when making comparisons, one must compare Goldfish of the same variety. Some Goldfish varieties are relatively large in size, including the Oranda, the Ranchu, and the Short-Tailed Pearl Scale. Other varieties are relatively small in size, including the Bubble Eye, the Celestial, the Butterfly Tail, and the Pompom. This is in keeping with the special characteristics of each variety. If one wants to evaluate the relative merits of large and small, it makes no sense to use fish from two different varieties as a basis of comparison, since there is no common basis upon which to make a useful comparison.

Second, one should only compare those fish that were raised in the same area. Fish that have been raised in different locations are the products of different environments and water qualities. These conditions produce variations in body size and plumpness, even among fish of the same variety. Goldfish from northern China tend to be delicate and slender, while those from the south are plump. With their differing body types, the style of their beauty is also not the same. Northern Goldfish are lithe and graceful, and sprightly in their movements. Southern Goldfish are gentle and refined in their bearing, and dignified in their movements. When all of these variables are considered, it is very difficult for a connoisseur to evaluate the relative beauty of different fish simply based on size.

BLACK ORANDA. PHOTO BY TUNG HOI AQUARIUM COMPANY.

Third, the beauty of size requires two additional qualifications: it only applies to young fish and to fish that have been raised naturally. If a fish has attained an extraordinary size naturally but is already in the twilight of its life, its potential for further growth is all but exhausted, and size is no longer really a mark of beauty. Also, by applying special methods of care and feeding, it is possible to produce fish of abnormal physical growth and development, inappropriate to their age. In either of the above cases, the largeness is flawed and cannot be taken into account when evaluating the fish's beauty. In other words, if in the single-minded pursuit of big, plump fish, one disregards the laws of natural growth and development as well as the special characteristics that define any given Goldfish variety, one will have lost sight of the beauty intrinsic to that kind of fish. As a consequence, the Goldfish's ornamental value will also be lost.

Another aspect of the criterion of size is future potential. One should not only judge the size and robustness of the fish, but also look for a fish that is growing well. Endowed with great potential for development, such a fish will be capable of providing years of enjoyment to its owner. The black Oranda above was born this year and has a large and nearly ideal body type. Its vigorous and lively movements are pleasing to the eye, and its wen is full and elastic. The fish is still quite young and has not yet reached its full size, so it still has

BLACK LIONHEAD. PHOTO BY TUNG HOI AQUARIUM COMPANY.

much potential for further development. For these reasons, its large body can be seen as a beautiful attribute.

This, however, can easily lead to the misconception that the younger a large Goldfish is the more highly prized it is. In fact, this is an oversimplification. If one compares a young fish to a fish in its twilight years, in most cases the younger fish will be more pleasing aesthetically. But youth and age are relative, and if one compares a yearling fish with one that is two years old, the situation is altogether different, since both fish qualify as relatively young fish. Because the two-year-old fish's growth rate has substantially slowed, its muscles and body are solid and powerful, meeting the criteria of beauty for this Goldfish variety, while the yearling fish has not had a chance to develop these characteristic traits. For precisely this reason, it is quite common in the commercial Goldfish business to find wide gaps in pricing among of fish of similar size and grade.

Now that we have clarified the meaning and aesthetic value of "largeness," we must next set about determining standards for measuring Goldfish size. We believe that the best standard of measurement is by length and weight. There are two standards of length: body length, the length from the mouth to the end of the caudal peduncle, and total length, which is the length from the mouth to the tip of the caudal fin. Weight is, of course, the total weight of the fish. The practical application of this standard of measurement will reveal one of the following three situations:

(1) Two fish of equal total length, as well as equal body length and weight, will be of equal aesthetic value.

(2) Two fish of equal total length are of different body length and weight, and the fish with the longer body length and greater weight will be of higher quality.

(3) Two fish of different total lengths, but with equal body length and weight, will be of equal aesthetic value.

When judging the size of the defining features of any particular variety of Goldfish, generally speaking we stress the harmonious and complimentary development of the body as a whole along with that of the distinctive features. As the entire body grows larger, the special features of the variety should also grow larger in proportion. There are also certain circumstances in which the body as a whole and the distinctive features of a variety are not growing in a balanced or harmonious way. During the process of development, the growth of one feature may be faster or slower, creating a distortion or imbalance—perhaps temporary, but perhaps not. For a connoisseur to pass judgment on the

RED-AND-WHITE HAMA NISHIKI. PHOTO BY TUNG HOI AQUARIUM COMPANY.

CALICO BUBBLE EYE. PHOTO BY TUNG HOI AQUARIUM COMPANY.

beauty of such a fish, he must grasp two principles. First, does the distortion cause the special characteristics of that variety to appear better defined and more pronounced? If so, then it is beautiful; if not, then it is not beautiful.

For instance, it is desirable for a Bubble Eye to have large bubbles; for a Pompom to have large pompoms; for an Oranda to have large headgrowth; for a Butterfly Tail to have broad, flat tail fins; and for a Pearl Scale to have big scales. If these features are highly prominent, even though they may appear "distorted," they can augment the fish's beauty. The Ryukin, on the other hand, should have a short, round body and small, pointed head. If its head is too large or the body too long, it is not a beautiful Ryukin. Second, one must determine whether the prominence of the distinctive feature adversely affects the symmetry or balance of the fish's body. For example, if one bubble of a Bubble Eye has grown normally and the other is unusually large, this will detract from the beauty of the fish's symmetry. If both of the fish's bubbles are exceptionally large as in the fish shown above, making the fish top heavy and shifting the center of gravity forward, this will also take away from the beauty of the fish's balance. Similarly, a Pearl Scale with large but uneven scales that are arranged haphazardly cannot be considered beautiful.

To sum up, the beauty deriving from the enlargement of the characteristic varietal features requires that the particular feature be prominent without affecting the symmetry and balance of the fish. There is an inherent contradiction in this, but one that often disappears as the fish grows older. It is a fact that large and beautiful fish with exaggeratedly developed special varietal characteristics are very rare indeed. The majority of Goldfish tend, as they grow older, to achieve corrections and adjustments to their features and proportions. Ultimately, many fish that have temporarily lost their symmetry and balance gradually become quite attractive. Conversely, there are fish with weak or undeveloped varietal characteristics that become more pronounced as the fish grows older. Generally speaking, a yearling Goldfish is at the height of its growth and development, and all of its proportions are undergoing a process of rapid change. At the same time, its future tendencies are also in flux. Hence, any beautiful attributes that such a fish possesses must be qualified by a certain instability, and new developments that are not in keeping with the keeper's wishes can occur at any time. On the other hand, a fish that is about two years old will already be growing and developing at a much slower rate, and its physical characteristics will be relatively stable. As a result, the attributes of a fish of this age group will be much more lasting and reliable than those displayed by a yearling. For precisely this reason, most Goldfish dealers and collectors find a large two-year-old Goldfish highly desirable.

The Beauty of Rarity

A rare thing is a precious thing. For that reason, rarity is one objective standard with which to evaluate Goldfish. Back in 1904 the Goldfish connoisseur Zhuoyuan Laoren, who called himself "The Old Man in his Garden," mentioned the beauty of rarity in his work *An Elegant Collection of Insects and Fish*: "After the tens of thousands of hatchlings have grown to the point that they are shaped like Goldfish, the rest depends entirely on selection. First, out of those ten thousand juvenile fish, one chooses one thousand; out of that thousand one picks out one hundred; and finally, out of that hundred one selects ten fish. Only thus can one obtain excellent, first-rate fish that outshine all others." The varieties of Goldfish that are available today are endowed with beauty of form, beauty of color, beauty of movement, and the beauty of charm; but there are very few that are both large and good. The perfect Goldfish does not exist. Hence, a Goldfish that boasts the attribute of rarity is precious indeed.

Judges in Chinese Goldfish shows always hope that participants will enter identical pairs of Goldfish. In fact, it is nearly impossible to find two fish of the same shape, color, and weight. Because high-quality Goldfish are rare specimens that have undergone a rigorous process of selection, it is extremely difficult to come up with two fish that are the same. In Chinese philosophy there is a saying, "No two leaves on Earth are exactly the same"; by the same token, no two Goldfish on Earth are exactly the same.

As Goldfish enthusiasts gain more and more experience in raising and caring for Goldfish, in conjunction with the rapid progress made in the science of aquaculture, some Goldfish breeders are applying modern technology and the laws of heredity to improve existing varieties or create new varieties of Goldfish. They may take an existing variety or even just a beautiful quality from a particular variety and make it more stable, intensify it, crossbreed it, or alter it. Through these means they hope to cultivate Goldfish that are more beautiful and "rarer" than ever. For example, twenty years ago less than five percent of Red Cap Orandas met the trade standard for "good." Today, thirty percent of this variety produced by reputable fish farms meet this standard. Not long ago, the Ranchu variety was relatively rare in China, but since 1983 we have several times brought Ranchus from Japan into China for breeding purposes, and today Ranchu are being bred in China on a large scale. Furthermore, Chinese breeders have bred a number of outstanding, "cream of the crop" fish, and these are no longer as rare as they once were.

TRICOLOR TELESCOPE.

RARE RED BUBBLE EYE WITH DORSAL FIN.

We should bear in mind that, first, rarity is not a fixed, unchanging quality. A fish that possesses the beautiful attribute of rarity can become commonplace almost overnight if breeding of that variety becomes widespread. That once-rare fish then loses the ephemeral quality of rarity and joins other established varieties as an example of the perpetuation of a particular ideal of beauty. Second, if we look at the process by which Goldfish are developing and evolving, we can see constant and continual improvements in the quality and beauty of Goldfish. As the fish have been placed in ever more controlled environments, moving first from the wild to the fishpond, and then to the modern aquarium, they have attained new levels of beauty and quality. We can see from all of this that there is a very important relationship between good equipment, good management, and good techniques on the one hand and maintaining and enhancing the quality and beauty of Goldfish on the other. Today, the famous fish farms in China have all mastered the principles of Goldfish heredity and mutation. They

are actively engaged in making improvements to existing varieties and in creating extraordinary new varieties. As a consequence, the famous fish farms breed high-quality fish with pure bloodlines and great potential for development. The farms keep meticulous, complete, and scientific records of breeding histories. When one buys a fish from a well-known fish farm today, one stands a good chance of buying a good-quality Goldfish, and one might even be lucky enough to buy a fish that possesses that elusive quality of rarity, the last of our criteria for judging the beauty of Goldfish.

In summation, the many diverse varieties of Goldfish, with their vast array of shapes and their various and splendid colorations, create for us an exquisite and touching living tableau. They offer us an inexhaustible source of beauty. As human life is boundless, beauty too knows no limits. In the future, humanity will continue to create and discover beauty. And so, when we speak of an objective standard of Goldfish beauty, we can only say that there is only better, there is no best.

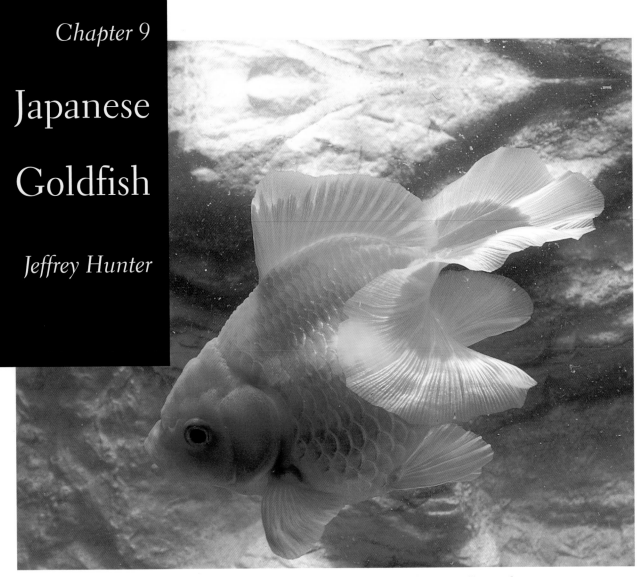

RED TOSAKIN. PHOTO BY HIKARU SHIRAISHI.

Many of us keep and enjoy varieties of Goldfish originating in Japan—the Ranchu, Edo Nishiki, Azuma Nishiki, Ryukin—or would like to keep some of the rarer Japanese varieties, such as Jikin and Tosakin. The Japanese have kept and raised Goldfish for centuries, and Japan is second only to China in its "Goldfish culture." While the details of Japanese Goldfish husbandry and their attitude toward Goldfish may differ from ours, it is certainly interesting to learn more about the origins of some of our favorite Goldfish varieties and the place they occupy in their home country. This chapter is devoted to a description of Japanese Goldfish, their history, place in Japanese culture, main varieties, and the Japanese Goldfish industry and hobby. I have included a pronunciation guide to help you say the Japanese names of varieties and other terms correctly, and make you a real *tsu* (expert) on the subject of Japanese Goldfish.

The History of Goldfish in Japan

Goldfish were first introduced into Japan about five hundred years ago from their place of origin, China. They were brought to trading ports in western Japan, especially the merchant city of Sakai, near Osaka, which was a center for trade with China at the time. It is thought that the first Goldfish to arrive in Japan from China were of the variety closely resembling what is now known as the Wakin—which means, ironically, "Japanese Goldfish."

For several centuries, Goldfish were expensive rarities available only to the nobility, the high-ranking members of the warrior (samurai) class, and wealthy merchants. They were called by many names, the most common being *kingyo*, or "golden fish," for gold, orange, and red fish, and *gingyo*, or "silver fish," for

Wakin. Photo by Hikaru Shiraishi.

white Goldfish. Eventually the name *kingyo* came to be used as the general term for Goldfish of every color.

About two centuries after their introduction, from the late 1600s, Goldfish began to spread to the common people in the major cities of Kyoto, Osaka, and Edo (modern Tokyo), though they were still an expensive and much sought-after luxury. The two and one-half centuries from 1600 to 1868 were called the Edo period, because Japan's capital was located in Edo. During the Edo period, Japan was almost entirely closed off from the world. Japanese nationals were not allowed to leave the country, and foreigners were prohibited from entering it. Trade was restricted to a few very carefully controlled ports. Yet during the Edo period Japan received a few imports of additional Goldfish varieties from China and, perhaps, Korea. One was the Maruko, or "round fish." This was probably an early type of Egg Fish or Lionhead, and the Japanese developed it into the Ranchu. Another was the Ryukin, or "Ryukyu Goldfish." The Ryukyu Islands southwest of Okinawa were another important trading center, through which Chinese and Southeast Asian goods and culture entered Japan. The third was the Oranda Shishigashira, or "Lionhead from Holland," which we know today as the Oranda. This variety is thought to have been brought to Japan on a European ship that departed from China and then stopped at Nagasaki. At the time, the Dutch were the only Europeans allowed to trade with Japan, so things associated with Europe were often described as being from Holland, which is pronounced "Oranda" in Japanese. "Shishigashira" means "Lionhead."

Partly because imports were so few and far between, the Japanese quickly began raising their own Goldfish. At first this was a hobby of the wealthy, as we have seen. Many of the feudal lords who governed Japan at this time were fond of Goldfish and encouraged Goldfish breeding in their local fiefs. This resulted in the creation of many distinctive local types of Japanese Goldfish, generically known as *jikin*, or "local Goldfish." The best-known local Goldfish is the Nagoya Jikin.[1] Others include the Tosakin, from the old feudal fief of Tosa (now Kochi), on the island of Shikoku; the Izumo Nankin, from Izumo, in Shimane Prefecture; the Osaka Ranchu; the Tsugaru Nishiki, from Tsugaru in Aomori Prefecture; the Yamagata Kingyo, also called the Sabao or Tamasaba, from Yamagata Prefecture; and others, most now extinct. Leading samurai retainers took up Goldfish breeding as a way to gain influence with their feudal lords who collected Goldfish; presenting a prize fish was a good way to secure a promotion or a favor.

Throughout the Edo period, the government tried to enforce strict regulations against luxury, and at one time it outlawed the keeping of Goldfish and confiscated every Goldfish that could be found. Needless to say, these went into the collections of the top government officials. A British envoy to Japan in this period also tells the story of a powerful government figure who, upon learning that the Englishman had two fine Chinese Goldfish, entreated and pressured him to give them to him as a gift. Toward the end of the Edo period, however, the wealth of the local feudal lords and the samurai class declined, and many were forced to encourage local industries to supplement their treasuries. Goldfish breeding was one such industry, and this resulted in greater availability of Goldfish and their spread among the common people.

At first most Goldfish were produced in western Japan, in the regions surrounding Kyoto and Osaka.

1. Though *jikin* started as a generic term for any local Goldfish, it is now almost always used to refer to the Nagoya Jikin, also called the Rokurin or the Kujakuo.

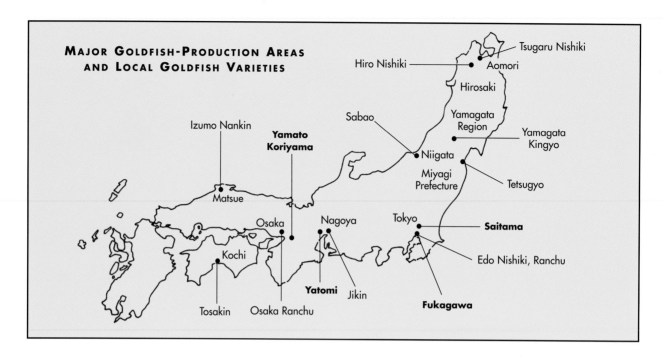

MAJOR GOLDFISH-PRODUCTION AREAS AND LOCAL GOLDFISH VARIETIES

Izumo Nankin
Yamato Koriyama
Hiro Nishiki
Tsugaru Nishiki
Aomori
Hirosaki
Sabao
Yamagata Region
Yamagata Kingyo
Matsue
Niigata
Miyagi Prefecture
Tetsugyo
Osaka
Nagoya
Tokyo
Saitama
Kochi
Edo Nishiki, Ranchu
Yatomi
Jikin
Tosakin
Osaka Ranchu
Fukagawa

Yamato Koriyama in Nara Prefecture, about an hour from Kyoto, was established as a center of Goldfish production at this time and it remains one to this day. Later, many Goldfish were produced in the Fukugawa district of the capital of Edo, which was built on flat land with a rich water supply. Goldfish are still produced in Tokyo and on its outskirts today, though land is so expensive that breeders are gradually moving farther and farther out, especially to neighboring Saitama Prefecture.

In the first centuries after their introduction to Japan, Goldfish were kept exclusively in ponds and large wooden tubs or ceramic pots. From the mid-1700s, the art of glassmaking was introduced to Japan, and eventually small glass Goldfish bowls were created. These were often so tiny that they could be carried around as a sort of fashion accessory, and many woodblock prints of the period show courtesans and ladies of fashion walking about with Goldfish in these "glass purses." The Goldfish, obviously, were very small, and no doubt they had very short life spans in these tiny quarters. Later, as glassworking technology advanced in the mid-1800s, Goldfish bowls and even aquariums similar to the ones we are familiar with were produced.

In 1853, American warships under the command of Admiral Perry steamed into Tokyo Bay and forced Japan to open its doors to the outside world. In 1895, Demekin, or "Popeye" Goldfish were imported from China for the first time, and the Japanese also developed new varieties through crosses with Calico Demekins, among them the Shubunkin and the Azuma Nishiki (a Japanese variety of Calico Oranda). At about this time the third major Goldfish-producing region in Japan was established on

CHILDREN IN CHINESE COSTUME PLAYING WITH GOLDFISH IN A TUB.

GOLDFISH IN A POND.

A COURTESAN WITH A GOLDFISH IN A BOWL.

flat land reclaimed from the sea in a region called Yatomi, near the city of Nagoya. Early in the 1900s, the first Celestials (Tenchogan) and Bubble Eyes (Suihogan) were imported. By the first two decades of the century, Japan had become a major world exporter of Goldfish of both native and Chinese origin. An export catalogue from the late 1920s includes illustrations of ten varieties: a Ryukin, a Calico Oranda, a Celestial, a Two-color Demekin, a Shubunkin, a Calico Ryukin, a Calico Demekin, a Calico Wakin, a Ranchu, and a Comet, in addition to minnows, eels, newts, and snails.

World War II wrought great destruction on Japan and, of course, the Goldfish industry as well. Several rare varieties were lost or almost lost, and it was some years before the Goldfish industry recovered. The postwar years were also marked by the importation of a second wave of new (to the Japanese) Chinese varieties, among them Blue Orandas (Seibungyo or Gingyo), Chocolate Orandas (Chakin), Pearlscales (Chinshurin), and, more recently, Butterfly Tails (Chobi), Pandas (Panda Kingyo), and Dragon-eye Orandas (Oranda Deme). Japanese breeders continued to cross local varieties as well. The most distinctive new varieties were bred by crossing Ranchus with other varieties to produce the calico Ranchu (Edo Nishiki) and, very recently, the production of red-and-white nacreous Ranchus (Sakura Nishikis). The Japanese claim to have developed the High-head Pearlscale in the postwar years, which they call the Hama Nishiki, though it seems to have been developed simultaneously, or nearly so, in China, and they have also independently produced several varieties that have also been bred in China. One is equivalent to the Chinese Pompom. Called a Hanafusa, it has a long body, lacks a dorsal fin, and may have either a short or long caudal fin. Another is a long-finned Ranchu, called a Shukin. Both of these varieties were produced in Japan by the early years of the twentieth century,

RYUKIN-TYPE GOLDFISH
IN AN AQUARIUM.

A 1920s CATALOGUE FROM KORIYAMA SHOWING TYPES OF GOLDFISH AVAILABLE.

BELOW TOP: CHOCOLATE ORANDA, OR CHAKIN. BELOW CENTER: EDO NISHIKI. BOTTOM: KYO NISHIKI. PHOTOS BY HIKARU SHIRAISHI.

but neither has ever become popular. Another uncommon Japanese variety is the Sabao (mackerel tail; also called a Tamasaba or Yamagata Kingyo), a Ryukin with a long, single caudal fin. It is said to have originated in Yamagata Prefecture, which is in northern Japan, and to withstand cold very well.

In the 1980s and 1990s, Japan experienced a major freshwater and saltwater tropical fish boom, and it seemed that Goldfish might be left behind, but in recent years, with increasing leisure time and renewed interest in traditional culture, there has been a resurgence, if not a renaissance, in Goldfish keeping. The Internet is beginning to play a role in linking hobbyists around the country, and a growing awareness of modern fish-keeping methods is also helping newcomers achieve success, though there is still much room for improvement (most Goldfish-care books in Japanese don't even mention the ammonia-nitrite-nitrate cycle, for example). New varieties continue to be developed, among them the "Muse," a cross between a Tosakin and an Azuma Nishiki, with the conformation of a Tosakin, black eyes, and white translucent scales; the "Aurora," a cross between a Shubunkin and an Azuma Nishiki, with the body conformation of the Shubunkin and coloration and long finnage of the Azuma Nishiki; Calico Jikin and Tosakin; and the Yanagi Demekin ("Willow"—meaning long and willowy—Popeye), a Popeye Comet or Shubunkin. In addition, extinct or nearly extinct varieties, such as the Osaka Ranchu and Izumo Nankin, are being redeveloped and reestablished within the hobby.

MUSE. PHOTO BY HIKARU SHIRAISHI.

Japanese Culture and Goldfish

SEASONAL ASSOCIATIONS

The Japanese cultivate a strong awareness and appreciation of the four seasons. There are many theories why this is so, and the Japanese love to expound on them; but for whatever reason or reasons, their food and clothing, religious customs and festivals, and literature and art all strongly reflect the four seasons.

Goldfish are affiliated with summer in Japan. It was in the summertime that the Goldfish vendors used to make their way through the residential neighborhoods of the cities, calling, *"Kingyoooo, kingyooo!"* They carried the fish in round wooden tubs suspended from a pole they carried across one shoulder. Summer is also the time of many festivals, most of them held in the evening, when temperatures drop a bit. Though summer festivals celebrate many different things, probably their main attraction to the populace is a chance to stroll out in the evening cool and enjoy the bustle and excitement of crowds, eat foods such as corn on the cob and fried octopus from vendors' stands, and enjoy the many games and amusements that the festivals offer, from fortune-telling to folk dancing to Goldfish netting, or *kingyo sukui.*

ABOVE: A RYUKIN IN A HANGING BOWL.
LEFT: GOLDFISH VENDORS.

A BOY BUYING A GOLDFISH FROM A TRAVELING VENDOR.

Netting Goldfish is a traditional carnival game in Japan, especially popular among children—and it is often a child's introduction to Goldfish as pets. The Goldfish, mostly small Comets or Wakins under 2 inches in length, are kept in a low tub and children try to net them with remarkably fragile paper nets. It takes a very dexterous child or adult to be a success, but it's a lot of fun and does result, with luck, in a new pet.

IN ARTS AND CRAFTS

The Goldfish lover who wishes to collect Goldfish memorabilia will find Japan a treasure trove. From the early 1700s, Goldfish have been a ubiquitous theme in Japanese arts and crafts. Pictures of Goldfish often decorate ceramics and tableware, and appear on lacquer-ware, folding screens, kimono, hair ornaments, and sword guards with great frequency. Goldfish are also depicted in many paintings and woodblock prints. Because of their association with summer, Goldfish are especially common designs on the light summer kimonos called yukata, folding fans, and the glass wind chimes known as *furin* (wind bells) that the Japanese hang from the eaves in summer to impart a feeling of coolness. Goldfish are also depicted as folk toys, because the color red was believed to signify health, and so red toys were a kind of charm for children's health. The figure of the Goldfish vendor was a common theme of children's dolls, too.

Because of the artistic license many painters take, it is not always possible to identify the variety of Goldfish appearing in arts and crafts, but red-and-white Wakins and long-tailed Ryukins and Demekins are seen most

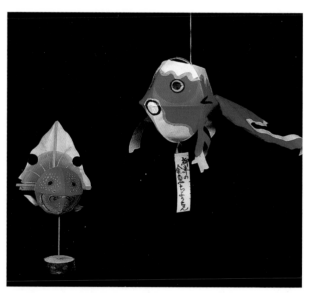

FOLK TOYS IN THE FORMS OF GOLDFISH.

DISH WITH GOLDFISH MOTIF; NOTE THE LACK OF DORSAL FINS.

A GOLDFISH-VENDOR DOLL.

RANCHU-TYPE GOLDFISH IN A GLASS BOWL.

OSAKA RANCHU.

GOLDFISH FROM THE *KINGYO FURYU MADARA SHU*.

frequently. There are also many interesting pictures of Goldfish lacking dorsal fins, which may be Marukos, the ancestor of the Ranchu, or Ranchus, Osaka Ranchus, Izumo Nankins, or related varieties no longer kept. Often these fish without dorsal fins have longer bodies and fins and less head growth than modern Ranchus. One particularly interesting painting shows three beautiful Ranchus, or perhaps Osaka Ranchus. Two are red and white in the very desirable pattern called *rokurin*—that is, red fins and mouth (one has red gill covers and another a red belly, both commonly seen variations of the *rokurin* pattern). Both these fish also have red eyes and nostrils, and an indication of good if not massive headgrowth. The third fish is black. It may be late in changing color, or a fiction of the artist's imagination, or perhaps there were black Ranchus in Japan at this time. At present no black Ranchus are produced in Japan.

Another interesting source is a woodblock book called *A Collection of Lovely Goldfish Patterns* (*Kingyo Furyu Madara Shu*), which contains pictures of beautifully patterned red-and-white Goldfish with elongated bodies and long, trailing fins, with the exception of the dorsal fin, which is very low. The descriptions of the patterns are fascinating. A white fish with the back half of the body and lips red is labeled "Red Pants," and "is popular in Osaka. The longer the tail, the higher the quality of the fish." Another with red lips, a red spot on the gill cover, red fins, and a blotch on the back is called "Saddled" and described as a "fine fish." A beautiful fish with red lips, red-and-white-striped fins, and a large red saddle dotted with white is described as follows: "Fish with a striped tail are called 'Imperial Stripes.' The more spots on the back the better." Another dramatically patterned fish is called "Wavy Beach. This is the best

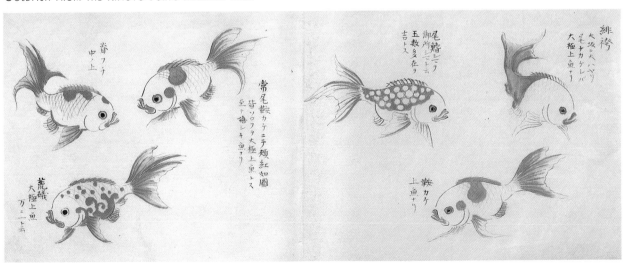

KABUKI ACTORS PORTRAYED AS GOLDFISH AND CARP.

of the best, one in ten thousand." Clearly, even at this early date the Japanese Goldfish hobby was booming and collectors were selecting fish for their beautiful and rare patterns.

Woodblock prints frequently show beautiful women, often courtesans, or children playing with Goldfish kept in ponds, wooden or ceramic tubs, or glass bowls. There was a lively comic tradition of woodblock prints, too, and a favorite ploy was to depict famous actors of the day as Goldfish, human faces grafted onto fish bodies. Another comic print is called "Goldfish Rafters" and shows two Goldfish in the foreground crossing a stream on a raft, vigorously poling along. In the background is a frog boatman. Popular woodblock artists such as Kuniyoshi depicted Goldfish as people going about their daily business—a granny Goldfish walking about with a cane, for example, and a mother Goldfish leading one Goldfish child by the hand and carrying another on her back.

Perhaps the most sensational woodblock print of Goldfish shows a large room with walls and ceiling made of a glass aquarium. This was based on a popular story of the time. In one version a feudal lord in Tokyo, and in another a rich merchant in Osaka, had this aquarium built as a display of his enormous wealth. The print shows the ladies of the household dressed in resplendent kimono and viewing the Goldfish swimming all around and above their heads. The "aquarium room" was, of course, a fiction; the technology to produce glass of the required strength did not exist at the time, and certainly not in Japan.

Other indications of the popularity of Goldfish are

LEFT: THE GOLDFISH HAIRSTYLE. BELOW: COURTESANS FEEDING LIVE FOOD TO GOLDFISH IN A CERAMIC VESSEL.

THE FABLED WALL-AND-CEILING AQUARIUM.

LEFT: GOLDFISH RAFTERS.
BELOW: IMITATING A GOLDFISH

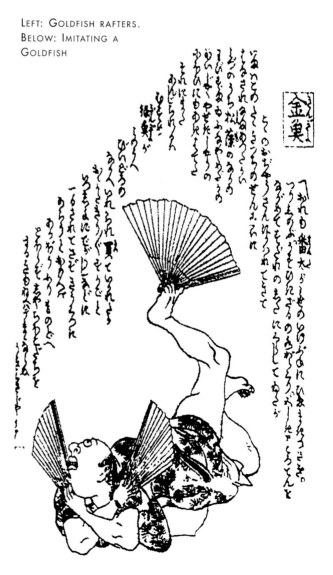

just as amusing. A fashion book from the 1770s illustrates a popular new hairstyle for young men called "the Goldfish." The hair at the back of the head is gathered into a kind of pony tail, then pulled up, with the end flipped forward—like a Goldfish's tail? And another delightfully silly illustration from about the same time shows a comic entertainer imitating a Goldfish at a drinking party, his mouth agape and folding fans spread out as fins.

IN POETRY

As Goldfish became more and more popular, they began to be taken up as the subject of haiku and short, lightly humorous poems called *senryu*. All Japanese poetry has a seasonal reference, and often the mention of Goldfish shows that the season depicted in the poem is summer. Here are a few Goldfish poems from then and now.

The Goldfish vendor:
Kind to the crowding children
Who buy nothing.

My memories
And the Goldfish bowl:
Both so cloudy.

How peacefully
Flow the days
Of my Ranchu's life.

The Goldfish seller
Stopped by a customer's call
Turns his tubs around.

The abandoned Goldfish
Flourishes
In the green paddy field.

The first graders
Compete
To be Class Goldfish Monitor.

In the spotless modern bank
A tank
Of Goldfish.

(*ABOVE*) GOLDFISH ON SALE AT A FLOWER SHOP AND (*CENTER AND BELOW*) AT FESTIVALS.

Lifting the lid
Over the pond:
Are the Goldfish all right?

"It's a Ranchu,"
He insisted,
Giving me the tadpole.

The Goldfish's life
Transparent
In its glass bowl.

The Goldfish
Nose against the glass
In its tiny bowl.

Swimming round
Its glass bowl:
The cat's desire.

The Goldfish vendor:
This one? Or this?
As he chases them around.

How cool the shade
At the Shinchuya
Goldfish Shop.

Just how naughty is he?
Buy him a Goldfish
And see how long it lasts.

How bright the moon at dawn:
It frightens
The Goldfish in his bowl.

Unique Varieties of Japanese Goldfish

Many decades ago, Yoshiichi Matsui, a pioneering Japanese Goldfish researcher, developed a chart showing the lineage of Japanese Goldfish varieties, but many are either extinct or kept in so few numbers that they are rarely available. There are also several types of Japanese Goldfish that completely overlap with Chinese varieties, and though they are now bred in Japan, they neither originated there nor are distinct from the Chinese variety, such as the Hama Nishiki (High-head Pearlscale) and the Demekins (Telescope or Popeye Goldfish). I have chosen to discuss in detail only the uniquely Japanese varieties that developed in the Edo period and are still bred and kept today: the Wakin; Ryukin; Ranchu and its related varities, the Edo Nishiki and Sakura Nishiki; the Oranda Shishigashira and its calico color phase the Azuma Nishiki; Jikin; Tosakin; Izumo Nankin; Osaka Ranchu; and Tsugaru Nishiki. At the end of this section I have listed extinct, very rare, or dubious varieties noted by Matsui and others with only a short identifying phrase.

WAKIN

Wakin means "Japanese Goldfish." The ancestors of modern Wakins were the first type of Goldfish imported from China, and were first known only as *kingyo* (Goldfish). The name Wakin was applied to it centuries later, in the mid-1800s, as other varieties such as the Ranchu appeared. This is the most common Goldfish in Japan. It has a torpedo-shaped body type very similar to the Crucian Carp, with a quadruple, triple, cherry-blossom, or single carp tail and short fins. Wakins with single tails are considered inferior. It is very strong and tough and is suitable for both pond and aquarium keeping. The prettiest Wakins are very vivid reds or red and white. Wakins can grow to a large size, easily reaching a foot in length.

RYUKIN

The Ryukin is so named because it was said to have arrived in Japan through the Ryukyu Islands that lie between Taiwan and Japan. References to this variety date back to 1833, but it is said to have arrived in Japan in the 1770s. In early texts it is also called Onaga (Longtail) and Nagasaki, probably because many foreign objects entered Japan through Nagasaki at this period. It is one of the most popular varieties in Japan, and has been highly developed there. In English texts it is variously and confusingly called a Japanese Ribbontail, Fringetail, Fantail, and Veiltail.

RED-AND-WHITE WAKIN. PHOTO BY HIKARU SHIRAISHI.

RED-AND-WHITE RYUKIN. PHOTO BY HIKARU SHIRAISHI.

The Japanese Ryukin has a pointed head and a deep body with a pronounced hump behind the head. The dorsal fin is high, and the caudal is long—often twice as long as the body. The caudal fin may have three lobes, four lobes, or three lobes with a slight indentation (what the Japanese call a *sakura*, or cherry-blossom-petal tail). Preferred colors are red and red and white. Ryukins have very deep red coloring.

Oddly, the Japanese have traditionally considered the Calico Ryukin a distinct variety, and call it simply "Calico." Perhaps this is because the calico color pattern has only been introduced to Japanese Goldfish strains in the past century, with the importation of the Calico Demekin from China at the end of the nineteenth century.

Ryukins are raised in all of Japan's Goldfish-producing regions and mature quickly. They can reach a size of 8 inches.

There is a single-tailed variant of the Ryukin called the Yamagata Kingyo (Yamagata Goldfish), Sabao (Mackerel Tail), or Tamasaba. It is said to have been developed in Yamagata Prefecture, which is in northern Japan, and to be exceptionally hardy in cold weather. It is red or red and white. An iron-colored variety called the Tetsu Onaga, or Iron-colored Longtail, also exists but is rarely seen.

RANCHU, EDO NISHIKI, SAKURA NISHIKI

The Ranchu has a short, round body and short fins—except for the dorsal fin, which it lacks entirely. The tail is set at a sharp angle to the back, and may have three or four lobes. The modern Ranchu has impressive headgrowth covering the entire head. It may be red, orange, red and white, or white.

The ancestors of the Ranchu were called Maruko ("round fish") or Chosen Kingyo ("Korean Goldfish"), and can be traced back to the late 1600s. These ancestral varieties had no headgrowth. Natural history paintings from the early 1800s show Ranchus called "Shishigashira Ranchu," or "Lionhead Ranchu," with small amounts of headgrowth, indicating that headgrowth was a new development at the time. Interestingly, some of these fish still have small knobs and bumps on the back, suggesting that the absence of the dorsal fin had not been completely stabilized. Written records suggest that these Lionhead Ranchus may have existed as early as 1765. Ranchu contests were held in Osaka as early as 1831. The Ranchu in the form we know today is really the product of the last seventy-five years. A painting of a Ranchu from 1909, included in Hugh Smith's book *Japanese Goldfish: Their Varieties and Cultivation*[2], shows a fish with a straight back and headgrowth indistinguishable from a Chinese Lionhead.

LEFT: RANCHU. PHOTO BY HIKARU SHIRAISHI. BELOW: SAKURA NISHIKI. PHOTO BY ROMAN SZCHETER.

EDO NISHIKI. PHOTO BY HIKARU SHIRAISHI.

2. Hugh M. Smith, *Japanese Goldfish: Their Varieties and Cultivation. A practical Guide to the Japanese Methods of Goldfish Culture for Amateurs and Professionals* (Washington, D.C.: W.F. Roberts) 1909. Out of print.

The Ranchu is often called the "king" of Japanese Goldfish, and is the focus of a very avid hobby.

The Edo Nishiki is a Calico Ranchu first produced in 1951 by Kichigoro Akiyama II, a Tokyo Goldfish breeder, by crossing a Ranchu and an Azuma Nishiki. It was further developed in the late 1960s and early 1970s by the Tokyo Fisheries Experimental Station. The ideal Edo Nishiki has the same headgrowth and body shape as a Ranchu, but this variety has not yet been perfectly stabilized, and fish with a good Ranchu conformation and strong calico color are rare. Part of the reason is that the Edo Nishiki lacks the avid hobbyist support that the Ranchu has, and far fewer people are engaged in perfecting the type.

The Sakura Nishiki is a recently developed Ranchu color variety with matte and metallic scales, the matte scales predominating.

Two long-tailed Ranchu varieties have also been developed, though they have never been popular. The Shukin is a long-tailed Ranchu, and the Kyo Nishiki a long-tailed Edo Nishiki.

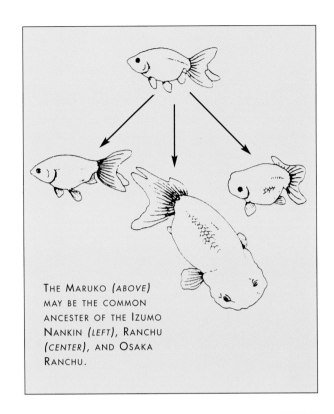

THE MARUKO (ABOVE) MAY BE THE COMMON ANCESTOR OF THE IZUMO NANKIN (LEFT), RANCHU (CENTER), AND OSAKA RANCHU.

(UPPER LEFT) A CROSS BETWEEN AN ORDINARY GOLDFISH AND A KOREAN GOLDFISH; (LOWER LEFT) KOREAN GOLDFISH; (CENTER) EARLY DEPICTIONS OF RANCHUS; (UPPER RIGHT) AN EARLY RANCHU WITH HEADGROWTH; (CENTER AND LOWER RIGHT) RANCHUS DEPICTED IN JAPANESE GOLDFISH.

ORANDA SHISHIGASHIRA AND AZUMA NISHIKI

The Oranda is a relative latecomer to the Japanese Goldfish scene, probably having arrived from China via the port of Nagasaki in the 1830s. From there it spread northward through Kyushu and into the Osaka area of Japan, but Orandas were not seen in the Tokyo area until the end of the nineteenth century. Some Japanese sources claim that the Japanese Oranda was produced locally by crossing a Ryukin and a Ranchu, but this theory is difficult to accept.

Japanese Orandas have traditionally had long bodies and tails, and are one of the largest Japanese varieties, reaching a foot in length. The back should not rise up in a Ryukin-style hump. Headgrowth is extensive and covers the entire head. The tail is four lobed and contracted when the fish swims, spreading out broadly when it stops. The caudal peduncle should be thick and long.

There are both orange and red-and-white Oranda, but red-and-white fish with intense reds are preferred.

The Azuma Nishiski was developed in the 1920s by crossing an Oranda with a Calico Demekin. It has the same conformation as an Oranda, but intense calico coloring. The preferred coloring is deep red on the head, intense sky blue on the body, and black on the tail. Azuma Nishikis do not show the concentrated spangling pattern of black and silver scales of many Chinese Calicos, but have a more open pattern of patches of intense color with black scales as accents, and because of the intensity and clarity of their coloring are far more beautiful than Chinese calico Orandas.

EARLY DEPICTION OF AN ORANDA SHISHIGASHIRA.

RED-AND-WHITE ORANDA. BELOW: AZUMA NISHIKI. PHOTOS BY HIKARU SHIRAISHI.

JIKIN

Jikin means "local Goldfish." It is also called the Peacock Tail and the Rokurin, or "six-scales," fish. The latter two names describe the main characteristics of the Jikin. It is a natural sport from a Wakin, and has the same torpedo-shaped body, but the four lobes of the tail fin are flattened so that they stand out behind the body like the tail of a displaying male peacock. The six scales or "points" are the lips and the dorsal, pectoral, ventral, anal, and caudal fins, which are all red. Gill covers may also be red. The body color should be white, though there may be some red on the belly. The perfect coloration of Jikins is achieved artificially. At about three months, any red scales on the body are either plucked off with tweezers or bleached with oxalic acid. This is very stressful for the fish, and as a result they are weak and delicate for the next year or so. Older Jikins tend to be stronger. Because of the shape of their tail, Jikins swim in a characteristically jerky manner. The Japanese believe that they are best viewed from above.

Jikins originated in the area around the modern city of Nagoya, Aichi Prefecture, and they are a specially designated Natural Treasure (Tennen Kinenbutsu) of that prefecture.

TOSAKIN

Matsui calls the Tosakin a "Curly Fantail" and believes that it is a natural sport of a Ryukin, which seems to be borne out by the body shape, with its pointed head and deep, round trunk. The distinctive feature of the Tosakin is its tail, which is undivided and spreads out horizontally so widely that it flips under at the front.

YOUNG JIKIN.

YOUNG JIKIN SEEN FROM ABOVE.

TOSAKIN. PHOTO BY HIKARU SHIRAISHI.

TOSAKIN SEEN FROM ABOVE. PHOTO BY HIKARU SHIRAISHI.

Seen from above, the tail is a flat half circle that curls under once or even twice at the front edge.

The Tosakin was first developed in the Tosa fief, now Kochi Prefecture, in Shikoku, and was a local variety cultivated by the lower-ranking samurai of the fief. It probably did not reach other parts of Japan in any numbers until the mid-twentieth century, but is now bred in various locales, including Tokyo, by fanciers and breeders.

Because of the shape of its tail, it is a weak swimmer and it is kept in shallow water with no current.

Tosakin come in red, red and white, calico, and iron color. They are relatively late in turning color from iron color, and some remain that color into adulthood.

IZUMO NANKIN

The Izumo Nankin is another local variety. It was developed in the Izumo area in Shimane Prefecture. It has an egg-shaped body and a narrow, pointed head. The fins are short, and it has no headgrowth. The preferred color is a white body with red lips and fins, but this pattern is rare and variously marked red-and-white fish are also acceptable.

This variety almost disappeared around the middle of the twentieth century but is now being revived by hobbyists across Japan and is no longer as rare as it once was. It can grow to be quite large.

OSAKA RANCHU

The Osaka Ranchu existed as early as the 1750s, and is frequently depicted in woodblock prints. It originated in the Osaka-Kyoto area, and remained popular there for centuries, but almost died out around World War II.

Hobbyists are now attempting to revive the variety, which is distinguished from the modern Ranchu by its lack of headgrowth, rounder, broader body, and longer three-lobe tail set almost horizontally, like that of a Tosakin.

Red and white is the favored color for Osaka Ranchus.

At present, this is a very rare and unstable variety, but depictions in art of the Edo period show that it was a beautiful fish that deserves to be revived.

TSUGARU NISHIKI

This is a local variety bred in Tsugaru, Aomori Prefecture, in northern Japan, from the 1800s. It resembles a long-finned Ranchu, but the headgrowth develops very slowly if at all. It is well adapted to cold climates. The preferred colors are red and red and white.

OTHER VARIETIES

Demekin. The Japanese version of the Popeye or Telescope Goldfish exists in black, red, red and white, and calico.

Deme Ranchu. A Telescope-Eye Ranchu. To my knowledge, these are no longer bred in Japan.

ABOVE: KINRANSHI, FROM *JAPANESE GOLDFISH*.
LEFT: IZUMO NANKIN. PHOTO BY HIKARU SHIRAISHI.

ABOVE: SHUBUNKIN.
RIGHT: SHUKIN. PHOTOS
BY HIKARU SHIRAISHI.

Hanafusa. A Pompom Goldfish. A Japanese Pompom with a dorsal fin is believed to have existed in the Edo period, but the present fish is probably from Chinese imports. Some have dorsal fins and some do not.

Kinranshi. A cross between a Ranchu and a Ryukin. Calico, with an elongated, somewhat heavy body, short fins, and no headgrowth. No longer being bred to the best of my knowledge.

Shubunkin. A calico fish with a long, deeply notched single tail, supposedly a cross between a Wakin and a Calico Demekin made around the turn of the twentieth century. The Shubunkin is a popular pond fish the world over and is bred in large numbers in Japan.

Shukin. A long-tailed Ranchu.

Tetsuo. An iron-colored Goldfish with a Wakin or Comet body type.

Watonai. A cross between a Wakin and a Ryukin, with a broader, deeper body and longer fins than a Wakin, but not to the extent of a Ryukin.

Yanagi Demekin. A cross between a Comet or a Wakin and a Demekin with a long, slender body, the long fins of a Comet, and telescope eyes.

KYO NISHIKI. PHOTO BY HIKARU SHIRAISHI.

The Japanese Goldfish Industry

The Japanese Goldfish industry is centered in three areas: Yamato Koriyama, in Nara Prefecture, near Kyoto and Osaka; Yatomi, in Aichi Prefecture, near Nagoya; and Tokyo and nearby Saitama Prefecture. Koriyama is the oldest Goldfish-producing area, going back to the mid-eighteenth century, when the feudal lord of the region encouraged Goldfish breeding as a cottage industry. In 1910 there were three hundred fifty Goldfish breeders in Koriyama producing more than ten million fish annually. There are about one hundred Goldfish farms in Yamato Koriyama today, producing about eighty million fish annually in 350 acres of ponds. The Fukagawa area of Tokyo is the second oldest Goldfish center, and in spite of soaring land prices and rampant urban sprawl over the last decades, Goldfish are still produced in small numbers in the northeast section of the city and in greater numbers in adjacent Saitama Prefecture to the northwest. Yatomi is an expansive area of flat land reclaimed from the sea in the last one hundred fifty years. It is the newest of the Goldfish-producing centers, but now the most important, with about two hundred twenty farms. It is also a major producer of Koi.

Individual farmers raise their fish and then take them to market, where they are auctioned off to wholesalers. Auctions are held regularly, usually on a weekly basis, from March through November, though the peak of the season is June, July, and August. This is because of the traditional association of Goldfish with summer in Japan. The auction at Koriyama is held in a roofed shed in the middle of a large pond and is attended by forty to fifty buyers. The Goldfish are kept in floating containers with mesh bottoms that look like flat-bot-

tomed boats. One container after another is poled into the shed, and buyers kneel to observe it closely as it floats down a central watercourse. The bidding and buying take place, and then the fish are poled out the other side, where they are bagged in plastic bags filled with water and oxygen and sent to their destinations, usually wholesalers' holding facilities, before they are distributed to the retail market.

BREEDING

Japanese methods of breeding Goldfish have changed surprisingly little over the last one hundred years, and the detailed descriptions provided by Hugh Smith in *Japanese Goldfish* matches almost exactly with my personal observation ninety years later, in 1999. The Japanese use outdoor mud ponds for breeding the hardier varieties of Goldfish in large numbers. When spring arrives—March or April in most of Japan—the ponds in which breeder fish have wintered are drained and the adult fish are netted and removed. They are kept in large floating containers in another pond while the breeding pond is prepared. The bottom is cultivated with a rototiller and the pond is divided in two compartments, one for males and one for females, with a divider made of net and bamboo. The bottom of the pond is sprinkled with charcoal.

At the same time, the breeder prepares ponds to grow out the fry. After draining and cultivating, he sprinkles the pond bottom with organic matter such as chicken or horse manure and vegetable waste. Then he refills the pond, which quickly swarms with daphnia.

In the meantime, the breeder sexes the fish based on the shape of the anal pore and the presence of sexual tubercles on the gill covers. At the same time, he selects for quality and type, excluding fish that will not improve the strain. The breeder fish are returned to the pond, each sex in its proper compartment. This allows the breeder to control the time of egg laying.

The breeder prepares two frames for a breeding platform. The lower frame is covered with a fine mesh to catch eggs that would otherwise fall to the pond bottom. It is attached to the pond bottom with poles about one foot below the water surface. He attaches spawning mops to the second frame, which floats on the surface attached to the lower frame.

When the fish and the breeder are ready—usually mid-April in the Tokyo area—the dividers are removed and male and female fish allowed to mix. After spawning is finished, the breeder removes the spawning mops and the mesh bottom and disinfects the eggs before placing them in lightly aerated hatching tanks.

After the fry have absorbed the egg sack and start swimming about searching for food, they are scooped out and placed in a daphnia pond to grow out. After they have consumed most of the daphnia in the pond, the breeder begins feeding a wheat-germ paste. At first the paste is rather watery, but as the fry grow it is made with less and less water. The food is set on trays or dishes that are suspended in the water.

When the fry are big enough to see the shape of the tail fin, the first culling takes place, together with a water change. As the fish grow, they are switched from a kneaded paste to a food of steamed cakes. After the first culling for tail shape, there are as many as five more cullings for body shape, color, and type.

Ranchu and other fancy varieties are usually bred on a much smaller scale in concrete tanks called *tataki*, about 6 feet by 9 feet and about 10 inches deep. Otherwise the processes are very similar, but on a much smaller scale.

THE PRESENT AND FUTURE OF THE INDUSTRY

At present, Japanese Goldfish breeders do not export nearly as much as they once did. There are a variety of macroeconomic reasons for this. First and foremost has been the opening of trade with China in the 1970s. China has been formidable competition for several reasons. It is the home of the Goldfish industry, with a long tradition of Goldfish production; it has much more flat land available for Goldfish ponds; a Chinese Goldfish farmer can easily undersell his Japanese counterpart, because China is a developing nation and Japan has a highly advanced industrial economy. The much higher cost of living in Japan means higher priced Goldfish for export as well.

Japan's increased industrialization also means that less people are working in agriculture, and the truth is that Japan is hard pressed to meet its domestic Goldfish needs. In the last decades, Japan has relied on imports of Chinese Goldfish to supply certain sectors of its market. Recently, Japan has periodically restricted or banned Goldfish imports from China, fearing disease. This has only further tightened the Japanese domestic market for Goldfish.

Japanese prefectural governments are making efforts to support the local Goldfish industry through research on disease control, diet, and breeding practices. In particular, they are working to establish strains of popular varieties that breed true in higher proportions, then supplying local breeders with those fry to increase their marketable product and promote the industry.

Still, high local demand and certain cultural attitudes mean that few Japanese Goldfish of high quality are available for export. First, because of the Goldfish shortage, the majority of young fish of all varieties are immediately snapped up by the domestic market, leaving none to grow to large size. Second, Japanese consumers traditionally buy small young fish and grow them out rather than purchase large, "finished" fish. As a result, most large fish available for sale and export in Japan are of lower quality or are breeders past their prime.

Finally, the active—one might even say fanatic—Goldfish hobby in Japan means that many hobbyists receive their fish from each other or other specialized sources, and this is where the true high-quality strains are to be found. This is especially true of the most prized varieties of Japanese Goldfish, such as the Ranchu, Edo Nishiki, Jikin, Tosakin, Izumo Nankin, and, to a lesser extent, Oranda and Azuma Nishiki.

The Japanese Goldfish Hobby

The most commonly kept Goldfish in Japan are without a doubt the Wakin and Ryukin, followed closely by varieties of Demekins and Orandas. But advanced hobbyists focus on other varieties. The Ranchu, of course, is most popular, but there are also very active groups for those who keep Tosakins and, to a lesser extent, Jikins, Izumo Nankins, and Osaka Ranchus. In this section I will provide information on those specialized varieties, their culture, breeding, and standards.

RANCHU

The Ranchu, by common agreement, is the king of Japanese Goldfish. Ranchu competitions have been conducted for more than a century, and there are numerous active associations of Ranchu fanciers all

across the nation. Ranchu hobbyists are responsible for the finest lines of fish. Let us examine some of their methods, and then go on to review the exacting standards they uphold in their pursuit of the ideal Ranchu.

Hobbyist Methods Ranchu fanciers are generally very conservative with regard to their methods of breeding, raising, and caring for their fish. Since they are conserving traditional methods, it is not surprising that their approach is what we would regard as exceptionally low-tech. They rely little on even the simplest equipment, and even less on medications other than salt. They leave much to nature, and to plenty of painstaking observation, attention to detail, and hard physical work. What follows is a general description of their methods rather than a prescription for Ranchu fanciers elsewhere.

Japanese Ranchu fanciers are fond of saying that Ranchu care begins and ends with water. For starters, it must be remembered that Ranchus are traditionally kept in outdoor ponds throughout the four seasons in Japan, which, in the main Goldfish-raising areas, has a relatively mild climate, similar to Seattle. The ideal water is a light green in color, often compared to the color of Japanese green tea. The green, of course, is the color of algae and other phytoplankton that grow in the sunlight. When the water starts to become too green, a water change is carried out—the frequency and amount depending upon the weather and the season. The secret is to keep the water the appropriate shade of green at all times, using water changes, shading of the pond, and reduction of the number of fish to achieve this goal.

Ideally, a Ranchu keeper reserves one out of every three ponds for storing and "seasoning" water. Newly

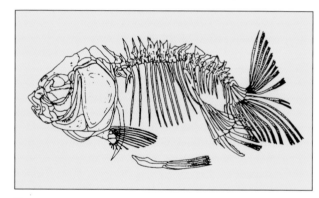

RANCHU SKELETON, SHOWING DISTORTION OF VERTEBRAE.

drawn water is seasoned by being left to sit, exposed to the sun, for two or three days before use. A standard (and simplified) schedule of water changes appears on the facing page. The feeding schedule is also included, because it is intimately related to water quality.

Ranchus have traditionally been kept in rectangular wooden or concrete ponds called *tataki*. There are two standard sizes, a rectangular pond about 9 feet by 6 feet, and a square pond 6 feet by 6 feet. The ponds have a sloped bottom, the shallowest part being about 10 inches deep and the deepest 13 inches. There is a drainage outlet at the deep end and a small bowl-shaped indentation for detritus to collect in before draining out.

The pond has no filtration—though occasionally I have seen a small airstone used for aeration. It is usually not heated in winter, either. Since the pond is outdoors, of course there is no lighting equipment necessary. Screen covers are a must to keep out cats, crows, snakes, and other predators.

One automated device that Ranchu fanciers seem to

use is the automatic feeder. Since it is important to feed fry regularly and fanciers have their own work to do during the day, automatic feeders are a great help. At the same time, dried food is becoming much more commonly used. Though live bloodworms (mostly imported from Taiwan and China) can be purchased at many tropical fish stores, frozen live food is increasingly used. Traditionally Japanese fanciers have sworn by live foods—especially daphnia, bloodworms, and mosquito larvae—and homemade foods, but that day is passing, if not yet entirely gone.

Fanciers separate their fish by size, age, and purpose. Interestingly, fish raised for shows are kept separate from and raised differently than those kept for breeding. Show fish are given as much as ten times more space than breeders—for example, only two or three show fish may be kept in a small pond of about 12 square feet, while twenty to thirty breeders are kept in another pond of the same size. Show candidates are pampered and grown to a large size. This reduces their interest in and capacity to breed successfully. It also shortens their lives, some breeders say. Breeder fish from the same line as show candidates display the same perfection of form, but remain much smaller. A good breeder fish will perform well for five or six years if cultivated correctly.

In recent years, with rising land prices and suburban sprawl in Japan, few people have the space for outdoor concrete ponds, but Ranchu fanciers have strongly resisted the switch to aquariums. Instead, they have adopted fiberglass tubs, which they place on balconies, porches, and rooftops. Though they have modified the scale of their fishkeeping slightly, the style remains the same. Part of their traditional outlook is that water over about 16 inches deep will not allow Ranchus to achieve their best form. They claim that the pressure exerted by water any deeper will deform the fish. In addition, they are averse to having any water current in their ponds. My observations in Japan have shown that fish in these still ponds are indeed much less active than fish kept in water with some flow, though I cannot say whether this actually affects the final form of the fish.

Japanese Ranchu keepers have a love-hate relationship with Nature. They insist on keeping their fish out of doors with no mechanical equipment for heating or filtration, yet they are always battling every little change in the weather. In an attempt to provide their fish with a relatively stable environment, they have tried to devise ways to deal with heat, cold, sudden temperature changes, sunlight, darkness, algae growth and lack of it, fallen leaves, wind, and rain. In spite of this, they remain firm believers in the necessity of subjecting their fish to the natural rhythms of the changing seasons and climate.

Standards The standards for Ranchus are very exacting, and they can be a little difficult for the Westerner to understand, because in explaining the ideals of Ranchu beauty, Japanese fanciers naturally refer to many concepts and objects that are a part of traditional Japanese culture. Though the Ranchu originated in the Chinese Lionhead, the aesthetic of the Ranchu is distinctly Japanese.

It is interesting to compare Ranchus to sumo wrestlers. People unfamiliar with sumo often think of the wrestlers as just big, fat, out-of-shape men with

SPRING. On a warm day in mid-March the first water change of the year is performed, replacing about 30% of the old water with new. As the weather warms in April, a 50% water change is made about every ten days, and as the water temperature climbs over seventy degrees, 70% water changes are made on a weekly basis.

Small amounts of food are given only after water temperature rises above seventy degrees. The amount is slowly increased as water temperature rises and the fish become more active.

EARLY SUMMER. The same rate of 70% water change is carried out on a weekly basis, and if the water is getting too green too quickly, the pond is partially shaded and the number of fish reduced.

This is the fishes' most active period, and they will eat as much as they are fed, but it's still preferable to keep them slightly hungry at all times.

MIDSUMMER. A 90% water change every four to five days. Again, if the water is still too green, reduce the number of fish.

Continue with moderate feeding, but reduce food when water temperature rises above eighty-five degrees.

AUTUMN. A 60% to 70% water change every five to six days.

It is important to feed the fish regularly so that they are ready for their period of winter dormancy, but overfeeding will spoil candidates for competitions. Stop feeding when the water temperature drops below fifty degrees.

WINTER. The last water change of 30% to 40% is carried out in mid-December, and then the fish are allowed to go dormant, or nearly so, until March.

RED-AND-WHITE RANCHU. PHOTO BY ROMAN SZCHETER.

CHAMPION SUMO WRESTLER CHIYONOFUJI, A *YOKOZUNA.*

funny hairdos. Similarly, many people who see a Ranchu for the first time often see only a big, fat, out-of-shape fish with funny headgrowth. But once you become more familiar with either the wrestler or the Ranchu, you learn to appreciate their unique styles. The ideal Ranchu (and wrestler) has an imposing, solid build made up of massed circles and squares; its (or his) body has a strict balance and proportion dictated by a very demanding and distinct aesthetic. Both Ranchus and wrestlers are supposed to comport themselves with dignity and move with grace and power. Not coincidentally, Ranchu contests are organized and judged in the same way as sumo tournaments, and sumo wrestlers' rankings are used to rank the fish, a topic we will explore further when we discuss Ranchu competitions.

The overall subjective principle by which Ranchus are judged is an elusive quality called *aji. Aji* literally means "flavor" or "taste," as in the taste of food, but aesthetically speaking it means richness, evocativeness, character, gravity, power, weight, and depth. It suggests that the Ranchu has a deep and lasting beauty with so many distinctive, fine qualities that the viewer must take time to savor it fully. The Mona Lisa has *aji,* while Andy Warhol's soup can, witty as it is, probably does not. Another quality often used in discussing Ranchus and other Goldfish is *hin,* "refinement or elegance," but *hin* also suggests a lightness that is not really appropriate to Ranchus. Other terms of praise for Ranchus are *takumashii,* or "big and strong"; *do-do shite iru,* or "bold and imposing"; and *yutaka* ("rich" or "full").

There is much talk among Japanese fanciers of the problems that arise from growing Ranchu too large too

fast, and many lament that this significantly shortens a fish's life span, resulting in a shortage of good older fish. But though they all lament this problem, they agree that big fish are more impressive and more likely to win in a competition. Still, some Ranchu clubs have gone so far as to establish separate categories for "Large-Size Fish" and "Normal-Size Fish" in the competitions they sponsor.

The most important objective principle of the Ranchu standard in Japan is not size, however, but balance and proper proportions. This is looked for first in the way the fish holds itself and swims, not only because the deportment of the fish is very important in itself, but also because it is believed deportment quickly reveals any faults in conformation that destroy the perfect balance and proportion that is the ideal.

It is impossible to overemphasize the importance that the Japanese place on the motion of the fish when swimming. It is a key element in judging Ranchus, and often the deciding factor in deciding contest rank. Every critical evaluation of a fish includes remarks about the way it swims. One of the words the Japanese use for the tail fin of a Ranchu is *suso,* which means the skirt or hem of a garment. They call the way the fish manages its tail fin *suso sabaki. Sabaki* means handling or management. *Suso sabaki* suggests the image of a woman gracefully managing the hem of her kimono as she walks with dignity and poise across a room.

A well-balanced fish holds itself evenly as it begins swimming in a smooth and effortless fashion. The tail fin should compress to move forward and then release, but the movement should not be strained or exaggerated. As it uses its tail to propel itself, it seems to be sliding gracefully yet powerfully through the water. A fish with faulty conformation will shake its body from left to right as it moves forward, or raise its tail and lower its head, even seeming to be pushing into the bottom of the vessel. Other faulty fish will have the head up and the tail down, or only be able to swim by frantically flapping their fins. These are all examples of unattractive deportment that also point to conformation faults.

In all discussions of the way a Ranchu swims, we must remember that they are judged in shallow bowls in which there is no current, and they are, as we have seen above, raised in ponds without current.

The Japanese are firm believers that the best view of Ranchus is from the top. The ideal Ranchu is often described as looking like an old Japanese coin called a *koban* with fins attached to it. This has led to a double misunderstanding in the West, where people speak of a coin-shaped back as a requirement for Ranchus. First of all, the *koban* (see below) is not a round coin. It is an elongated oval, almost a rectangle with rounded corners. Second, Japanese Ranchu fanciers are saying that the fish should look like a *koban when seen from above, not from the side*. This misunderstanding has created puzzlement among Western Ranchu collectors, who look at side views of Japanese champion fish and find their backs too long and not curved enough. The round fish with the excessively deep body that uninformed Western collectors regard as the ideal Ranchu, and which Chinese breeders are producing in large numbers, would be rejected as fat and graceless by the Japanese connoisseur. They disparagingly call such a fish a "potato."

When describing a Ranchu's back seen from the side, the Japanese compare it to a traditional Japanese comb, which comes in two shapes: rather long, with rounded corners—like the *koban* coin—and shorter and rounder,

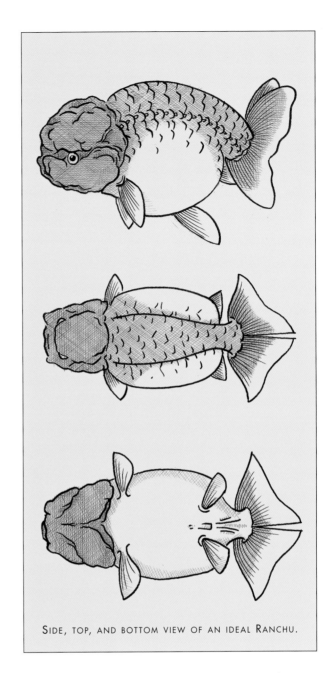

SIDE, TOP, AND BOTTOM VIEW OF AN IDEAL RANCHU.

TWO TAIL TYPES:

STANDARD TYPE.

MAEGAKARI TYPE.

TWO JAPANESE COMBS AND THE LONG BLACK TYPE.

THE *KOBAN* COIN.

YEARLING RED RANCHU WITH NEAR IDEAL CONFORMATION.
PHOTO BY ROMAN SZCHETER.

TWO ADULT RED RANCHUS WITH EXCEPTIONAL HEADGROWTH.
PHOTO BY ROMAN SZCHETER.

closer to a round coin seen from the side, but still not as round as a quarter, dime, or nickel. Both of these shapes are accepted, the first known as "the long style" (*nagate*) and the second as "the round style" (*marute*).

Perhaps the most prominent feature of the Ranchu is the head (*kashira*). There must be sufficient space between the eyes, and from the eyes to the front of the head, and the gill cover should be "deep"—that is, extend quite far toward the tail. Headgrowth should seem to start from the bottom of the gill cover and move upward. Fish with broad foreheads and square noses generally produce better headgrowth.

Several different terms are used to describe headgrowth of different shapes.

• A dragon head (*tatsugashira*) Ranchu has imposing growth between the eyes, projecting forward symmetrically in two rounded shapes resembling traditional depictions of dragons in Chinese and Japanese art.

• Grape head (*budogashira*) describes headgrowth consisting of large, uniform, round growths over the entire head.

• A *tokin* is a kind of round cap worn by certain religious practitioners in medieval Japan; it looks a little like a pillbox hat. Fish with pronounced growth on the top of the head are described as *tokingashira*, or "cap head." The presence of this *tokin* in young fish is believed to mark them as eventually growing to have the ideal, all-round head growth called *shishigashira* (see below).

• *Binhari* (also pronounced *bimbari*) describes a fish with heavy growth on the gill covers. It takes its name from a hairstyle popular in Japan in the 1700s, in which a woman's side locks were puffed out by placing a whalebone support inside them.

• Finally, the *shishigashira*, or lion head, takes its name from the *shishi*, the mythical lion-dog of China and Japan (which looks a little like a giant Pekinese). A fish with heavy growth starting from the bottom and covering the entire head is called a *shishigashira*.

The eyes of a Ranchu should be placed evenly, neither facing up or forward, and should be small and cute, looking out from the headgrowth.

The stomach should sweep down in a smooth curve from the gill covers to the end of the abdomen (*hara no tomari*), in a rounded shape.

The back of the Ranchu, seen from above, should be broad and full, suggesting a heavy bone structure. The scales on the back should be regular and well aligned, and very shiny, with no dull areas. The width of the back should be uniform to the point called the *koshi*, or "hip" in Japanese—this is the point even with the end of the belly, just before the back starts to curve down to the tail—and then pull in just a bit. The *sesagari*, the curve from the *koshi* on down to the caudal peduncle (*otsutsu*), should be even and balance with the upward curve of the belly at this point.

The caudal peduncle should be short and thick and give the appearance of strength. The curve to the tail joint will differ depending upon the curve of the back up to the *koshi*, but the curve of the caudal peduncle has a very important effect on the balance between it and the curve of the tail. The angle of the curve of the caudal peduncle is one of the most unique and expressive features of a Ranchu. When the curve is too shallow, the peduncle appears too long, and the length of the caudal peduncle tends to grow as the fish does, with undesirable results. In contrast, a fish with a strong, definite curve that continues down to the tail joint, which is also thick and strong, is unlikely to become unsightly as it grows.

The tail joint (*ozuke*) must be symmetrical when viewed from above, thick, and strong. The tail seat (*ozara*) is the small round area of scales underneath the tail fin, which can only be seen by turning the fish upside down. A large tail seat is desirable, because it means, of course, that the tail joint is thick. The scales of the tail seat should be small and regular, with the appearance of a brilliantly sparkling necklace. It is undesirable

RED-AND-WHITE RANCHU. PHOTO BY HIKARU SHIRAISHI.

for the tail core or central ray (*oshin*) to extend into the tail joint more than one and one-half scales. This is called an "inserted" (*sashikomi*) tail core. But this is not a serious fault and is found on many champion fish. It is true that when the tail core does project into the tail joint and the core is relatively thin, the tail often sits at a better angle and the fish has more of a feeling of stability. The tail core should be straight and symmetrical in both above and side views. An overlapping tail core is a fault.

The tail fins in general should be small but well displayed. Three tail shapes are acceptable: a triple tail (three lobe), a quadruple tail (four lobe), and what the Japanese call a "cherry-blossom tail" (*sakurao*), which is essentially a triple tail with a slight indentation in the middle, so that the tail fin resembles the petal of a cherry blossom. The split of a quadruple tail should be narrow, so that the two halves remain close together. "Triple" and "quadruple" refer to the number of lobes of the tail. Some Western standards specify that a triple tail (an unsplit tail with three lobes) is a disqualification, though this is not true in Japan.

Though the precise angle of the tail will depend on the curve of the fish's back, in general it should be close to 45 degrees. The fins on either side of the tail core must be symmetrical. The tail should be of medium width, and each tail shoulder (*okata*) should be gently rounded, just about touching the end of the belly. When the fish swims it should compress its tail, and when it stops swimming, the tail should open again immediately, demonstrating a combination of firmness and beauty.

Though fish with single anal fins are acceptable in many contests in Japan, dual anal fins are preferred. A lack of anal fins is a disqualification. The two anal fins should be the same size and shape and set straight. They should not project beyond the caudal fin or the line of the belly.

Traditionally, color has not been a major factor in judging Ranchus. The most orthodox colors are pure red with clear or white tail-fin tips (*su aka*, or plain red), and completely red, down to the tail-fin tips, which is called *shojo*. (The *shojo* is a mythical animal, a kind of mischievous sprite that loves to drink saké, and turns bright red when it gets drunk—making it a perfect name for an all-red fish.) But in recent decades fanciers seem to be showing more interest in red-and-white Ranchus in various patterns.

Finally, it is important to mention that different Ranchu clubs have slightly different standards. Some may prefer a certain kind of headgrowth, for example, or a certain back shape. The standards discussed above, however, are the most generally accepted. I have also simplified them for the present discussion. One interesting Japanese work outlines "the sixty-three possible faults in a Ranchu," which should give the reader an idea of the detail with which Japanese observe and appreciate their fish.

Competitions The Japan Ranchu Association (Nihon Ranchu Kyokai) has fifty-five local branches or affiliated clubs, and the larger clubs sponsor their own Ranchu

PROGRAM FOR THE ADULT FISH DIVISION OF A RANCHU COMPETITION.

contests, which are held in the autumn. The fish are shown in three categories: fish born in the current year (*tosai gyo*); fish over one year old (*nisai gyo*), or adult fish; and breeders (*oya gyo* or *oya uo*).

The fish are displayed in shallow, round, galvanized bowls with white interiors. The bowls are lined up on tables, and the primary judging takes place from above, though fish are also examined from the side. The ranking of fish is, as mentioned earlier, taken from sumo wrestling. Though there are no teams in sumo, the wrestlers are divided into East and West sides for a tournament. The East takes precedence over the West. The top-ranking wrestler in modern sumo is the *yokozuna*. Nowadays there is almost always at least one active *yokozuna*, but this was not true in earlier sumo history, and Ranchu contests follow the earlier convention: they only award the rank of *yokozuna* in very special cases, such as when a fish wins the first prize three years in succession. More often than not, no fish is judged to be worthy of that highest rank. As the Japanese are fond of saying, "There is no perfect Ranchu."

The second highest rank in sumo is called *ozeki* ("great barrier"). The top-ranking Ranchu at most contests, then, is the East *ozeki*. West *ozeki* is the second rank, followed by the *tachi gyoji* ("senior referee"), then the *torishimari* ("director") of East and West. These five fish are the "grand prize" (*yutosho*) winners.

There are six first-prize winners: *sekiwake* ("across the barrier") of East and West, *komusubi* ("little ball") of East and West, and *kanjinmoto* ("tournament sponsor") of East and West. There are five second-prize winners: first, second, and third *gyoji* ("referee"), followed by *wakegyoji* ("junior referee") of East and West. Finally, there may be as many as twelve third-prize winners. They are all called *maegashira*, a junior sumo rank, and they are numbered East *maegashira* 1, West *maegashira* 1, East *maegashira* 2, West *maegashira* 2, and so forth.[3]

In total, then, twenty-eight Ranchus are recognized with ranks and prizes. Breeders, two-year fish, and yearlings are all judged separately, so at a full-fledged show there may be eighty-four winners. There may also be special awards such as the Governor's Prize or the Mayor's Prize.

Just as breeders of pedigreed dogs and cats name their animals, competitors give their Ranchus fanciful names, often with a literary flavor. Here are a few examples, in translation only, of the names of competition winners in Japan from 1976 through 1985: Great Gem, Heavenly Gem, Regal Commander, Great Dragon King, Celestial Dragon, Dragon Light, Flying Dragon, Scarlet Plum, Imperial Palace Cherry, Double Cherry, Hope, Peace, Infinity, Determination, Morning Sun, Beautiful Spring, Eastern Cloud, Bright Heavens, Golden Star, Pine Peak, and Five Seas.

The contests are very competitive, and there is often strong partisanship among clubs and active dispute about the ranking of fish, as well as "tricks of the trade" in displaying fish to the judges that can help a fish win a higher rank. The contests also take their toll on the fish. Since there is a series of increasingly important contests in the fall, a winning fish may appear in many contests. The travel, the handling, and the exposure to other fish seriously weaken the champions, and they sometimes expire at the end of the season.

Contests are also important social events for Ranchu hobbyists. In previous decades, raising show Ranchus was a gentleman's hobby and Ranchu clubs were usually sponsored by wealthy businessmen, landowners, or political leaders. Though those days are past and now most members are ordinary citizens, some clubs are still centered around a hereditary leader, the "Head" (*soke*), a term used in Japan for the leader of a traditional art such as tea ceremony or flower arranging. The Head may no longer be a wealthy patron, but he still governs many of the club's activities.

Ranchu breeders also observe a strict gentleman's

3. Only *yokozuna ozeki*, *sekiwake*, and *maegashira* are actual sumo ranks. The others are loosely derived from sumo history, but are unique to Ranchu contests.

code of behavior. Here are a few rules of good behavior for Ranchu fanciers from a club in the Tokyo area:

Don't walk on the raised area between ponds with your shoes on.
Don't handle another's fish without permission.
Don't tap on the container to make the fish swim.
Don't give a fish you have received as a gift to a third party.
Don't leave your fish in the care of others.

The clubs also conduct educational efforts in the form of monthly "study meetings" at which experienced senior members instruct newer recruits in the skills of raising and breeding Ranchus. Quite commonly, the Head or other leading breeders in the club will give or sell baby fish at the size of about three-fourths of an inch to club members at the beginning of the summer. At monthly meetings thereafter, the new members bring their fish together, discuss their development, and receive advice and constructive criticism from club members and leaders. This teaches them to care for and evaluate Ranchus at all stages of their growth.

The creative aspect of Ranchu raising is strongly emphasized in Japan, where hobbyists enjoy "building" their own fish through careful and creative care. In fact, tiny baby Ranchus, called *kuroko*, or "black fry," because they are still iron-colored, are regularly sold at the beginning of summer at Japanese pet shops and fish stores. Though large adult fish are also available, prices are very high and most Japanese fanciers are not very interested in owning a "finished product" that they had no hand in creating.

In Japan, raising Ranchus is regarded as a refined and relaxing hobby, as described in this brief essay by Aoki Reibo, a Japanese bamboo flute player and Living National Treasure, which appeared in a Japanese newspaper recently.

"I don't care if you cook for me, but don't forget to feed the Ranchus." I've been saying that to my wife for more than forty-four years.

That's how precious my Ranchus are to me. They are the jewel of Goldfish, a manmade wonder. Their headgrowth may seem like nothing more than a lump to most people, but unless you feed them fresh bloodworms, they will not develop a beautiful, well-formed head.

Each morning I place some bloodworms on my palm and lower it gently into the water. My Ranchus swim halfway onto my palm and slowly

RED TOSAKIN. PHOTO BY HIKARU SHIRAISHI.

suck in one tiny worm at a time. No matter how hungry they may be, they don't devour their food. How elegant! I never tire of watching them. I sit in front of my pool and watch the Ranchus swimming gracefully back and forth, and before I know it, an hour has passed.

Ranchus are most beautiful when they are about 4 inches long. If their pool is too long, they swim so strongly that their bodies lengthen, and if it's too deep, the water pressure changes their appearance, too. That's why Ranchus are always kept in a pool 3 feet by 4 feet, with only 4 inches of water.

I keep several such pools, filling them with water and letting it sit in the sun for a week, so that when I change the water in my Ranchus' pool I can avoid shocking them or harming their delicate scales.

Some people keep their Ranchus in garden ponds, and they spend so much time crouched in front of the pond looking at them that they often develop lower back trouble. But that doesn't stop them; they switch to sitting cross-legged, but they keep on gazing at their Ranchus.

TOSAKIN

The Tosakin was developed in the old Tosa fief on the island of Shikoku, near modern Kochi. Tosa is also the home of the famous long-tailed Japanese chicken called the *onagadori* and the fighting Tosa dog (Tosa *ken*). There is some disagreement about the origins of the

ADULT RED-AND-WHITE TOSAKIN. PHOTO BY ROMAN SZCHETER.

SAME FISH FROM ABOVE. PHOTO BY ROMAN SZCHETER.

Tosakin. The first picture of a Tosakin, dating from the mid-1800s, reputedly shows a fish with a body shape resembling a Wakin, but with the distinctive Tosakin tail. A later source states they were produced by crossing a Ryukin and an Osaka Ranchu. Still others suggest they are a natural sport of a Ryukin. However they originated, they became popular in the Kochi area, and by 1910 competitions were being held there. Then as now, Tosakins were bred by hobbyists, not Goldfish farmers.

U.S. air attacks on Kochi in 1945 and an earthquake the following year were thought to have wiped out the variety, but an avid hobbyist who was devastated at having lost all his fish scoured the area and found six fish—two breeders and four two-year-old fish—surviving at a restaurant. He begged the owner to part with them, and offered a large sum of money. "I don't need money," the restaurant owner said, "I need liquor." In the last years of the war and afterward, money became worthless, but he could carry on his restaurant business if he had liquor.

The hobbyist searched the countryside, and finally came up with a big bottle of sweet-potato vodka, which he traded for the fish. These six fish are said to be the origin of all Tosakins in Japan today. The variety was revived first in Kochi, and brought to the Tokyo area several decades later, in 1971, where a small group of young, avid hobbyists have worked hard to propagate and popularize them, with enough success that they can now be purchased at pet shops. In 1969, the Japanese government declared the Tosakin a Natural Treasure (Tennen Kinenbutsu) of Kochi Prefecture, and a few years later a Tosakin Preservation Society was founded.

Hobbyist Methods The Japanese regard Tosakins as weak fish, and attribute it to inbreeding—after all, all the fish in Japan today derive from six fish. They are thought to be especially susceptible to water-chemistry changes, and year-old fish are regarded as the weakest. Japanese

sources give conflicting advice about the water best for keeping Tosakins. Some suggest green water rich in algae, in various combinations with clean water, depending upon the season. This seems to vary considerably from breeder to breeder, however; some recommend the use of clear water all year long, and even go so far as to say that clear water is more important to successfully raising Tosakins than any other Goldfish.

Up to their first autumn, fish are kept in a round mortar bowl called a *marubachi*. These are especially made for Tosakins, and are about 2 feet in diameter, with sloping sides. The Japanese believe that Tosakins should be raised in a relatively small, shallow container to prevent the body from growing too large and to allow the tail to keep growing. If their tank is too large, they are too active, and if too many are kept together, they school, which increases their activity and harms desired fin development. They use no current and no filtration, though some are now using aeration.

After the first fall, fish may be moved to a square container about 36 inches by 24 inches. Stocking recommendations from a leading breeder in Tokyo are as follows:

15 gallons	10–13 year-old fish
	3–4 two-year-old fish
	2–3 breeders
20 gallons	15–20 year-old fish
	5–6 two-year-old fish
	4–5 breeders
35 gallons	too large for year-old fish
	11–13 two-year-old fish
	7–9 breeders

Though the amount of water seems quite small for the number of fish, the containers are shallow, holding only about 6 to 8 inches of water, so there is a large water-surface area.

YEARLING RED TOSAKIN. PHOTO BY RICHARD HESS.

SAME FISH FROM ABOVE. PHOTO BY RICHARD HESS.

Whatever the container, sunlight and good ventilation are necessities. Since most Japanese hobbyists use no filtration, they carry out a regular regimen of water changes. Their insistence on "good ventilation" (in raising all fancy varieties) also probably stems from the fact that they have traditionally used no artificial aeration (though it's doubtful that there would be a significant difference in dissolved oxygen among unaerated outdoor ponds, "poorly ventilated" or otherwise). From May to July they change the water every four to five days. In July and August they perform water changes every other day, making sure that the water never gets cloudy. Up through the end of October, water changes are made with clear water; in winter, with all green water. From mid-June to mid-September they cover half the bowl or aquarium with a board to provide shade — remember, they are keeping their fish outdoors and exposed to Japan's very hot summer sun. They believe that the heat of summer will cause the gills of breeder fish to open and stay that way.

The breeder of Tosakins is faced with a dilemma. Three-year-old fish are preferred as breeders, but many three-year-old fish have such extensive tail growth that they don't swim very well, and as a result many eggs are infertile. If two-year-old fish are used, however, there is a preponderance of single-tailed fry. The unsatisfactory choice is between fertility and single tails.

Beautiful show specimens are equally the result of breeding and culture, so they are not necessarily the best choice as breeders. It is best to select fish that have one extremely strong point, and to distinguish faults that are the result of culture from those that are genetic. For example, a fish that has good traits but has lost an eye or bent its tail through an accident is fine as a breeder. Two males are usually mated with one female in a 36 by 24-inch tank. It is important to make certain that the males are ready, with conspicuous breeding stars on their pec-

toral fins. If using live plants for breeding, a fine, soft-textured species is preferable, or the breeders' tail fins can be severely damaged, and the plants should be secured in a corner of the tank. When the belly of the female fish is a little soft, she is ready to spawn. The temperatures in the spawning tank are kept warm.

Tosakins are often quite slow to spawn, and the breeder may be tempted to give up and remove the fish from the spawning tank. It is necessary to be patient, however, and leave them in the breeding tank until they do spawn, and then separate them. They can be artificially spawned if necessary, following the standard technique for the practice. Standard methods for hatching the eggs and feeding the fry are used. After six weeks, the fry will begin to grow scales and look like tiny Tosakins. At this point Japanese breeders place the Tosakins in the round mortar *marubachis*. The Japanese believe that young fish are more active in a round bowl, because they can't settle down into a corner. Active swimming at this period, they think, helps produce good tails, while later, after the tails have developed their main shape, activity is restricted so the tails may grow large while the body remains small.

It is culling that actually produces the Tosakin. The first culling takes place when the fish are the width of a matchstick. At this point, all fry with single tails or asymmetrical tails are culled, and all those with symmetrical tails, preferably with a small split in the middle (a sakura tail), are kept. The second culling is very important. It takes place at about six weeks, when the scales begin to appear. At this point, fish with tails that have distinct outer ribs and are open from 90 to 60 degrees are kept. Thick caudal peduncles and large tail seats (*kinza*; for the Japanese names of the parts of a Tosakin, see the drawing on page 156) are also desirable traits. Fish with tails too closed or too open are culled. Those with tails open to more than 90 degrees tend to become unable to swim, as the front edge of the tail grows to flip over the main tail (*ushiro*) rather than below it, in the standard Tosakin conformation.

From this point on, culling occurs every time the water is changed, eliminating fish with defective tails, asymmetrical stomachs, or deformed dorsal fins. Fish that show one excellent quality even if they are lacking in others (as long as they don't have a serious fault) are kept. As mentioned earlier, these may become good breeding stock. In addition, since so much of the Tosakin's final shape depends on culture, they may develop into fine fish as they grow.

Standards The most distinctive feature of the Tosakin is its beautiful tail that spreads out like a fan and curves under and back on itself at the front. More than any other variety of Goldfish, perhaps, Tosakins must be viewed from above to be appreciated. From the side, they have the deep body of the Ryukin, but their tail, which rests horizontally in the water, can hardly be seen.

Let's begin with the terminology for the parts of the Tosakin, starting with the tail. The very first ray of the tail fin on each side is called the *maebone* or *oyabone*—the front ray or the parent ray. The first ray should be flexible yet strong and straight. The point where the tail fin turns underneath itself is called the turn, or *hanten*. The part of the tail fin that is underneath the main part of the tail fin is called the front, or *mae*. In adult fish, the *mae* may turn back on itself once, which is called singlefold (*ichimai gaeshi*) or twice, which is called doublefold (*nimai gaeshi*).

The width of the tail fin when seen from above is called the *watari*. In general, the wider the *watari* the better (as long as it remains in proportion to the fish, discussed below). The main section of the tail is called the back, or *ushiro*. Older fish sometimes develop a scalloped edge to the tail, which is considered very desirable. It is described as looking like a Japanese paper umbrella. The tail should have no creases, pleats, or folds in it, and the color must be clear. The tail core or central ray (*oshin*) must be straight both vertically and horizontally.

The caudal peduncle (*otsutsu*) should be heavy and short. The few rows of scales just before the start of the tail fin are called the "golden seat" (*kinza*) if they are red, orange, or gold, or "silver seat" (*ginza*) if they are white or silver.

The Tosakin's body should be egg shaped. The distance from eye to nose (*mesaki*) should be long, and the distance between the eyes (*mehaba*) should be short. In other words, the face should be narrow and pointed. Many otherwise fine fish tend to have a short, heavy face and heavy gill covers, but this is regarded as "inelegant' (*hin ga nai*). *Hin*, or "elegance," is perhaps the ideal

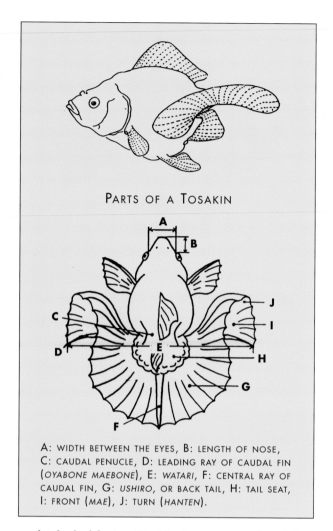

PARTS OF A TOSAKIN

A: WIDTH BETWEEN THE EYES, B: LENGTH OF NOSE, C: CAUDAL PENUCLE, D: LEADING RAY OF CAUDAL FIN (*OYABONE MAEBONE*), E: *WATARI*, F: CENTRAL RAY OF CAUDAL FIN, G: *USHIRO*, OR BACK TAIL, H: TAIL SEAT, I: FRONT (*MAE*), J: TURN (*HANTEN*).

quality looked for in a Tosakin, in contrast to the *aji* that is the mark of a great Ranchu.

Tosakins have round, medium, and long body types, and round bodies are considered best for show. Unfortunately, round-bodied fish tend to flip as they get older and larger, and so breeders keep both round-bodied and medium-bodied fish. They use the former type for showing and the latter type for breeding. Ideally, when seen from above the entire fish should fit into a circle. The width of the *watari* is the radius of the circle. From the tip of the nose to the end of the *kinza* should be half the radius, and the back tail (*ushiro*) should be the other half of the radius.

Red and red-and-white fish are equal in rank, but intense colors are preferred. Red-and-white fish that are predominantly red are generally preferred over red-and-white fish that are predominantly white, and completely white fish are last in line. Some Tosakins change color quite late; even champion breeders may still be "black" (actually an iron-gray color). This is not a disqualification, and these fish eventually do turn red or orange.

Many winning first-year fish are iron colored. In addition, first-year fish should not have a very conspicuous front fin (overlap), because as they grow older they will develop imperfect finnage. It is a mistake to hold first-year fish to the tail-fin standards of two-year and breeder fish. The front of the fin, whether single or double fold, continues to develop as the fish grows, and premature development does not bode well for the future.

Though no one would enter Tosakin in a swimming competition, they are judged by their swimming as well. They should be stable and horizontal as they swim and at rest. They should not list up or down. When they move forward, the front ray of the fin should be flexible, bending backward in response to the water's resistance and then returning to its proper straight posture when the fish stops.

Hobbyists perform minor operations on Tosakins, though a fish which has not been operated on is preferred. A fish that has been manipulated is not faulted in competition as long as no scars are visible. Tosakins tend to develop reverse gills in warm water. This is sometimes "remedied" on young fish by using baby fingernail clippers to cut off the reverse edge. Young Tosakins make have a *sakura* tail—that is, a back tail with a slight indentation in the middle, so that the tail resembles the petal of a cherry blossom. Some hobbyists "repair" this by clipping the edge of the tail back to the depth of the indentation. The tail may grow back with the indentation, and it may not. This operation is performed more than once by some hobbyists.

Another common defect is a tail with pleats—in other words, there is more tail tissue at the edge and in the mid-region of the tail than at the base. This can sometimes be corrected by slicing out a thin pie-piece section of the tail. The tail usually grows out without the pleat.

The Tosakin can be—actually demands—to be kept in a small aquarium or bowl, which gives it an edge over the Ranchu as a pet in urban Japan, where the notion that Ranchus must be kept in ponds still predominates. The number of Tosakin enthusiasts is growing, and clearly this variety is now firmly established. Annual shows are held in both the city of Kochi and in Tokyo, and some reports suggest that a slight difference is developing between fish in Tokyo and Kochi, the Kochi fish growing larger and longer than their Tokyo counterparts. The Tokyo group in particular actively promotes Tosakins, recruiting new members by donating baby fish to interested hobbyists in spring and then holding "study groups" throughout the summer to help them learn the ropes, followed by a show in the fall.

Recently, some Chinese breeders have begun to produce fish like the Tosakin, but it is unknown as yet what the ancestry of these fish is and whether they breed true. If they do, it is certainly a welcome development, since

RED-AND-WHITE TOSAKIN FROM ABOVE. PHOTO BY ROMAN SZCHETER.

new and vigorous blood could overcome the hurdle of this variety's delicacy, which is its only drawback.

If Tosakins become popular outside Japan, they may change our fishkeeping habits, making aquariums that can be viewed from above more popular. Once established, they are easy fish to care for and one of the loveliest creations of Japanese Goldfish breeders.

JIKIN

The Jikin is said to have originated in the early 1600s, when a samurai named Amano Shubo no Kami, living in what is now Gifu Prefecture, succeeded in establishing a strain of fish with the Jikin's characteristic flat tail from the Wakin. Because people at the time thought that the flat tail of this new fish resembled the tail of the mythical dolphin of Asian art (*shachi*, not to be confused with the real animal of the same name), they gave it that name. Coincidentally, the dolphin is often depicted head down and tail up, a stance which larger Jikin tend to adopt at rest. For two centuries, this variety was raised mainly in the Nagoya area, mostly by samurai retainers of the Owari fief, but by the last decade of the 1700s, it had spread to Mikawa and Hamamatsu.

It was around this time that another samurai fishkeeper discovered a method of using the extract of the wax begonia to bleach the body of the fish white, leaving only the fins and the lips red. From this point, the fish came to be known as the Jikin (local fish) or Nagoya Jikin. Around 1850, Makita Magobei discovered that the same effect could be achieved with tartaric acid, and he made a fish with a mallow-flower pattern on its side. The mallow flower was the official symbol of the ruling Tokugawa clan, and Makita was arrested for lese majesty and sentenced to beheading. He was eventually pardoned when he offered the fish as a gift to the authorities. He lived near Juo Hall in Nagoya, and after this incident, the Jikin came to be known as the Juo or the

ADULT JIKIN. PHOTO BY ROMAN SZCHETER.

ADULT JIKIN. PHOTO BY ROMAN SZCHETER.

Jio (*Ji* as in Jikin). The Jikin is also called the Peacock Tail (*kujakuo*), and the Cherry Tail (*sakurao*). The Rokurin Hozon Kai, the society founded in 1941 to propagate and preserve this variety, wanted to standardize these names in order to popularize the variety outside the Nagoya area and across Japan. They gave it yet another name: Rokurin, or "six scales." "Six" refers to the six red places on the fish's body: the mouth, the dorsal fin, the pectoral fins, the ventral fins, the anal fins, and the tail. "Scales" refers to the fact that the original red scales are removed so that the fish's body is white. Though fanciers sometimes use the name Rokurin, the most widely known name remains Jikin.

In 1958, the Jikin was declared a Natural Treasure of Aichi Prefecture.

Hobbyist Methods Jikins are raised and kept like other fancy Goldfish, except that breeders prefer to use fish four years and older as breeders, believing this results in offspring of better type. Jikins are regarded as pond fish, not aquarium fish in Japan, and the Japanese believe that they are to be viewed from above. With the high contrast of red and white—festive colors in Japan—their beautiful tails, and characteristically perky swimming movements, Jikins are a beautiful sight in a pond.

The crucial aspect of Jikin cultivation is the process of producing the distinctive *rokurin* coloration. The young fish must first change color, which usually takes place in about August. Then fish with more white on the body, or with white in the appropriate places, are selected to be made (*tsukuru*). Though historical lore mentions begonia juice and tartaric acid used to bleach the

fish, this practice is not used today. Instead, small areas of scales are removed with a fingernail or a flat, thin bamboo shim. Only five or six scales are removed at a time, and the fish is returned to the pond to recuperate. After a number of such sessions, the fish is finished.

Obviously, impeccable water quality is crucial to success, since the de-scaled fish are susceptible to bacterial invasion. After the fish have recovered, however, they are kept in green water. The breeders believe that this intensifies the red coloring and that the fish prefer aged, green water. In fact, some breeders use the water they remove from their Ranchu tanks during the water changes for their Jikin tanks. (This refers to Ranchu breeders who raise fish outdoors and change water when it becomes too opaque with algae growth.)

Since the color pattern is man-made, there is no reason to use only "made" fish for breeding, and breeders will also keep "unmade" fish with fine conformation for this purpose.

The Jikin also has a reputation in Japan for delicacy, but this usually only applies to the period around which the fish are made. Once established, they are vigorous, healthy fish, no doubt due to their Wakin ancestry.

Standards The Rokurin Hozon Kai organizes its standards into five categories: general appearance and comportment, head, body, tail, and fins. Whether relatively long or short, in general appearance the fish should be balanced and elegant. It should be able to swim freely in any direction. When it stops in the water, it should remain on an even keel, the head neither down nor up in the water. It should swim with its tail, each push with the tail fins resulting in a forward movement. It shouldn't shake its head or body from side to side to make its way through the water. When a superior fish is at rest in the water, its tail fins will move up and down in small movements, as if the fish is preparing for its next push forward.

As far as the head is concerned, the red on the mouth should be a small and well-defined area. The measurement from the eyes to the nose should be long and the head pointed. Some fish have slightly protruding eyes, and this is a fault because it is inelegant. Red gill covers are not a fault, but the coloring of this area must be well placed and not disrupt the visual balance of the fish as a whole. The head of the fish cannot turn to one side or the mouth open unevenly. The eyes should be evenly placed on the head. When any of these faults disrupt the balance of the fish, it is disqualified in competition. The gill covers should be tight to the head.

From above, the body should have the double-crescent shape of a bamboo leaf. The back should be a gentle, even curve. Excess fat near the pectoral fins will detract from the bamboo-leaf shape. The caudal peduncle should be thick, because this helps the fish swim well. An all-white body is best, but the fish may have red on the abdomen if it is not visible when viewed from above. The line of the stomach should be a gentle curve up to the caudal peduncle, and the fish should have a bamboo-leaf shape from the side as well as from above. The caudal peduncle must not stretch out too far, and there should not be too much space between the end of the dorsal fin and the tail. Finally, the scales should be regularly aligned in neat rows.

PRONUNCIATION KEY

Japanese is actually very easy to pronounce. The vowels are exactly like those of Spanish or Italian.

A is pronounced like the o in hot.
I is pronounced like the ee in fee.
U is pronounced like the ue in due.
E is pronounced like the e in bed.
O is pronounced like the o in go.

Every consonant is pronounced. The only difficult one for English speakers is r, which is pronounced somewhere between r and l, like a Spanish r without the trill—the tongue just touches the roof of the mouth at the start of the sound.

Breaking the words into syllables helps. Give each syllable equal weight and don't leave out any sounds. Though there are subtle accents in Japanese, you can pronounce it well enough without worrying about accents or pitches. Just treat each syllable like a metronome beat on a single tone. The following very simplified pronunciation guide won't pass muster in a language class, but it will get you closer to the original pronunciation.

Azuma AH ZUE MAH
Azuma Nishiki AH ZUE MAH KNEE SHE KEY
Chakin CHA KIN
Chinshurin CHIN SHOE RIN
Chobi CHO BEE
Demekin DAY MAY KIN; no accent: not dee MEE kin.
    Actually the "e"s are shorter than the English long "a."
Edo E (as in "Ed") OH
Edo Nishiki E (as in "Ed") OH KNEE SHE KEY

Gingyo GIN (hard "G", NOT like the cocktail) GYO
Hamanishiki HAH MA KNEE SHE KEY
Izumo IS UE (as in "rue") MOE
Izumo nankin IS UE (as in "rue") MOE NAN (like the Indian bread) KIN
Jikin GEE KIN
Kingyo KIN GYO
Koriyama KOE REE YAH MAH
Kyoto KYO TOE
Maruko MAH RUE KOE
Nishiki KNEE SHE KEY
Oranda OH RON (not "ran," past tense of "run") DAH
Osaka OH SAH KAH
Osaka Ranchu OH SAH KAH RON CHEW
Ranchu RON CHEW
Ryukin RYU (NOT RAH-YOU) KIN
Ryukyus RYU KYUSE
Sakura SAH KUE RAH
Sakura Nishiki SAH KUE RAH KNEE SHE KEY
Seibungyo SAY BOON GYO
Shikoku SHE KOE KUE
Shishigashira SHE SHE GAH SHE RAH
Shubunkin SHOE BOON KIN
Tetsugyo TETSUE GYO
Tosa TOE SAH
Tosakin TOE SAH KIN
Wakin WAH KIN

And a few extras thrown in for fun:
Hara-kiri HAH RAH KEY REE
Hibachi HE BAH CHEE
Karaoke KAH RAH OH KAY

YOUNG JIKIN SEEN FROM ABOVE. PHOTO BY ROMAN SZCHETER.

The tail is the most distinctive feature of the Jikin. It must be symmetrical right to left, and it should be as close to flat as possible, at a 90-degree angle to the body. The lower lobes of the tail in particular should open and close in tandem as the fish swims. The tail must be red to the tip, though a small amount of transparent fin at the tip is acceptable for breeders. A large amount is a fault. The outer edges of the tail fin should be flexible to assist in swimming. All of the leading rays of the tail fin must be completely red. The opening and closing motions of the upper portions and the lower portions of the tail should not be too different. The tail should not be so large that it unbalances the fish visually and destroys its comportment as it swims. Tail fins that fold outward at the tip are a disqualification; those that fold inward a small amount are only a fault.

The other fins are also important in judging Jikins. They must also all be red to the tip, again with a slight exception for breeders, which may have a thin transparent edge. The leading ray of each fin must be red or the fish is disqualified. A slight band of transparency at the attachment of the fins to the body is not a fault, and in fact in the case of the dorsal fin it can make for a more elegant appearance. The dorsal should stand straight up. A sagging dorsal gives the appearance of an aging fish. Jikins must have double anal fins, which should be

close together, straight, and even. It is a fault if the anal fins are not aligned and one projects when the fish is at rest. This is also true of the ventral fins.

IZUMO NANKIN

The Izumo Nankin was developed in Shimane Prefecture. "Izumo" is the old name for this region, and "Nankin" is the Japanese pronunciation on the Chinese city of Nanjing (sometimes written as Nanking). The origin of the name is obscure, but "Nankin" was a general term in old Japan for rare and precious things.

Goldfish were first bred in the old Izumo fief from about 1750, and one of the lords of Izumo took an active interest in Goldfish production—remember, at this time Goldfish were a luxury item in Japan—as a means of local economic development. Though Goldfish of the same body shape and general coloration of the Izumo Nankin appear in many old Japanese prints and paintings of Goldfish, at present there is no documentary evidence dating the time at which this variety was developed.

The first modern record of the Izumo Nankin is by Matsui, who states that on a trip to Shimane in 1927 he saw Izumo Nankins, fine specimens of which were being bred by one Hiroshi Sato. Matsui also says that the variety was on the verge of extinction. In later publications he writes that the variety was being bred in

Shimane from at least the late 1800s, though he offers no documentation.

Today Izumo Nankins are bred by small numbers of hobbyists around the country, and there is a society to preserve and promote the variety that has held annual competitions since 1988. Izumo Nankins are seasonally available from better Goldfish dealers.

In appearance, they resemble the Maruko (round fish), a variety regarded as the ancestor of the Ranchu. (The Maruko, no longer bred in Japan, was probably a Korean or Chinese egg fish.) They have pointed heads like a Ryukin, and egg-shaped bodies. They lack a dorsal fin, like the Ranchu, but have no headgrowth. Their fins are short to medium in length, and they are predominantly white, with red markings. The ideal Izumo Nankin has red fins, lips, and gill covers, like Jikins, but other patterns are also acceptable.

Standards The head of the Izumo Nankin must be small and pointed, that is, narrow between the eyes but long from eye to nose. A blunt or rounded face is a disqualification, and there must be no headgrowth of the type seen in Ranchus. The trunk should be symmetrical and egg shaped without projecting in an exaggerated fashion. Thin fish have an underfed look and are not considered elegant. The curve of the back seen from the side should be smooth, like the curve of a traditional wooden Japanese comb. The caudal peduncle must be thick and longer than a Ranchu's, extending gracefully to the tail fin. The outer rays of the tail fin should project strongly to right and left, at a minimum of a 60-degree angle to the body. The tail core (central ray) should be strong and prominent. The Izumo Nankin must have a twin tail, split at least 50% of its length.

A CALICO JIKIN, ALSO CALLED EDO JIKIN. PHOTO BY HIKARU SHIRAISHI.

The ideal coloration is a pattern of white body with red fins, mouth, and gill covers. This is the same *rokurin* pattern sported by Jikins, but it is not produced by artificial methods in the case of Izumo Nankins. A red head is a disqualification. Attractive red-and-white patterns are also acceptable, and a dappled pattern on the lower half of the body is regarded as especially beautiful. Though in competition beautiful coloration may compensate for other faults, nevertheless body and fin conformation should take precedence over coloration, and even completely white fish are acceptable.

Each body part should conform to standard and at the same time the fish should display a balance as a whole. The scalation should be regular, and the smaller the scales the better. Both white and red coloration should be bright, clear, and shining. The fish should present an elegant appearance and swim "lightly." The tail fin should move gracefully when swimming, and then open fully when the fish stops.

In judging Izumo Nankins, the line of the body from tip of the nose to the tail, as seen from above, is crucial. The fish should be straight, balanced, and the body outline should seem to flow in graceful curves from nose to tail. Izumo Nankins can grow to be quite large, but they must display this conformation whatever their size.

OSAKA RANCHU

The Osaka Ranchu was probably the first Japanese Ranchu-type variety to be developed from the imported Chinese egg fish, or Maruko. As the name indicates, it originated in the Osaka-Kyoto area, probably from the mid-1700s. The first record of an Osaka Ranchu competition is from 1831.

Today the variety is being revived by fanciers, but it remains very rare and as yet unstable.

Standards The head of the Osaka Ranchu is narrow and short, in contrast to the Tosakin and Izumo Nankin, which have heads that are narrow and long. There should be little if any headgrowth and no dorsal fin. The ratio of body length to width should be a minimum of 2 to 1.2. Length is measured from nose to end of caudal peduncle.

The tail should be broad with rounded edges. It should be open, and set nearly horizontally, like a Tosakin or Butterfly Tail. The central ray of the tail should not rise up, but be straight and horizontal. A three-lobe tail is preferred, though a slight notch is also acceptable. A four-lobe tail will make the fish unstable in the water.

The color must be deep red and clean, shining white. The preferred pattern is red mouth, mustache, eye sockets, and fins, red on the lower half of the body

from the mouth to the caudal peduncle, and white from the head to the back.

Visiting Japan

Though the unique varieties of Japanese Goldfish are occasionally imported, it is difficult to find them in the United States. It is much easier, of course, to see them in Japan. The most convenient places to see Japanese Goldfish are the major department stores in Tokyo and Osaka. Most department stores have a pet department on the roof, and three Tokyo department stores have good selections of high-quality Goldfish. Seibu Department Store near the Ikebukuro train station has the best, followed by Odakyu, near Shinjuku Station, and Isetan, also in Shinjuku. All of these stores sell Ranchus, Jikins, Tosakins, Azuma Nishikis, and a wide variety of Orandas, Ryukins, and Telescopes.

Though some Goldfish are available year-round, the best selection can be found from May through October. The department-store pet departments are mostly open air, and can be pretty cold in the winter months, when stock is also low.

There are a few specialist Goldfish shops in all the major cities as well, listed in the phone book and in Japanese fish hobbyist magazines.

It is much more difficult to visit the smaller breeders of the Fukagawa area in Tokyo, and even more so to visit those in Saitama, Yamato Koriyama, and Yatomi. The breeders in the Fukagawa area, which is now highly urbanized, can be visited without appointment—if you can find them! Though their addresses can be found in telephone books and on the Internet, even Japanese have a hard time locating them in the serpentine hodgepodge of Tokyo's streets and neighborhoods. A Japanese contact is indispensable in locating these breeders.

Yamato Koriyama is about one hour from Kyoto by train, but the Goldfish breeders are spread about around the town and countryside, and you will need a knowledgeable taxi driver to visit them. Some are private, wholesale operations, but there are also retail stores open to the public. Yatomi, near Nagoya, is even more rural and cannot be visited without a car and introductions to the breeders. Though there are a handful of retail shops in the area, they don't offer the best fish. The breeders do not sell retail, and an introduction is required to visit them. Japanese etiquette also requires that if you trouble the breeder, you had better buy, and he may not necessarily have good stock available, so you can end up paying a high price for mediocre fish.

Few if any of the breeders speak English, and for the

AZUMA NISHIKI. PHOTO BY HIKARU SHIRAISHI.

tourist the department store pet shops are by far the best bet. If one hits the right season, in a few hours one can see a good sampling of fine Japanese Goldfish. In addition, if you visit the Tokyo area in October, you might be able to attend one of the many Ranchu competitions, which are open to the public. The dates change from year to year, but are available on the Internet (in Japanese). The Internet has a wealth of information about Japanese Goldfish and hobbyists, including breeding tips, clubs, shows, and Goldfish farms, but most of it is in Japanese.

Japanese Goldfish have a special and unique beauty, and I hope this brief introduction helps more U.S. Goldfish keepers and collectors appreciate it. Though of course Goldfish are also a business in Japan, keeping, breeding and raising them are also very much a hobby, and individual breeders play an important part in establishing and preserving standards and keeping varieties alive. This makes it a pastime that offers both aesthetic and social rewards, which I hope more American Goldfish hobbyists may experience and share in the future.

REFERENCES

Ishikawa, Kamekichi, et al., *Ranchu Hiden* (Tokyo: Midori Shobo, 1985).
Kaji, Sumio, *Yasashii Kingyo no Kaikata* (Tokyo: Yuki Shobo, 1997).
Kingyo no Kaikata, ed. Masajiro Nakamura (Tokyo: Narumido Shuppan, 1997).
Nagasawa, Heijiro, *Genshoku Ranchu: Miroku no Subete to Shiikuho* (Tokyo: Midori Shobo, 1977).
Ranchu Kaden (Tokyo: Midori Shobo, 1993).
Ranchu Meikan, vol. 1 (Tokyo: Midori Shobo, 1999).
Rokurin Hozon Kai, *Rokurin* (Nagoya: Tanaka Kosaku, 1993).

Saishin Kingyo to Ranchu Catarogu, ed. Tadamasa Ishikawa (Tokyo: Narumido Shuppan, 1996).
Sakurai, Ryohei, *Kingyo no Tanoshii Kaikata* (Tokyo: Takahashi Shoten, 1999).
Shiraishi, Hikaru, *Kingyo: Kaikata, Sodatekata* (Tokyo: Seitosha, 1999).
Smith, Hugh M., *Japanese Goldfish: Their Varieties and Cultivation. A Practical Guide to the Japanese Methods of Goldfish Culture for Amateurs and Professionals* (Washington, D.C.: W.F. Roberts) 1909. Out of print.
Suzuki, Hiromi, *Kingyo to Nihonjin* (Tokyo: Sanichi Shobo, 1999).
Tamaka, Fukaki, Tanoshii Kingyo no Kaikata, Sodatekata (Tokyo: Nagaoka Shoten, 1995).
Tanaka, Kunie, *Tosa Kingyo no Bi* (Tokyo: Midori Shobo, 1994).

Chapter 10

Breeding Ranchus

Izhak

Kroshinsky

The introduction of Chinese Goldfish into the U.S. market brought the import of Japanese Goldfish to a halt. The quality of the Chinese imports was excellent with one exception—the Ranchu. Recently I have seen Chinese Ranchus of good quality, however, which indicates that the Chinese are working to improve their strains. The main difference between the two strains even now seems to be the shape of the caudal fin, the caudal fin of the Japanese Ranchu being more curved.

The raising of high-quality Ranchus requires patience and a long-term commitment. It takes from two to three years to raise a Ranchu to breeding size in the climate of southeastern New York State, where I live. This makes Ranchu breeding a much slower process than, for example, breeding Guppies, which can be bred when a year old or even younger, and can as a result produce several generations in the time it takes to produce a single generation of Ranchus.

Selection of Breeding Stock

A Ranchu must look like a sumo wrestler, large and powerful. My standards are the same as those used in Japan, but here I stress the points that seem more important to me. The head should be a little wider than the body width. The lower part of the body must be deep and wider than the upper part of the body. A smoothly curved back should slope down from the highest point at an angle of about forty-five degrees to meet a thick caudal peduncle.

In breeding my line, I pay special attention to the shape of the caudal fin. I accept fish with a four-lobe tail, a three-lobe tail, and a three-lobe tail with a slight indentation at the tip. The upper lobe or lobes of the caudal fin should be set at about a 90-degree angle to the caudal peduncle. When seen from behind, the two sides of the caudal fin projecting out and down should

164

be set at a 90-degree angle to each other, appearing like a roof with a 90-degree peak. When seen from the side, the central ray of the caudal fin should gently curve down in a graceful arc. The lower lobes should also curve gently upward at the end.

Inbreeding is the only way to achieve good, consistent results in Ranchu breeding. One may get lucky and obtain very good fish out of a cross of unrelated fish or even an uncontrolled spawn of poor-quality fish, but following spawns will be poor and completely undependable. Over the long term, the hobbyist can only control the shape of his fish through line breeding.

It is important to start with Ranchus of good quality, preferably obtained from a breeder who line breeds. Fish obtained from such a breeder, even if not perfect

specimens, will carry the genotype required to produce high-quality Ranchus. It is my experience that line-bred Ranchus produce a much larger percentage of high-quality fish than a cross of high-quality Ranchus from different strains. In the latter case, both fish possess the genes to produce the desired phenotype, but the arrangement of the genetic material must be different, resulting in inferior offspring or lower percentages of high-quality Ranchus.

If a cross of different lines is made, the F-1 fish should be crossed back to the parent of the line that the hobbyist is pursuing. In such situations, it is a mistake to breed F-1 to F-1.

At times even a good line should be crossed out in order to reintroduce vigor, which can decline with long-

term line breeding. A one-time outcross is enough to achieve this. The penalty is that some undesirable characteristic may be introduced, which will then have to be worked out of the strain. After outcrossing, always mate the F-1 progeny back to the parent line.

My criteria for selecting fish for breeding each spring is simple: I select the best all-round fish. The exception is when I am trying to enhance a particular characteristic. In that case I may choose a fish that shows that trait even though it may be lacking in others.

If I am satisfied with the status of the line I will breed the same fish again—that is, if it is producing at least 10% of high-quality fish per spawning. The best way to improve on the line is to inbreed, and it is acceptable to breed brother to sister if the line is producing a large number of high-quality fish. If the line is not producing 10% or better high-quality fish, one should breed back to older fish.

If you are breeding large numbers of fish, it's a very good idea to keep breeding records. For various reasons, I keep my breeding limited to a small number of fish, so I can easily recall their relationships.

Although I have had one-year-old fish spawn, the eggs are small and few. Normally, I prefer to use two-year-old males and three-year-old females, though at times I may breed back to an older male if he is of exceptional quality or if I want to enhance a particular trait that he possesses.

Preparing Stock for Breeding

I recommend giving Ranchus a period of dormancy before breeding. I do this outdoors, but it can also be achieved by keeping your fish in a dark, unheated basement. With fish outdoors, the dormancy period lasts about five months. Indoor hibernation can best be achieved in an unheated basement or garage. The temperature should ideally be dropped below 50 degrees. I advise low light for about nine hours a day for two months. Then increase the period of light by one-half hour a week until, after an additional two months, it reaches thirteen hours a day and at the same time raise the temperature gradually to about 68 degrees.

In spring, when breeding preparation begins, the metabolism of the fish is geared to prepare for spawning—which in the female means egg production. Overfeeding at this time may result in bulging ovaries, and egg binding may occur if spawning does not take place due to low temperatures or other factors. It is best to feed enough to condition for spawning but not more. Live food at this time is highly beneficial if a clean source is available.

When the temperature rises to the mid-sixties degrees, usually in late April or early May in my locale, I move this year's breeders indoors and place the female in a spawning tank of about 40 to 50 gallons, with 12 inches of water. This size tank also insures that very young fry have easy access to food. I place the male in a separate tank. I keep the temperature at sixty-

eight degrees; in my experience, this results in the fewest mutations. I also try to maintain the pH at neutral. I feed both fish large amounts of live food, and within a week place the male with the female. I prefer to place the pair together on Friday with the hope that spawning will take place over the weekend, when I can observe it and remove the fish as spawning is complete.

Spawning

Spawning can often be induced by making large water changes with cooler water. As the cooler water warms up in the tank, the breeders respond to the natural spring rise in water temperatures.

I prefer to use one male per female, as this allows me to better control the genetic background of the spawn. I may use an additional male to stimulate a female slow to respond and remove it once the chase gets started by both males.

I find live plants such as anacharis hair grass the best spawning material, but artificial spawning mats made out of prewashed polyester or nylon yarn work, too.

Spawning usually takes place during the early morning and is completed in about two hours. I find that there is usually little damage to the female, perhaps because Ranchus don't have long finnage and they aren't vigorous swimmers. I let the fish breed naturally, but at the end of the spawning process I may strip them. Stripping fish that are not ready is dangerous and ineffective.

The breeders can be moved back to the pond if pond temperatures are within four degrees of the indoor tank temperatures; if not, wait until they are to return the breeders to the pond.

Care of Eggs

About an hour after spawning, I take several steps to minimize the growth of fungus. I increase aeration and restart mechanical filtration. I have also used methylene blue at 2 PPM to inhibit fungus with good results. Fungus attacks unfertilized eggs but will spread and engulf fertilized eggs as well, preventing them from hatching.

At a temperature of sixty-eight degrees, the fry hatch in about five days. Temperature has an effect on the male to female ratio; at temperatures higher than sixty-eight degrees, more males are produced. A day or so before hatching, I stop filtration and decrease aeration, to reduce turbulence at hatching. I also lower the water depth to 6 inches, so that the young fry hatch in shallow water. This is critical, as they must fill their swim bladders with air at the surface, and deep water will hinder this.

Care of Fry

When the fry become free swimming, which occurs in about two days after they have absorbed their egg sacs, raise the temperature to seventy-four degrees for quicker growth. Feed the fry fresh-hatched brine shrimp twice a day for about three weeks. I feed the amount of brine shrimp that the fry can consume in about two hours, which is about how long brine shrimp remain alive in fresh water. Siphon out any dead shrimp after each feeding. I also provide light feedings of finely crushed flake food after the first week.

After the first week, you should begin making water changes, being careful not to damage the fry.

At about two weeks of age, I start to feed soaked crushed pellets, homemade food, and chopped tubifex worms. Though tubifex worms introduce the possibility of bacterial infections, this risk is paid off in increased growth rates. With two feedings a day, the young Ranchus reach two inches in length in about four months.

Culling

Culling—the rejection of fish with undesirable characteristics—is a very important process in raising Ranchus. Culling should be started as early as possible. I start it as soon as defects are detectible. In a good spawn, culling begins at about four weeks. In poor spawns, culling may begin after the first week, eliminating fish with single tails and back deformities. I cull any fish with the slightest visible defect. This has the benefits of reducing competition for food among the remaining fish and making it easier to maintain high water quality. In my strain, I begin culling based on the angle of the caudal peduncle.

While slight imperfections in the smooth curve of the back may improve with age, I recommend culling out any fish with such imperfections, which I view as a serious defect. Breeders of different strains will cull different kinds of fish. No strain is perfect; each displays a weakness at one point or another. The difficulty in fixing a strain of Goldfish to produce a high proportion of almost identical fish, as has been done with many tropical fish, may be an indication of high genetic variability in the Goldfish.

Feeding

Feeding plays a large role in the production of the perfect Ranchu. Young fish from the best of strains will not amount to much if not fed properly. Young Ranchus must be fed heavily, and with the correct diet, from an early age. From about three weeks, I recommend the use of a homemade gelatin-based food that includes fresh vegetable matter such as spinach, peas, red peppers and carrots for red pigment, wheat germ for carbohydrates, and eggs and ground fish for protein. Adding powdered vitamins to the food will ensure that the fish do not suffer nutritional shortages, which can result from exclusive feeding of some pellet foods.

My recipe for homemade food is as follows:

2 lb	Smelts or other fish
24 oz	Frozen peas and carrots
3–4	Large red bell peppers
24–30 oz	Frozen chopped spinach
16 oz	Plain wheat germ
5 tsp	Dog vitamins
32 envelopes	Plain powdered gelatin (each envelope usually contains 1/4 oz)

You may also add up to a dozen eggs.

Liquefy the first four ingredients in a blender, adding sufficient water for blender operation. Place the

mixture in a large pot, add the wheat germ, and heat until warm, stirring continuously. When warm, add the gelatin gradually, stirring continuously to avoid lumps. Stir in vitamin powder, then cool and refrigerate.

Once the mixture is solid and rubbery, cut into three-sixteenth-inch-thick sheets and freeze. Defrost the sheets lightly as required, cutting into one-fourth-inch cubes prior to feeding.

This recipe makes about 2 gallons.

I offer a variety of food types, because no single type contains all the required nutrients. Pellets of good quality are convenient and could be used as one of the feedings in warm weather. Large-size flake foods can also be offered. Live foods such as earthworms or black worms are important, and must be fed at least once a week to maintain good growth and vigor. Frozen brine shrimp are not as rich in food value but do contain carotene for

red pigment, and when frozen fresh do contain important nutritional elements.

The amount and frequency of feeding depends upon the temperature. When it is between sixty-five and eighty-five degrees, feed twice daily. Between sixty and sixty-five degrees, feed once daily, and below sixty degrees observe the fish closely and feed according to their behavior. If they do not appear hungry and do not attack their food, don't feed them. Observation is always very important. Under natural conditions fish are constantly looking for food, and will feed as much as possible when a concentrated food source is found. The food available under natural conditions is not as rich in carbohydrates as what we feed in captivity. With that in mind the hobbyist must realize that the fish will consume as much food as they can at any one feeding and they also will feed on very concentrated food when fed

pellets only. As such the amount of food and type must be closely regulated. Feeding homemade foods offers the opportunity to add vegetable matter, which will help the fishes' digestion. Adult Goldfish are largely herbivorous, and as such must be fed large amounts of vegetable matter, but they also require animal protein for the best growth and development, especially when young. Protein could be offered in homemade food in the form of ground fish or eggs, or as live foods such as black worms, daphnia, brine shrimp, and bloodworms.

With experience the hobbyist gains the ability to feed correctly based on observation of the fishes' behavior and appearance. Close observation will enable the hobbyist to spot problems early enough to take corrective measures before there is any long-lasting impact on the fish.

Water Quality

Good water quality is a must for raising quality Ranchus. Although they are adaptable to a fairly wide pH range, it is very important to keep ammonia levels at zero. Goldfish are heavy feeders and produce large amounts of waste, partly due to the large proportion of vegetable matter in their diet. Closed canister systems are not usually suitable for filtration. Open systems that can be easily cleared of trapped material are better. Filters that incorporate sponges for mechanical filtration and also provide biological filtration are best. Frequent and large water changes are a must. With good tap water quality, up to 90% of the water should be changed on a weekly basis, the amount and frequency depending on the

number of fish, water temperature, and on the type of filtration.

I highly recommend the use of ultraviolet sterilizers in ponds. They eliminate suspended algae and bacteria, resulting in clear water. The use of ultraviolet sterilizers will not eliminate all pathogens, but probably does cut down the number of the free-swimming ones.

Good water quality is especially crucial in raising Ranchus because it enables the hobbyist to feed them heavily in order to achieve the round body shape and large headgrowth of a well-raised Ranchu. Many hobbyists start with very good young Ranchus and are surprised that they do not achieve the growth rate or the quality of young Ranchus from the same spawn raised by the breeder. The main reasons are always water quality and diet.

Headgrowth

In Japanese Ranchus, headgrowth is larger than the body when viewed from above, but is smooth in texture as compared to the Chinese Lionhead or the Chinese Ranchu. The headgrowth is visible by four months of age and reaches its prime after about three years. The growth should not be so excessive as to interfere with the fish's vision and mobility. Headgrowth is mainly genetically determined, but it is also influenced by environmental conditions. Falling autumn temperatures encourage fat accumulation and increased headgrowth—which is fatty tissue. The amount of live food, degree of crowding, and water conditions also influence headgrowth. Fish raised in crowded conditions and in water of poor quality will display earlier and larger headgrowth. At the same time, crowded conditions will result in smaller fish. It seems that as the fish directs its growth towards body size, headgrowth slows down. The same phenomenon occurs with other types of Goldfish, in which fin development is delayed in favor of body growth.

There is no difference in the size of headgrowth between the sexes, though white Ranchus often have smaller headgrowth than all-red fish.

Some manufacturers of pellet foods claim to incorporate headgrowth enhancers. I have used Hikari's lionhead pellets, and they do seem to accelerate headgrowth.

Overwintering Fish

As water temperatures begin to drop and daylight hours become shorter in early autumn, fish raised outdoors in ponds respond by slowing body growth and accumulating fat. They also look in their prime condition in early fall, which is a good reason to hold Goldfish shows in late summer or early fall. As the temperature drops the fish also become less active, and the amount of food must be reduced accordingly. Below fifty degrees the fish should be fed sparingly or not at all, and as the temperature drops lower all feeding should be stopped. The fish will enter hibernation, during which they will swim around very slowly or become nearly motionless.

I do not hibernate fish in their first winter, but I induce hibernation in all my fish from the second winter. While hibernation is not necessary to raise Ranchus, I find it makes breeding easier because Goldfish seem to still respond to the natural seasonal cycles that ruled the lives of their ancestors.

The pond must also be thoroughly cleaned up in late fall and one last water change made before shutting down for the winter. As the nights grow colder, I cover the pond with plastic sheeting over a wood frame. This helps maintain water temperatures at about ten degrees higher than the ambient temperature. The frame should be pitched to shed rain and snow. This extends the warm season for the fish and, in deep winter, minimizes the amount of ice that forms on the pond. The cover will also eliminate leaves from falling into the pond; leaves and other detritus will contribute to poor water quality in the winter or early spring.

Aeration should continue until the water temperature drops to about forty degrees. Aeration at temperatures below forty degrees prevents stratification of the water, and stratification helps restrict ice formation to the top of the pond rather than the bottom. As you may recall from your high-school physics lectures, water at thirty-six degrees is heavier than water at thirty-two degrees, which is one reason that ice forms on the water surface. By mixing the water through aeration, you run a greater risk of the pond freezing solid.

I maintain ultraviolet sterilization and filtration until there is a danger that the lines will freeze up, at which point I remove both devices for storage until spring. I leave a heater in the pond as a precaution against prolonged low temperatures that may lead to extensive ice buildup, which can result in cracking a concrete pond or building up a thick layer of ice. A thin layer of ice will not harm the fish.

Winter offers a chance for both the fish and the hobbyist to rest, though on warm days the cover should be removed and the pond given a quick inspection.

Spring is the most critical time for Goldfish in the pond. The fish have lost about 20% of their body weight during hibernation, their immune system is weak, and as the water temperature starts to rise so do the activity levels of bacteria and parasites. At this time, give the pond a thorough clean up. Reinstall filtration, aeration, and ultraviolet sterilization systems.

Feeding should be resumed very gradually when the temperature rises above fifty degrees. The digestive system of the fish has almost completely shut down over winter and will take time to reestablish. Start feeding with homemade food and live food, and by late April, you are ready to begin another breeding season.

Predators and Disease

When keeping Ranchus outdoors, you may face the problem of predators. Herons, sea gulls, and other birds can be discouraged by covering the pond with a net over a frame. Cats, raccoons, and other similar predators can be kept away from the pond with a perimeter wire about 6 inches high around the pond, attached to a low-voltage transformer. This device, manufactured primarily for Koi ponds, is very effective and has minimal visual impact.

Ranchus are very hardy if kept under proper conditions. Problems may arise on occasion, however, due to neglect or carelessness. Newly purchased fish must be quarantined in a separate tank for about a month before introducing them to the rest of the stock. The key to disease prevention is the quarantine of all new introductions. Treating the entire stock can be expensive and frustrating, as your established stock, kept under healthy conditions, is likely to be very susceptible to newly introduced diseases.

Closely observing new fish in quarantine to spot early signs of disease is critical to their survival. Delay in diagnosing any troubles that crop up may mean complications or even a lost battle.

Gill flukes are a very common problem on newly acquired fish. It seems easier to eradicate flukes on fish from Japan than from China. Gill flukes are so common on imported fish that treating the fish even before they display any symptoms is recommended. Various protozoan parasites may also be introduced with new fish. Bacterial infections are less common. Diagnosis and treatment of all of these potential threats are described in part 1 of this book.

Breeding Ranchus is a rewarding hobby because there are so many variables in the fishes' genetic makeup that the pursuit of perfection is never ending. To really accomplish anything in line breeding, one has to start with the best stock available and keep at it over the years. One of the more interesting aspects of the hobby is that while you are perfecting your fish, you are also perfecting your eye. This creative aspect of Ranchu breeding is what makes it such a satisfying pastime.

I hope that more Goldfish hobbyists will take up Ranchu breeding, so that in the future the United States may have the kind of community of Ranchu fans that makes the hobby as interesting and involving as it is in Japan.

About the Authors

DR. ERIK L. JOHNSON, a world-renowned veterinarian with a clinical specialty in fish medicine, speaks and conducts seminars regularly throughout the United States. He is the author of *Koi Health & Disease* and the producer of the videotape of the same title.

RICHARD E. HESS, as the proprietor of The Goldfish Connection, imports thousands of the highest quality goldfish annually and has decades of experience keeping fish and helping others to select the best and keep them healthy.

JACKIE AND LOUIS CHAN are the owners of Tung Hoi Aquarium Company in China, annually producing over 2.5 million fancy goldfish in 50 varieties and colors.

JEFFREY HUNTER is a translator, a long-time resident of Japan, and a collector of Japanese goldfish.

IZHAK KROSHINSKY is a leading American Ranchu breeder.